Local colour

Figs - 95

Nation among HE soldiers   102B (106)

Cz Legion & Nat'l Pride   111

THE GREAT WAR'S FORGOTTEN FRONT
A SOLDIER'S DIARY
AND A SON'S REFLECTIONS

JAN F. TRISKA

EAST EUROPEAN MONOGRAPHS, BOULDER
DISTRIBUTED BY COLUMBIA UNIVERSITY PRESS, NEW YORK
1998

EAST EUROPEAN MONOGRAPHS, NO. FIVE HUNDRED

Copyright © 1998 by Jan F. Triska
ISBN 0-88033-397-9
Library of Congress Catalog Card Number 98-70324

Printed in the United States of America

For Carmel

TABLE OF CONTENTS

ACKNOWLEDGEMENTS		ix
FOREWORD BY DAVID M. KENNEDY		xi
PROLOGUE		1
I	PREPARING FOR WAR	
	Meeting in Vienna	5
	Basic Training Olomouc, November 16, 1916–February 23, 1917	12
	Artillery School Vienna, February 24–March 30	18
	Field Artillery Training Imst in Tyrol, April 3–May 3	22
II	THE ITALIAN CAMPAIGN: THE ISONZO FRONT	
	Baptism by Fire Mount Barbara, May 6–May 10	25
	Battle in Earnest Avšje, May 11–26	27
	"Slaughter" Monte Ermada, May 31–July 6	34
	Retreat under Fire Mount Liesl, July 11–August 22	41
	The Italians Advance Koren, August 23–September 14	48
	Victory at Caporetto Kanalski Lom/Ravne, September 15–November 6	53
	Drills and More Drills Slap ob Idrijci, November 6, 1917–January 12, 1918	62
III	THE ITALIAN CAMPAIGN: THE PIAVE FRONT	
	The Magic Castle From the Isonzo to the Piave, January 12–February 6	66
	Buckling Under Milies, February 7–May 5	69
	Preparing for a Final Victory From Milies to San Michele di Piave, May 5–June 14	77
	The Battle of the Piave Montello, June 15–23	82

IV	RETREAT AND CAPTIVITY	
	Killing Time	
	From the Piave to San Giovanni, June 24–October 28	94
	Retreat	
	San Giovanni to Grions, October 28–November 4	101
	Prisoner of War	
	Grions to Camponogara, November 4–20	104
	About the Czechoslovak Legions	112
V	CZECHOSLOVAK LEGIONNAIRE	
	The Czechoslovak Legion in Italy	
	Legnaro, Saonara, Padova, Vicenza	
	November 24–December 27	117
	The Czechoslovak Legion in Czechoslovakia	
	Těšín Silesia and Southwestern Slovakia	
	December 27, 1918–November, 1919	122
	Discharged from Service: A New Life Begins	
	Olomouc, November 3, 1919	137
VI	EPILOGUE	
	The Great War Reconsidered	141
	The Great War and the Twentieth Century	145
	In Sum	155
PHOTOGRAPHS		157
MAPS		164
SELECT BIBLIOGRAPHY		177

TABLE OF CONTENTS

PHOTOGRAPHS OF JAN

1. Bugler in Sokol uniform, Olomouc, fall of 1908, age 18.
2. Journeyman cabinet maker, Olomouc, July 1910, top row, second from left.
3. Private (*Soldat*), basic training, Infantry, Olomouc, December 16, first row, third from left.
4. Private First Class (*Vormeister*), Mountain Artillery, on leave, Vienna, August 1917.
5. Sergeant (*Zugsführer*), with Božena, on leave, Vienna, July 1918.
6. Sergeant (*Četař*), Czechoslovak Legion from Italy, now Czechoslovak Army Corps from Italy, Heavy Field Howitzers Group No. 1, in Slovakia, 1919.
7. With other Czechoslovak legionnaires from Italy in Slovakia, 1919, seated, first from right.

MAPS

I   Jan's Journey to the Isonzo Front
II   Area of the Isonzo Front
III   Detail of the Banjška Plateau/Bainsizza
IV   The March to the Piave
V   The Battle of the Piave
VI   Italian Prisoner of War
VII   From Italy to the Czechoslovak Border
VIII   The Czechoslovak Legion from Italy in Czechoslovakia
A   East Central Europe, 1910
B   World War I, 1914-1918
C   East Central Europe, 1918-1923
D   East Central Europe, ca. 1930
E   East Central Europe, 1992

ACKNOWLEDGEMENTS

I am grateful to the dear friends and generous colleagues who have helped to bring this volume to completion. The intellectual debts I have accumulated are numerous: I have been fortunate in obtaining able advice and valuable, thoughtful assistance from a great many. Without them this book could not have been published.

Those who deserve my thanks the most include: at Stanford University, David B. Abernethy, Professor of Political Science; Irina V. Barnes, Assistant Director, Center for Russian and East European Studies; Grant A. Barnes, Director Emeritus of the Stanford University Press; Gordon A. Craig, J.E. Wallace Sterling Professor of Humanities Emeritus; Milan L. Hauner, Visiting Professor of History, 1993-1994; David M. Kennedy, Donald J. McLachlan Professor of History; Hubert R. Marshall, Professor Emeritus of Political Science; Eliska Ryznar, Catalogue Librarian Emerita, School of Law Library; and Kurt Steiner, Professor Emeritus of Political Science. In the vicinity of Stanford, Maria Cuevas, former resident of Northern Italy; George L. Dickey, Capt., U.S. Navy (Ret.); Timothy Goode, retired teacher at Santa Clara High School; and Rachelle Marshall, editor and proofreader. At the University of California in Berkeley, Andrew C. Janos, Professor of Political Science, and Barbara A. Voytek, Executive Director, Center for Slavic and East European Studies.

In the Czech Republic, I am grateful to Dr. Bohumír Klípa, Institute of History of the Czech Armed Forces and the staff of the Institute; Zdenek L. Suda, Professor Emeritus of Sociology, University of Pittsburgh, presently Dean, University of Silesia, Opava; and my sister, Božena Řeháková.

In Slovenia, my heartfelt thanks go to Vasja Klavora, Prim. Dr., Nova Gorica, and to the staff of the War Museum in Kobarid/Caporetto; in Austria, to Hofrat Dr. Reiner Egger, Director of the Österreichisches Kriegsarchiv, Vienna, and Dr. Karel Stefec; in Italy, to Giovanni Galvagni, Museo Storico Italiano della Guerra, Rovereto; and in Germany, to Wolfgang Schuller, Dr. iur., Professor of History, University of Konstanz.

In addition, my research in Europe was supported by a grant from the International Research and Exchanges Board, with funds provided by the U.S. Department of State (Title VIII program) and the National Endowment for the Humanities. None of these organizations is responsible for the views expressed. Paul Robert Magocsi, Professor and Chair of Ukrainian Studies at the University of Toronto, kindly permitted the reproduction of Maps 36, 37, 38, 44, and 50 from his unique *Historical Atlas of East Central Europe* (University of Washington Press, Seattle, 1993).

Last but not least, I am indebted to my family: to my son Mark for his warm and sustained encouragement; to my son John for his generous offer to draw Maps I to VIII and for his patient labor; and to my wife Carmel, who aided and abetted me at every step of the way.

Jan F. Triska

FOREWORD

DAVID M. KENNEDY
Donald J. McLachlan Professor of History
Stanford University

War is the prolific womb of stories—not for nothing do we call them "war stories"—and the Great War of 1914-1918 was among the most fecund of them all. Paul Fussell has even argued that the task of telling the tales of World War I fundamentally altered the English-language narrative form, making the ironic voice forever after the story-teller's requisite tone.

Yet in *The Great War's Forgotten Front* the voice we hear is not cleverly ironic but disarmingly candid. It is the voice of an observant and unpretentious Czech cabinet-maker improbably swept up in a series of sometimes grisly, sometimes comic trials by arms. The soldier Jan Tříska's tale, translated with warm affection and scrupulous accuracy by his eponymously named scholar-son, a distinguished political scientist who has long taught at Stanford University, may lack the literary adornment one finds in accounts by Robert Graves or Erich Maria Remarque or Ernest Hemingway. But *The Great War's Forgotten Front* has an eloquence of its own. Professor Triska has assembled the mundane details of his father's three years of military service into a deeply moving story of one man's confrontation with the great cataclysm of the First World War. Against the son's deftly drawn historical backdrop, the soldier-father speaks to us in these pages with chilling authenticity, and often with stunning directness.

The unusual provenance of Jan Triska's tale is a special boon for readers in English. For those who know little more of the Austrian-Italian front than what they may have read in Hemingway's *A Farewell to Arms*, this book will come as a revelation. Here the action is seen from the Austrian side, through the eyes of a young husband and father, a Czech cabinet-maker quietly plying his trade in the great imperial capital of Vienna, until in late 1916 he was drafted into the Austro-Hungarian army—an army mustered from such a polyglot mixture of the Austro-Hungarian Empire's peoples that it had to develop a special language of command called "Army Slav," some eighty essential German words that the Czech, Polish, Slovak, Slovene, and other ethnic minority recruits were compelled to learn. After just thirteen weeks of basic training and five weeks of artillery training, Jan found himself on the Isonzo front, facing a battle-seasoned Italian army. Six months later, his artillery unit had suffered fifty percent casualties. Two men died in Jan's arms in one day. In the see-saw of battle along the Isonzo, the Austrian forces at last forced the great Italian retreat from Caporetto, about which Hemingway wrote. But the caprices of war then dictated that the Austrians surrender and Jan become an Italian prisoner of war—until he was recruited to fight for the Czechoslovak Legion and sent off to Silesia and Slovakia to defend the new state of Czechoslovakia against Polish and Hungarian incursions. Jan's war did not end with the Armistice of November 1918, but only a year later, with his newly independent homeland finally secure.

Throughout this bizarre military odyssey, Jan repeatedly, sometimes furtively, returned to Vienna to his wife and daughter, seeing in the crumbling capital on his periodic visits the inexorable decay and eventual collapse of the Habsburg Empire. At all points he attentively recorded not only the drama of combat and the accumulating signs of political decline, but also the prosaic aggravations and joys of the soldier's life—from wretched weather, bad food, and ubiquitous lice to occasionally kind officers, wondrous discoveries of caches of wine, and ineffable precious visits to his wife and child.

Professor Triska has done students of the First World War a service. Few if any accounts in English offer as rich a portrait of the human face of the Great War on the Austrian side of the Italian front, or into the reverberations in individual lives of the end of the Austro-Hungarian Empire and the birth of the Czechoslovak republic. The son has honored the father by so faithfully re-telling his story, a tale which is by turns terrifying, tender, and touching.

PROLOGUE

This is the story of a front-line soldier in World War I, a conscript in the Austro-Hungarian Imperial and Royal Army. The soldier underwent a terrible ordeal in the hopeless war between Italy and Austria-Hungary, a sideshow of the Great War. The story is based on a terse but meticulously recorded war diary the soldier kept, hoping to transcribe his wartime notes later if he survived, when he could sort things out at leisure. He did survive, but did not return to his diary for many years.

At the end of the war Austria-Hungary, a multinational empire, "that motley holdover of the middle ages...," was defeated. It collapsed and was broken up into its major ethnic parts. Czechoslovakia, the country of Czechs and Slovaks, a historical part of which was Moravia, the soldier's birthplace, emerged as a free and independent state, the Czechs liberated after 300 years of Austrian Habsburg domination and the Slovaks after a millennium of Hungarian hegemony. In the middle of this cataclysmic turn of events, the soldier returned from the war to his wife and small daughter. The world he had left behind no longer existed. There was no time to look back then nor for many years to come.

The soldier was my father. Forced into retirement some thirty years later, after the communist coup d'état in Czechoslovakia in 1948, he finally had the time to sit back and reflect. Czechoslovakia was a healthy democracy for the first twenty years of its existence, from 1918 to 1938. Then came six years of Nazi German occupation for the Czechs and Nazi puppet statehood for the Slovaks during World War II, from 1939 to 1945. The period of renewed high hopes that followed, from 1945 to 1948, was short-lived. The country's geopolitical location in the heart of Europe led to its downfall once again in the communist coup of 1948. Czechoslovakia, the last of the eight European satellites to orbit around the Soviet sun, became demoralized and degraded under the rule of its Stalinist leaders. Stripped of his dignity and his means of earning a living by the new communist government, his property and business confiscated and nationalized, my father took the time in the late 1950s and early 1960s finally to confront his wartime diary. Working on it became a welcome diversion from the depressing realities of the day.

In 1948, soon after the February communist takeover, I was about to be arrested for my student political activities at the Charles University Law School in Prague. I escaped to West Germany. Six months later I left for the United States, where a fellowship awaited me at the Yale Law School. After studying at Yale and then at the

Harvard Graduate School of Government, I taught at Harvard, the University of California at Berkeley, and at Cornell. In 1960 I settled with my American wife and two small sons in the San Francisco Bay Area, at Stanford University.

Shortly before his death in 1970, my father sent me a copy of his World War I diary. The single-spaced, laboriously typed, legal-sized manuscript was a careful transcript of the original diary, which occupied several small notebooks, one of which my father always kept in the right breast pocket of his military tunic. Whenever he could, he made daily entries with indelible pencil in tiny, spare script. On each home leave he would exchange the old notebook for a new one.

I remember those notebooks well. When I was a small boy, sometimes my father read me excerpts from them, transforming the notes from memory into stories of excitement and suspense. In order to make the diary more intelligible to me than the sketchy, elliptical phrases written in haste on the battlefield, my father in his sixties "recollected in tranquillity" his wartime experiences, amplified and edited the entries, and with the advantage of hindsight updated some of the events and developments of World War I.

I found the manuscript captivating. It offered perceptive insights into the crucible of war and the trauma of a front-line soldier, one vulnerable man among tens of millions of other vulnerable men. With bated breath I took part in the merciless battles, suffered their terrible din, smelled the acrid stench of gunpowder, shared the fear, boredom, and misery of Father's long days on the front.

When I was a small boy I loved Father's bedtime stories about his war adventures. I always begged for more. I had no idea, of course, how grisly was the reality behind the fantasy of his thrilling accounts. Now I know. For me Father's diary gave war a human dimension. It made me see for the first time his war as it truly was in time and in place.

The object of war is clear: defeat the enemy. A soldier kills in order not to be killed. What could be more simple, basic, or desperate? As a fellow gunner in Father's battery pointed out during a battle on the Isonzo front in Slovenia, "When I was in prison back home before the war, I had enough to eat, a warm cell to sleep in, and no fear of losing my life. I was safe. I hated it then, but how I wish I was back in that cell right now!"

My father's war was truly Everyman's war. To men like my father—the hundreds of thousands of Czechs, Poles, Slovaks, Ukrainians, Slovenes, Croats, Bosnians, Serbs, Albanians, Italians, and Jews, the second and third class citizens of the Dual Monarchy—

but also to many Hungarians and German Austrians (*Deutschösterreicher*), the preferred citizens of the Empire, the war had no meaning other than as a brutal interruption in their lives. They wanted the war to end, win or lose, and go home. Loyalty to the Empire became meaningless; it did not last much past the first firefight, the first battle, the first offensive. Survival was what mattered. A self-inflicted wound guaranteed rest, food, and safety in a field hospital. Remaining alive was the chief and overwhelming concern. All else was irrelevant.

Historians tell us that helplessness leads to hopelessness, a process that ultimately decides the outcome of wars. They speak of the significance of loss of hope on the part of the warring decision-makers. Maybe so. There are no opinion polls or statistical surveys documenting the feelings of soldiers in the trenches, only anecdotal evidence such as my father's diary. If we had such data, we might find that loss of hope in front-line soldiers is more than a little significant in determining the outcome of a war. Had such data been available in World War I, that war would have been considerably shorter, and countless wasted lives would have been saved.

It was some years after I received the manuscript that I was able to give it my full attention. To start with, I translated the diary from the original Czech. Very quickly I realized that to be able to understand the whole of my father's story within the context of its time and place, I needed to learn more about my father's war. I researched the subject in Stanford's libraries. I visited all the places mentioned in the manuscript, including all the battlefields; I also visited museums, archives, memorials, and cemeteries having to do with the Great War in Slovenia, Italy, Austria, and the Czech and Slovak republics, the sites of my father's war. I talked to scholars and interviewed experts in all these countries.

What makes my father's diary valuable, I discovered, is its design: It is organized around dates and names of places. This simple framework endows the diary with a discipline that attests to the authenticity and honesty of the day-by-day entries.

After this kind of immersion, my first major question took form: How do the observations, perceptions, opinions, and attitudes of the soldiers in the trenches jibe with the historians' evaluations of World War I and its signficance? And what is the relationship, if any, between the soldier, who sees the war from a snail's eye view, and the big picture, encompassing the Italian front, the Habsburg monarchy, the Central Powers, the Allies, and the Great War itself? Some say that history viewed from the top is an illusion leaning on constructs composed of masses of details whose essential nature historians sometimes do not fully understand. Others maintain that the eyewitness point of view may be sharp because it is narrow but worthless because its is limited.

I believe that to understand the meaning and significance of World War I it is important to know both the broad historical overview as well as the discrete details revealed by perceptive observers. It is true that the macro point of view has an explanatory power and value that the micro level lacks. The micro point of view is not trivial, however. It supplies intimate background knowledge that is otherwise unobtainable, it furnishes the historical evaluation with an independent proving ground, and it endows the macro level with evidence provided through hands-on experience.

I was pleased to discover that the two insights, the micro and the macro, are here in agreement, complement each other, reinforce each other's arguments and conclusions, and are congruent. Both condemn the war for its enormous costs, the arrogance and lack of imagination and purpose of its leaders, and its immorality and senseless savagery.

Finally, my concern and involvement with World War I led me, it seemed inevitably, to two other related questions: First, comparatively speaking, what kind of war was World War I? How similar or different was it from other wars? And second, what significance, if any, does World War I have for us today, eighty years later? Did "the war to end all wars" leave any enduring imprint on the twentieth century, and if it did, what kind of imprint? I attempt to answer these intriguing questions in the Epilogue.

I
PREPARING FOR WAR

Meeting in Vienna

On July 2, 1914, exactly one month after the assassination of the Austrian Archduke Franz Ferdinand, the nephew and heir-apparent of Emperor Franz Josef, and his morganatic wife, Countess Sophie von Chotek, the Austro-Hungarian Habsburg Empire declared war on Serbia and ordered general mobilization. Jan Tříska, a young Czech from northern Moravia, was living at that time in Vienna, where he had come to seek his fortune four years earlier. On October 17, 1914, he married Božena Kubizňáková, an attractive twenty-year-old cook's assistant from eastern Bohemia. He had met her the winter before at a dance sponsored by Sokol, a Czech all-national gymnastic organization of some 150,000 enthusiastic members. Sokol ("Falcon") was an ethnic and social club of mostly young people dedicated to physical fitness. But it was also a patriotic symbol of awakening Czech ethnic and civic pride, whose hope was the eventual liberation of the Czech people—a proud nation whose origins went back to the ninth century and the good King Wenceslas, the patron saint of Bohemia—from Habsburg oppression.

Jan was a strong and healthy man, twenty-four years old and thus immediately subject to the draft. But he was lucky. Since he was a certified cabinet-maker by trade, it was easy for him, when the war started, to get a job in a large Viennese factory making railroad cars. Because the Simmeringer Maschinen und Waggonfabrik was an industry essential to the war effort, Jan was exempt from the draft.

Before the war Vienna was a legendary city of Baroque grandeur and elegance located between the romantic Vienna woods and the perennially blue Danube. A city of two million inhabitants, it was the rich and important capital of an empire that was the second largest European power in terms of territory (Map A) and the third largest in population. Few other cities in Europe could boast of a more beautiful combination of magnificent buildings interspersed with fine gardens and large public parks. The gaiety of its carnivals and balls (*Faschings*), its cosmopolitan flavor, the quality of its music and high culture, and its stylish people were renowned throughout Europe. Poets and artists, royalty and commoners alike were captivated by Vienna.

This was the city where Jan and Božena met and married. Both were children of poor peasants from small, remote villages in the hinterlands of the Empire. Both came to Vienna to find a new life.

Jan, a tall, handsome, neatly-dressed young man with a quick smile and a carefully trimmed mustache, knew well how to work hard. His father died of meat poisoning when Jan was a small boy. While attending the village elementary school in Klopina, Moravia, where he was born, Jan, like his four brothers and four sisters, planted and harvested the grains, potatoes, sugar beets and alfalfa on the family plot of land. They also tended the kitchen garden and looked after the livestock. In addition, they all hired out to help other villagers with their chores as well.

When Jan was fourteen his mother secured for him an apprenticeship in a nearby village, Pískov (Map VIII), with a friendly but demanding master cabinet-maker. At the same time he was enrolled part time in the local two-year vocational school. In his free moments Jan was expected to help his master's wife with her chores. At the age of sixteen, Jan moved to the city of Olomouc, the district metropolis. There, hired as an apprentice journeyman in a thriving cabinet-making establishment of three masters and fifteen journeymen, Jan entered again a trade and vocational school. Evenings and Sundays he worked for the masters' families—gladly, when they had pretty daughters about his age.

When he was twenty, in 1910, with his precious journeyman certificate in hand and a little money in his pocket, Jan left for Vienna, the capital of the Empire. He was proud of himself; his hard work, discipline, and diligent application to his duties had paid off. Vienna was the culmination and fulfillment of his dreams from childhood. How many times had he heard that "...the timid stay at home, the daring go to Olomouc, and the bold end up in Vienna?" He was ready to work harder than ever before, to learn his trade to perfection, to avoid mistakes, and to do whatever it took to improve his station in life.

And he was not disappointed. In Vienna good, well-paying jobs in carpentry and woodworking were plentiful. Jan now had an incentive to improve his German, the language of the Empire. In Sokol he could relax a bit, exercise, socialize, and make new friends. To top it all, he met Božena and was never lonely from then on.

A peasant with high aspirations, Jan admired the conventional bourgeois values and the good life Vienna stood for. He was determined to achieve such a life—a job with good prospects, a decent place to live, a family of his own, and the chance to enjoy the cultural and social amenities of urban life that Vienna offered in abundance. Like hundreds of thousands of other young men and women from the backwaters of the Empire, this young Czech was fully primed to succeed.

Jan was not an idealist, a reformer, or a crusader. An active and dedicated member of Sokol and a Czech patriot entirely within the frame of reference of the Austrian Empire, Jan was not a Czech nationalist. That revolutionary ideological ferment was taking place outside his sphere of limited knowledge. As it was to many other Czechs, conversion was to come to him only later, toward the end of the war, and then he embraced it firmly, fully, and with enthusiasm.

Božena's background was similar to Jan's. Born in Bohemia in a small village, Bratčice, Božena, like her brother and three sisters, when not attending school helped her parents with the vegetable garden, small animals—goats, pigs, rabbits, geese, ducks, and chickens—and kitchen chores. Her father, the village horticulturist, was an artist with flowers, a florist well-known for his unique, resplendent bouquets, corsages, and floral arrangements for weddings, funerals, and other formal occasions. He grew exotic flowers under glass, grafted fruit trees expertly, raised exquisite long-stemmed roses, and was a master beekeeper as well. He was devoted to his flowers but scorned farming. Alas, in the community of small villages, these pursuits did not bring in enough money to support a family.

Fortunately, Božena's mother was a businesswoman. She walked from village to village peddling women's apparel such as aprons, head scarves, skirts, blouses, underwear, stockings, slippers, and other dry goods. Too busy with their household chores to go shopping, farmers' wives eagerly awaited her visits with the newest acquisitions and the latest gossip. She purchased her merchandise in Čáslav (Map VIII), the district market town, and carried it in a peddler's pack on her back. When she was older, Božena begged to accompany her mother on her day trips. She loved the buying and selling part of the excursions and was glad to help her mother carry the load.

When Božena was sixteen, she pleaded with her mother to send her to Vienna. Through her many village contacts, her mother arranged for Božena to be placed in a respectable Viennese German-speaking family "to learn how to cook," a euphemism for working as a live-in maid. Two years later, as a reward for exemplary demeanor and devotion to duty, she was advanced to cook's assistant. Like Jan, Božena was upwardly mobile and ready to work hard to achieve her goals.

Jan fell in love with Božena at first sight. She was his great love, but more than that: she was his soul mate. She was as eager to improve her lot as Jan was and as willing to work unstintingly. Together, they were an unbeatable team. For them Vienna was the magnetic center of the universe, whose attraction had lured them away from family and tradition.

Once there, however, they also learned the other side of the picture: that in Vienna appearance was often illusion, that in this seemingly enchanted city all that glittered was not always golden. The Czechs who lived in Vienna, some 30 percent of the city's population, were considered inferior to the German Austrians, fit only to serve as tailors, cobblers, gardeners, tradespeople, domestic servants, shopkeepers, and the like. Still, the Czechs were much better off in Vienna than were the Slovaks in Budapest, and considerably better off than some of the other ethnic minorities in the Habsburg empire. In fact, these minorities lumped together were more numerous in the Empire than the two ruling nationalities combined, the German Austrians and the Hungarians. Of the 51 million people of the Dual Monarchy, there were 12 million German Austrians, 10 million Hungarians, and 29 million members of lesser ethnic groups.

In this huge social cauldron with its clearly defined strata of the ruling classes—the Court, the nobility, the officers' corps, the bureaucracy, the Church, and the German Austrian industrialists—and those beneath, the Czechs on the whole tended to have more opportunities for social advancement than other minorities. There were more Czechs—six and a half million of them—than any other subordinate nationality group; historically and culturally they were closer to the Austrians than any other group save the Hungarians; as a group they were known to be technologically advanced and had the reputation of being industrious, skilled, quick to learn, and reliable. The more ambitious and daring among them were thus more likely to become upwardly mobile than were members of some other ethnic groups in the less than porous Viennese society.

Jan and Božena fit neatly into the scheme of things in Vienna. Anticipating the increasing importance of food in a wartime economy, Božena, now a married woman without employment, suggested that they open a small neighborhood food store. Božena would be in charge, and Jan would help in the evenings and on Sundays. There was some risk. They were inexperienced, their savings were small, and their mastery of the German language was far from perfect. Jan thought it over. Why not?

They found the ideal location in a busy, established neighborhood in the Fourth District at Heumühlgasse No. 6, a little food store that included a modest one-room apartment immediately behind it. They moved in and after a few weeks opened for business.

The store, fronted by a double door and a display window, was a typical neighborhood shop, small but before long fully stocked with the usual basic foodstuffs—bakery goods delivered fresh every morning, dairy products, staples such as potatoes, flour, sugar, coffee and tea, fruits and vegetables in season, delicatessen meats and pickles, canned goods, chocolates, as well as wines, spirits, household cleaning supplies, and more.

Božena's kitchen was a narrow space set off from the store proper, which opened to the public hall in the rear. Prominent was a large ice-box which contained a 150-liter stainless steel vessel for milk, various dairy products, and other small perishable goods sold in the store. On the table was a two-burner gas stove, which Božena used to boil water as well as to prepare the couple's meals.

The one-room apartment was simple but contained what they needed: a matrimonial bed (two single, side-by-side beds), two small bedside stands where the chamber pots were stored, two large wardrobes, a dining table with four chairs, a linen chest, and a small, low coffee table, all lovingly made by Jan before their wedding, when he was working as a cabinet maker. Three small upholstered chairs, a coal-burning stove, a floor lamp, brightly patterned small carpets on the wooden floor, and traditional holy pictures on the wall completed the furnishings. The couple shared a cold water faucet and a toilet with the other tenants on the ground floor. There was no bathroom, but public baths were within reach.

When the war broke out, after nearly fifty years of relative tranquillity, people were slow to grasp its effect on their daily lives. Given "the dastardly deed of bloody assassination in Sarajevo," the Austrian declaration of war on Serbia was viewed in Vienna as legitimate and just. Even sworn pacifists like Rainer Maria Rilke, Oskar Kokoschka, Sigmund Freud, Stefan Zweig, Ludwig Wittgenstein and Arnold Schönburg applauded. The autumn of 1914, when Jan and Božena married, was a golden time in Vienna with people dancing in the streets, coffee houses teeming with celebrants, and theaters, concert halls, and opera houses filled to capacity. The Serbs would be punished, the newspapers declared, and the glorious old Empire, rejuvenated by the war, would be preserved for all time. It was anticipated that the war would be short and victorious, and the good life, soon to return, would go on forever.

By the fall of 1916, however, the German Austrians had long lost their early enthusiasm for the war, and the patriotic fervor that had swept Vienna in 1914 was only a memory. The war was going badly for the Dual Monarchy; it was becoming a costly, dangerous affair. In fact, Austria-Hungary was slipping into increasing dependency on Germany, which had come to its rescue in Serbia and in

Galicia. Now Italy had joined the conflict and was fighting the Austro-Hungarian army in Slovenia in full force.

As the war grew exponentially in scope and in intensity on all three Austrian fronts—Russia, Serbia, and Italy—it began to chip away at the strength of the Empire and its beautiful capital. The splendor of the palaces, some of which were now unheated, was fading, and a feeling of falling from greatness was in the air. The spontaneous food riots of 1915 grew, despite early food rationing, into mass food demonstrations in 1916. The rich supplies of farm products from rural Hungary—flour, pork, poultry, eggs, fats—that formed the basis of the famed Viennese cuisine, were fast diminishing, and the production of Austrian cereal crops fell by half due to the lack of manpower in the countryside. Along with food shortages there were dwindling supplies of shoes and clothing, soap, medicine, and raw materials.

Rationing was administered by local authorities. The coordination of supply and distribution, never entirely satisfactory or efficient in the best of times, deteriorated into spiraling prices and inflation, black markets, corruption, and profiteering.

The Austro-Hungarian army had many problems of its own. Despite the pretensions of its vast and anachronistic professional officer corps, the army's military history was unimpressive. When the new universal military conscription was put in place after Austria's defeat by the Prussians in 1866, it provided an army of civilians in uniform more numerous and less expensive to maintain than the professional army it replaced, and thus more suitable for the defense of the Empire's vast frontier. At the same time, however, the ranks lost their former homogeneity, efficiency, and effectiveness. The multinational composition of the Empire did not ensure the citizen-soldiers' loyalty, allegiance, or devotion to the Crown. And the fact that 75 percent of the ranks were subject ethnics while 75 percent of the officers were German Austrians did not help matters.

And yet, this disparate collection of national, ethnic, and religious groups did somehow endure the shock and stress of a long war. In fact, by the end of 1916 the Monarchy had mobilized almost 3.5 million men out of a total population of 51 million, and with its very limited industrial capacity managed to equip, more or less, this huge military force.

On the Italian front, which by late 1916 was turning into the major Austrian battleground, the Italian offensives were becoming more and more costly for the Austrians. Italy had declared war on her historic enemy Austria in May, 1915. But the declaration, in typical Italian fashion, was made more for the figure it would cut with the

Entente powers—especially France and Great Britain—and with its own populace, than for the threat it posed to the Central Powers, especially Germany. In fact, Italy had tried to avoid an open break with Germany; it did not declare war on Germany until fourteen months later, in August, 1916.

Austria, however, was for Italy a different matter. The Allies had promised Italy not only the Trentino and South Tyrol (Alto Adige), Trieste, Istria, and a part of Dalmatia—regions containing Italian populations or having cultural or historical ties to Italy—but much more, including the port of Valona, special rights in Albania, Rhodes, and the Dodecanese, some islands in the Adriatic, and possibly Smyrna and territories in Africa, as well as a loan of 50 million British pounds. Italy could not resist entering the war.

The Italian army was not ready for a difficult frontal attack on the Italian-Austrian frontier, a mountainous region that presented awkward strategic obstacles for offense and, as the Austrians soon found out, for defense as well. Despite the rapid Austrian reinforcement of their border forces—the High Command dispatched some five divisions there from the Serbian front—the Italians had an overwhelming superiority in numbers. Nevertheless, with the exception of the city of Gorizia, which the Italian armed forces reached and conquered in August, 1916, their repeated efforts to break through the Austrian defenses proved futile again and again. The Italian-Austrian front froze into the trench warfare typical of World War I.

By the fall of 1916 the Italian efforts had amounted to little, and Italian losses, reportedly some 300,000 men, were almost double those of the Austrians. The Austrian High Command, in turn, felt it could not endure the stress of many more defensive battles; their troops were strained to the limit, and the casualties were rising steadily. More and more new conscripts were needed. On November 13, 1916, Jan was ordered to report to his draft board immediately.

Jan's three brothers were already serving in the Austrian armed forces: the oldest, Karel, with the Eighty-fourth Infantry Regiment; the second oldest, František, with the Twelfth Cavalry Regiment; and the youngest, Ludvík, with the Thirteenth Infantry Regiment. Jan was ordered to report to Ludvík's Thirteenth Landwehr Infantry Regiment in Šumperk in northern Moravia, not far from Klopina, his and his brothers' birthplace, located in the Administrative District of Zábřeh.

The Landwehr, the Austrian army reserve force, was created when the Hungarians had insistently demanded of the Austrians, and ultimately received, the concession to raise a separate, Hungarian-administered military force under Hungarian command known as the Honved. Its Austrian counterpart, separate but equal, was the

Landwehr, or Home Guard, the territorial defense force of Austria proper, to which the Thirteenth Infantry Regiment belonged.

Jan left Vienna on November 15, 1916, leaving behind his twenty-two year old wife and his two month old daughter, also named Božena. It was a tearful, painful parting. The young mother would now be in sole charge of the food store in the Fourth District, in addition to caring for a small baby.

Basic Training. Olomouc, Moravia
November 16, 1916 - February 23, 1917
Imperial and Royal Landwehr Infantry Regiment No. 13

From Vienna the train trip to Šumperk should have taken six hours at most, but it took Jan almost twice that long. Civilian trains were overcrowded and were shunted aside, again and again, to permit priority military trains to pass through. Jan had to stand all the way from Vienna to Šumperk. The train stations along the route were in wild disorder. When Jan arrived in Šumperk, he was told by the military police at the station that his destination should have been Olomouc, a major military garrison town and former fortress in central Moravia, not Šumperk, and Jan was ordered to report there at once (Map I).

Weary, sleepless, and chilled to the bone, Jan arrived in Olomouc in the middle of the night. He knew the city well from his four years there as an apprentice journeyman cabinet maker before coming to Vienna. But he and the other recruits arriving in Olomouc that night had not been expected. All the military barracks were full. The new arrivals were sent to cold, dirty, unfinished shanties to sleep—or sit—on the dirt floor. They were miserable.

After two days of general chaos and bumbling, a semblance of routine was introduced and gradually established. The recruits took showers, were divided into squads, platoons, and companies, and were placed in temporary housing. They were issued used uniforms (including some blue army uniforms that had been discarded years earlier), old boots, mended underwear, used bedding, and other second-hand equipment, but no rifles. Then they were vaccinated and photographed.

On November 22 the regimental commander informed the recruits standing more or less at attention on the parade grounds that the Emperor Franz Josef had died. The men were not unduly surprised. It had been rumored for several days that the Emperor had expired but that his death was being kept secret for security reasons. After a short memorial ceremony eulogizing "His Majesty, Franz

Josef I, by the grace of God, Emperor of Austria, Apostolic King of Hungary, King of Bohemia, Dalmatia, Croatia, Slavonia, Galicia, Lodomeria, and Illyria, King of Jerusalem; Archduke of Austria; Grand Duke of Tuscany and Krakow; Duke of Lorraine, Salzburg, Styria, Carinthia, Carniola, and the Bukovina; Grand Prince of Transylvania; Margrave of Moravia; and Count of Habsburg and the Tyrol"—the recruits swore allegiance to the new Emperor, Charles I, and were dismissed.

Under the vigilant eyes of their drill corporals, the recruits were being transformed ("very, very slowly," according to their new masters) from unruly civilians into obedient soldiers. The methods of transformation were rigorous: tough and frequent drills, simple as well as complex; forced marches; lectures and seminars (mostly in German, which the majority of Czechs did not understand); and interminable cleaning, washing, and scrubbing of everything in sight, including the latrines. They all had to memorize the "Army Slav," an unofficial but widely used lexicon of army jargon, some eighty basic German words of command. Their rifles arrived then, too, used weapons of obsolete vintage, Model Werndl, 11 mm caliber single-shot capacity. The men wondered what had happened to the previous owners of these rifles—were they wounded, killed, captured? The mess was of war-time quality and the amounts of food barely adequate. Fortunately, many men were receiving packages from home, which they shared with their new comrades. All in all, the raw recruits were beginning to look and feel like soldiers, whether they liked it or not.

Who were these men, these new soldiers in the Imperial armed forces? They were mostly sons of peasants, men with little education and simple needs, used to obedience and working long hours for small wages. Basic military training, however harsh and exhausting, was just another job for them. They took it in stride.

The rains came, and with them penetrating dampness, mud and cold. Jan's platoon commander, Staff Corporal Müller, was tough but, all in all, reasonable. There were worse NCOs, some much worse. Being strict and tough on recruits was important: Drill corporals who were reputed to be tough and strict kept their jobs in the rear, while those who were milder and kinder did not last long; more often than not they were dispatched to the front in short order.

This rule, universally observed and respected, applied to the officers as well. It was confirmed to Jan when their new company commander, a recently promoted Reserve Captain Rohner, a German industrialist from Bohemia, came one grey day to inspect the company on the parade grounds. To show how tough a disciplinarian he was, the captain took over and ordered the company to stand at attention in full marching order in the heavy rain and cold wind, with full packs and rifles. At the rapidly snapped commands "nieder" and "auf," he forced the men to prostrate themselves in the mud and spring up at full attention again and again and again, until many were unable to pull themselves up any longer, despite the shouting and cursing of their NCOs. Only then did the captain stop and dismiss the company. The men returned to barracks, and the cleaning, scrubbing and polishing routine started all over again. Fortunately, after having proved his mettle, Captain Rohner never showed up again. Many years later Jan found out that toward the end of the war Rohner, too, in spite of his strictness with the ranks, had been sent to the Italian front. He had not been heard from since.

Reserve Lieutenant Novotný, the Assistant Company Commander, a school teacher, a Czech, and like Jan a member of Sokol, was considered by his men to be a good soldier and a decent human being. Rather than punishing the slow learners, he rewarded the fast ones. The men liked him, and the feeling was reciprocated. The lieutenant gave Jan his first evening leave pass, to which Jan was not really entitled, to visit his two brothers, Karel and Ludvík. Severely wounded at the Serbian front, Karel had been discharged from his regiment and returned to his family in Olomouc, where he worked on the railroad. Ludvík, on home leave from the Italian front, was staying with Karel.

A food package from Božena, his first, awaited Jan at Karel's home. They parceled out the goodies and celebrated, with many a toast of slivovitz (plum brandy), and Jan barely made it back to the barracks that night. A few days later, completely unexpected, Božena showed up at Karel's apartment. "A miracle!" thought Jan. How had she managed it? Lieut. Novotný, obviously partial to Jan, issued him a 24-hour leave pass then and there. In addition, he gave Jan a block of ten precious evening passes, dates to be filled in by Jan when needed, "within reason, of course." Best of all, a week later, on December 23, Jan received his first three-day home leave pass, the most generous Christmas present he could have imagined.

The time was short and the trip to Vienna long (Map I). Upon arrival in Vienna, Jan had to report to the crowded Military Command Post in Hütteldorferstrasse—all of which did not leave much time for the cherished conjugal reunion; but the brevity made the time Jan and Božena had together even sweeter. Sorely missed was their little daughter Božena, barely three and a half months old, who was by then being cared for full-time by her maternal grandparents in Bohemia. Clearly, running the food store without Jan was proving to be almost more than Božena could manage.

For Jan this first home leave was a most useful learning experience. He discovered that with luck and a little daring, he could spend a full day, Sunday, with his wife without the precious home leave pass. Less than a week later, on December 30, he decided to test out his hunch. He received a "Sunday one-station pass," a military permit that entitled the bearer to travel from Olomouc Saturday evening to the next closest railroad station, in any direction, but no farther; and to leave Sunday evening in time to be back for duty early Monday morning.

Saturday evening Jan took the train all the way to Vienna. At the first station, Prostějov, he left the train with those getting off, hid in the darkness behind the train, and after the military police had passed through his railroad car, he jumped back on and returned to his compartment. When his fellow passengers on the crowded train found out what was going on, that this poor, lonely soldier was trying to visit his forlorn wife, they were eager to assist in every way possible. Whenever the warning came that a military patrol was approaching, Jan either jumped off when the train was at a station and waited out the inspection behind the train or behind the crowded platform, or, if the train was moving, hid beneath the long wooden benches of the third class carriage, protected from view by the voluminous, floor-length skirts of the kind and generous peasant women. In Vienna, Jan jumped off the train just as it was slowing down in the central station and disappeared in the crowds.

At home in the Fourth District he was warmly greeted not only by the happily surprised Božena but also by her younger brother Alois, who was stopping by on his way back from his leave in Bohemia en route to the Italian front. After a brief but joyful visit on Sunday, December 31, Jan left in the evening for Olomouc the same way he had arrived from there that morning. At 5 a.m. on Monday, New Year's Day, he reported back to the barracks, tired but happy.

It rained or snowed almost daily. From sun-up to sun-down the drills continued. The recruits' old Model Werndl single-shot rifles were replaced by brand-new, five round, magazine-fed rifles, 8 mm Mannlicher Model 95. The pressure to complete the basic training and have the troops depart for the front was mounting. In the barracks, on the parade grounds, on the large exercise grounds in the suburbs, and during the long forced marches in the countryside in full battle dress, the need to accelerate the process of preparedness and readiness for the front was constantly emphasized. Crawling in the mud under a barrage of live ammunition was now almost a daily occurrence, as were bayonet charges against straw dummies, exercises with live hand grenades, extended target practice with rifles and light machine guns, practicing wearing gas masks for lengthening periods of time, and horseback riding.

The stress and strain on the troops was beginning to show, and the numbers of men reporting sick grew. The diminishing food rations were not as yet a problem because food packages from home kept coming relatively often, but the pay and cigarette rations—6 kreuzer (about 15 cents, U.S.) and five cigarettes a day—did not go far. Come what may, Jan did manage to leave for Vienna on "Sunday one-station" passes as often as he could, thus escaping, incidentally, the obligatory regimental attendance at Catholic mass.

In the middle of January there was a call for volunteers for basic artillery training with heavy howitzers in Klosterneuburg, a town close to Vienna. Jan applied on the spot, not only to be closer to Božena but also because in a shooting war, the artillery was considered a much safer place than the infantry. When he found out that the training was only a temporary assignment and that, once trained, the volunteers would be returned to the infantry regiment, he felt cheated. He had made a bad mistake.

As luck would have it, Jan's body came to the rescue. His right heel began to swell and became increasingly painful. Jan could not walk and reported sick. In the infirmary the medics lanced the swelling, bandaged the foot, and confined Jan to barracks. When the order came for the volunteers to report for transport to Klosterneuburg, Jan was certifiably unable to comply.

Staff Sergeant Steiner, who was responsible for the Klosterneuburg detail, was "truly disgusted" with Jan, "the shameful malingerer." In order to find a replacement in a hurry, Steiner said that he had had "to pay a considerable bribe" to find a new "volunteer," which, of course, Jan was compelled to pay back. He never did.

A week later there was another call for volunteers, this time for permanent transfer to the mountain artillery regiment in Vienna. The need for artillery reinforcements at the Italian front was serious. Clearly, artillery was rapidly becoming more important than ever before. At the outset of the war the Austrian army was poised to continue to follow the German doctrinal model of mobile warfare: quick, strong, and sustained opening attacks on broad fronts. Highly trained and experienced career officers and NCOs, the backbone of the Imperial army, were ordered to mold the recruits and reservists into an efficient and effective part of a highly mobile war machine. However, the Austrian army lacked both the tradition of victories as well as the national homogeneity of the German army. Hard-pressed before long on all fronts, the Austrian High Command was forced to trade its offensive strategy of forward mobility for a defensive game plan of strong fire power. The need to build an artillery much larger in proportion to infantry than ever before became overwhelming. At this point it filtered down to Jan's infantry regiment with calls for volunteers to join the artillery. Jan volunteered again, in spite of his bandaged foot. Fed up, Staff Sergeant Steiner turned Jan down, "the nauseating cheat and swindler." What now?

The next day Božena, accompanied by Ludvík, arrived unexpectedly at the base to visit the ailing patient. The two were sent directly to the canteen, where Jan, on crutches, came to join them. Over coffee he told them the whole story. This time Ludvík came to the rescue. He knew well his own company commander, Lieutenant Venos; Ludvík and Venos had, in fact, been in business together before the war. It just so happened, luckily, that Venos was in charge of the volunteer artillery detail. Perhaps the lieutenant would help.

Venos could and did. Jan reported to him the next day, January 20. The lieutenant, over Steiner's vehement objections, assigned Jan to the volunteer detail and ordered him to report, together with the other nineteen volunteers, to the transfer and transport depot, from which they would leave on February 23 for Vienna. Jan could not believe his good fortune.

When his foot healed, he rejoined his platoon and resumed basic training. Steiner tried his best to make soldiering as tough for Jan as possible; he had the power and was diabolically inventive. Fortunately, Novotný was apprised of what was going on and kept a close eye on Steiner. One morning when Jan had to remake his bed 23 times without success, the lieutenant suddenly appeared like a *deus ex machina*. He sent Jan off and had it out with Steiner. From that day on, Steiner ignored Jan, and Jan's life was just about back to normal.

Several companies of the regiment, certified ready for the front, were leaving, one after another. To replace them new recruits arrived. For the rest, the drills continued. The weather became worse; the heavy snow melted during the day and froze solid at night. The company's new acting drill sergeant, König, a bear of a man who had been a game warden in civilian life, had a nice sense of humor. At a mock fixed bayonet attack in a large field near a wooded hill, the sergeant, leading the company, turned to the men and shouted, "Company! Advance in the direction of the man shitting in the field!" (*"Schwarmlinie vorwärts, Direktion der scheissende Mann!"*) And they all complied, delighted, despite the fact that "shit" was not in their Army Slav dictionary. The man in the field nearly suffered a heart attack.

In the final weeks before his departure for Vienna, Jan's soldiering in Olomouc went well. He had to obey Steiner's orders—orders were orders and had to be obeyed—but the two avoided each other as much as possible. Jan and Božena saw each other almost weekly, mostly in Vienna but also in Olomouc. Božena had problems with the food store and with the accounts. Food rationing was a headache for all concerned. Customers had to present proper ration cards to the shopkeepers for all the foodstuffs purchased, and the shopkeepers, after hours, had to process the cards, glue them into official ration books according to kinds and number codes, and present them, like cash, to the state-controlled food companies. Jan helped all he could, in person or by mail.

From her little village some fifty kilometers from Olomouc, Jan's old, widowed mother came to visit her two sons, Karel and Ludvík, their married sister Josefa, and Jan when she could, which was not often. To the delight of all, she invariably brought a suitcase full of koláče, the sweet buns topped with plum jam or other fillings that were the specialty of the region. In the evening the siblings often took their mother to a movie, a memorable treat for her.

Back at the base, thanks to Lieut. Novotný, Jan was now often assigned to kitchen duty. The chores were relatively easy and the food portions larger. Jan was almost sorry to leave Olomouc. (Jan found out later that the Thirteenth Landwehr Regiment had fought on the Eastern Front until July 1917, when it was transferred to Romania. In September 1917, it was transferred to Italy. It suffered severe losses on all three fronts.)

Artillery School. Vienna, February 24 - March 30
Imperial and Royal Landwehr Mountain Artillery Regiment No. 1, Third Reserve Battalion, Second Cannon Battery

Then came the departure. Except for their sidearms, the men turned in their rifles, cartridge boxes, ponchos, and other infantry equipment and reported ready. After rigorous basic training lasting thirteen weeks, the twenty volunteers were leaving for Vienna and five weeks of training in mountain artillery. They were excited. Not only was their imminent departure for the front postponed, but they were about to be trained for a less dangerous war assignment, or so they thought. The men considered themselves fortunate.

Jan knew the overnight train trip to Vienna by heart. This time they all slept the entire way; three eight-person, third class compartments had been reserved for them on a war-priority basis; they had plenty of space on the crowded train. In Vienna the volunteers were warmly greeted at the station by a Czech billet corporal, who marched them to their new regimental quarters, Kaiser Franz Jozef Kaserne, 3 Steinbruchstrasse in the Thirteenth District on the outskirts of the city. The barracks were recently built, one-story wooden structures, clean and heated.

With the assistance of the corporal, the new arrivals went through the necessary paperwork and orientation and were assigned their new billets. They received blankets and mattress covers to be filled with clean straw. They took showers and were for the first time deloused, a procedure which they did not need as yet. They were issued used artillery uniforms distinct from their old infantry tunics, which they were ordered to turn in mended, cleaned, and pressed. Their new uniforms had to be adjusted for size and fit, and mended, laundered, and pressed as well.

As the volunteers, all Czechs, soon discovered, the regiment was composed almost entirely of German-speaking Austrians, mostly Viennese, a basic difference from Olomouc, where the regiment was composed of Czech enlisted men only. Formally, this was no problem—in both places all commands and instructions were in German; but effectively the difference was enormous. Its impact on the twenty Czech newcomers was chilling. Their perception of the new setting as not entirely friendly was not completely wrong. They clung to each other like exiles in a foreign land.

For Jan, who was used to living among the Viennese, this was an opportunity to be of help to his Czech comrades as well as to the German-speaking majority, particularly the NCOs. Also, being older than most of the enlisted men and at 26 closer in age to the NCOs, he became the unofficial translator, communicator, and spokesman for his group.

The Third Battalion of the First Regiment of the Imperial and Royal Landwehr Mountain Artillery was composed of three separate batteries, each capable of independent engagement in battle. Each was provided with four 75 mm mountain cannons Model Škoda 1915, which were considered a technological triumph for the Škoda factory in Pilsen, Bohemia; reputedly they were the best mountain guns of that caliber in the world at that time. They were able to fire faster, farther, and more accurately than their opposite numbers, and they were relatively light and thus appropriate for mountains, where transport was difficult and targets were mostly within easy range. Their weight was 620 kg in battle position; their gun barrels were 1,155 mm long and their maximum range 7,000 meters. They were transported on two-wheel carts drawn by single horses; in the mountains, they were disassembled to fit into eight special leather saddle bags that were strapped and mounted on eight pack horses or mules. Two additional horses carried the ammunition for each cannon, twelve shells weighing 6.5 kilos each, packed into four three-shell boxes weighing almost 20 kilos each. Later, this supply of ammunition proved completely inadequate in battle conditions, when often each gun routinely fired 400 shells or more a day.

Each battery consisted of a full complement of men, pack animals, carts, and wagons. There were about 86 men total (later augmented to as many as 130 men). Sixteen were in charge of the four guns and eight in charge of the 36 pack animals, this comprising the first or front line. The reserve or support line, usually positioned behind the front in a well-sheltered area, consisted of four medics; a changing number of men in charge of ammunition, repairs, supplies, inventories, and provisions; cooks; telephone operators; field observers; various clerks; and, of course, the officers, normally a captain and two lieutenants, in command of the battery and in charge of administration.

Jan was assigned to the Second Battery. The daily routine now included lectures, seminars, and hands-on training with the guns; working with the horses; training in field telephone communication; basic medical and first aid training; working with different kinds of field glasses as field observers who would direct and monitor the battery fire; and participation in the Chargenschule, an NCO training school for enlisted men chosen for possible advancement in function, position and/or rank, in which Jan was included. All this was in addition, of course, to the daily drills on the barracks parade grounds, forced marches, exercises with their new/used carbines (a shorter and lighter Mannlicher Model 1895K), kitchen duty, and the never-ending sweeping, cleaning, scrubbing, washing and polishing. Sundays were free, except for the obligatory attendance at mass, a welcome difference from Olomouc. Jan received permission, as did all the other Viennese, to sleep at home when not on duty, a privilege he cherished. Home was a mere streetcar ride away from the base, and soldiers traveled free.

On March 21, the battalion's First Battery left for a four-week field exercise in the Austrian Alps. The Second Battery was to follow in ten days. The men received new uniforms and new field gear, including backpacks, blankets, and new dog tags. Jan's dog tag, an identity document folded and tucked into a small, flat brass case 3 x 5 cm., was to be carried in the uniform's left breast pocket. Jan filled in the required information in indelible pencil: name, rank, serial number, birthplace, birthdate (March 4, 1890), religion (Roman Catholic), year of induction into the army, regiment and battery number, the name and address of closest relative (Božena), and whether inoculated against cholera (yes). There was also space for a short message. Jan wrote: "Please send my notebook, wallet, and my watch to my wife." In addition, the document included spaces to be filled in later in the event the bearer was killed: the date and place of burial and the volume, page number, and date of the army official Book of Death where this information was recorded.

The schooling and drills continued and now included numerous inspections—of the men, of the guns, ammunition, horses, carts and wagons, field kitchens, telephones, medical and surgical supplies, among others. The enlisted men were then divided, according to their responsibilities, to serve in the first (battle) line or second (supply) line. Jan was assigned to the first line as a gunner.

The battery was scheduled to leave Vienna on March 30. On the 28th and 29th the men were to be confined to barracks with no communication with the outside. In the evening of March 27 Jan went home for the last time. He did not have the heart to tell Božena of his impending departure, but would she guess it from his new field uniform? Fortunately, she did not. Early the next morning Jan made himself a small food packet, filled his field water bottle with red wine, kissed Božena good-bye, and left as usual. He forgot the canteen at home.

On March 30 the battery marched to the Penzing Railroad Station with all its guns, horses, carts and wagons. A friend and future brother-in-law, Franz Dubový, a butcher with the regimental slaughterhouse, which remained at the base, came to the station to say good-bye to Jan. In conversation Jan mentioned the forgotten wine. Right away Dubový took the streetcar to the couple's home, picked up the field bottle without alarming Božena, and delivered the wine to Jan. From the station Jan sent Božena a postcard which said farewell as gently as he could.

But Božena had begun to suspect the truth and acted quickly. She took the streetcar to the base, only to learn that the Second Battery had already left for the station. Panicked, she took the streetcar to the station, only to discover that the transport train had come and gone. Devastated, Božena returned home. Why hadn't he told her?

Deep in her heart she knew why, as she told Jan later. Surely the departure of the battery was a secret, and "the enemy might be listening." She knew instinctively that Jan did not want to spoil their last time together to sadden her unnecessarily—the Austrian Alps, after all, were not the front. But the most compelling reason of all, she was certain, was that her strong, dependable, stalwart Jan could not bear the sight of her tears, was in fact terrified by them. She knew, too, that she would hear from him soon. And she did.

Field Artillery Training. Imst in Tyrol, April 3 - May 3

Traveling in boxcars on a freight train—men, guns, horses, carts and wagons—it took the Second Battery two full days and two nights to cross Austria from east to west, from Vienna via Salzburg and Innsbruck to Imst (Map I). The town, a lovely, bucolic Alpine center, was located in Tyrol, a high mountain region in Western Austria not far from the Swiss border, which at that time was an Austrian Crown Land. It was selected by the Austrian High Command as a suitable field training base for the kind of operations a new mountain artillery unit was expected to perform in the upcoming battles on the Italian front.

The battery was billeted in a local school. After getting settled, the men, under the direction of their NCOs, sorted out their equipment and prepared alphabetical lists of the personnel, those who would be involved in which parts of the battle line as well as the supply and reserve line units. On paper, at least, the component parts of the entire battery—men, animals, equipment, supplies—were identified and consolidated for the common purpose of starting the field training in earnest.

By engaging in mock battles in the adjacent valleys, hills, mountains and forests, the overriding purpose of the battery command was to forge the battery into a single, integrated, independent, efficient battle unit. When the need arose, the men in the reserve line—including cooks, telephone operators, clerks, orderlies, horse drivers, and other auxiliary personnel—were expected to serve as combatants, not only assisting the gunners but performing as machine gun crews, sappers, field observers, sharpshooters, and even gun and ammunition carriers, should horses not be available.

The men now put to use what they had learned in theory in Vienna. Dismantling and assembling the guns; digging slit trenches, dugouts and foxholes; and skillful handling of the packhorses became part of the daily, and often nightly routine. The battery was beginning to shape up as a unit.

The weather was good for an Alpine April. The low-lying meadows, freshly green again, glistened in the sun, and colorful wildflowers were beginning to show. The air was cool. There was still plenty of snow and ice above the valleys. Whenever he found the time, Jan liked to hike in the surrounding countryside and marvel at the views, panoramas very attractive to a flatlander, which he was. One day on a long walk in the foothills, he came upon a large eagles' nest built of twigs and short branches, perched on a tall fir tree growing at the top of a cliff. There were three or four very young eaglets in the nest, their downy heads bobbing up from time to time. Drawing closer, quietly and unobtrusively Jan was able to observe the patience and gentleness of the parents in feeding their hungry young. From then on, armed with a pair of field glasses he found the way to his secret observation point often. He loved the wonder of that rare experience and told no one of his precious discovery.

Meanwhile, the reality of the approaching front was beginning to take hold. Like many others, Jan bought himself a pocket watch in an iron case with an alarm mechanism and a fluorescent display, which served him well later on. He had left behind with Božena the beautiful silver pocket watch which his oldest brother, Josef, had bequeathed to him, his favorite little brother, when he committed suicide with his girlfriend Marie. Her parents had forbidden Marie to marry Josef because he was too poor; the young couple chose death over separation. At the time Jan was a boy-apprentice cabinet maker in the village of Pískov. He treasured that watch.

Like many others, Jan had his handlebar mustache recut into a short, practical version. In fact, when Božena came for a week-long visit on April 18, "to see what Tyrol looked like," as she put it, without his "Franz Josef" mustache she could not recognize him at first in the crowd of soldiers waiting at the station. They all looked alike.

Like other young wives and girlfriends, Božena stayed in a village hotel, and the two spent as much time together as Jan could spare away from the demands of the battery. When he showed her the eagles' nest, she was as delighted and awestruck as he was. It made them both homesick for their little daughter, whom Božena had decided by then to leave for the duration of the war with her parents in Bohemia. Early on she discovered, to her dismay, that even with hired help it was difficult if not impossible for a single mother with a small baby to run a store in war-torn Vienna, in a food-rationed economy with all of its voluminous and involved paperwork. She visited her baby daughter as often as she could.

In the morning of April 27, the name day of the Austrian Empress Elizabeth, the battery marched to the village church for a solemn mass. In the afternoon the soldiers stood at attention on the parade grounds and listened to the speech of the battery commander, Captain Müller, celebrating the Empress on her special day. Jan chafed at the length of the ceremony. He was impatient to be with Božena.

Early the following morning, with his sergeant's permission Jan took Božena to the railroad station and saw her off. The long-awaited week with his beloved now seemed incredibly short. He fully appreciated the effort it must have taken her to make all the necessary arrangements to leave the store and come to Imst. He was grateful. The visit gave him new strength and helped him to clear his mind. He was apprehensive about the battery's impending departure for the front, of course; they all were. But strangely enough, in a sense he was also looking forward to it. After six months of intensive training, he felt fit and ready to face the unknown. Deep down, however, he wondered how he would react to the challenges on the battlefield; would he have the stamina to endure the hardships and emerge alive and well to return to his wife and child? He was almost eager to put his character and his manhood to the test.

And yet, Jan was in some ways a loyal skeptic. It was in his character to want to be conscientious, reliable, responsible, and trustworthy in whatever endeavor he was committed to, cabinet-making or soldiering. At the same time he was a watchful observer. He performed conventional roles and fulfilled traditional expectations with patience, but often with a twinge of self-deprecating humor. Like many others in the spring of 1917, he had his doubts—about the war, its conduct, its duration, and frankly its purpose. Could the glittering pomp and circumstance of the old Habsburg Empire cope with the sobering reality of a drawn-out, uncertain war? Jan was not sure.

Six days later, early in the morning of May 3, while engaged in complex, holistic battle exercises in the mountains above Imst, the Second Battery received urgent orders to depart immediately for the Italian front. By late afternoon they were already packed into boxcars on a freight train and moving toward their destination. The departure drill worked without a hitch.

II
THE ITALIAN CAMPAIGN: THE ISONZO FRONT

Baptism by Fire
Mount Barbara, May 6 - 10

From Imst the battery traveled east by way of Innsbruck and Schwarzach-St. Veit, where both men and horses were fed the following morning, May 4. The train then continued south via Villach into Slovenia to Santa Lucia/Most na Soči and Baška grapa, which was adjacent to the Klavže railroad station, the major Austrian war depot in the area for supplies, storage, administration, and reserves (Map I). Baška grapa and Podmelec, Jan soon discovered, were the key entry points for the Austrian armed forces fighting along the Isonzo/Soča River perimeter on the Italian front in the rugged area of the Banjška planota/Bainsizza. This was a large, hilly plateau, a maze of low mountains and high ridges on the Austrian side of the Italian-Austrian border located about 50 km west of Ljubljana/Laibach, the capital of Slovenia, and bounded by the towns of Grgar in the south, Čepovan and Lokve in the east, S. Lucia in the north, and the Isonzo River in the west (Map II).

The whole Isonzo front was some 86 km long and extended from the Adriatic Sea to the town of Bovec/Plezzo/Flitsch north of Kobarid/Caporetto, and from the Banjška Plateau south to the strongly fortified area of Gorizia/Gorica/Görz, and from there south to the plateau of the Carso/Kras/Karst, a vast badlands of hills and sharp rocks adjacent to the Gulf of Trieste (Map II). Only two railroads, the one that Jan arrived on from Imst in the north, and the other from Ljubljana to Trieste in the south, and a few narrow roads connected the Isonzo front in Slovenia with the major artillery depots of the Dual Monarchy in Austria north of Slovenia.

In Baška grapa after midnight, the men unloaded all the equipment and horses from the train and marched some fifteen hours south to the reserve line at Špilenca/Špilnik in the region of Čepovanska dolina, where they slept (Map III). In the morning of May 6 the battery left for the front. The men sent the bulk of their gear and supplies by aerial cableway to Dol, a hamlet located near the village Kal nad Kanalom, the intermediate reserve line just below the designated battle position of the battery and thus protected from enemy shelling.

The wartime mountain aerial cableways were installations in which one or several cars traveled on an inclined cable track hauled by a steel wire cable that was driven by an engine at one of the two cable stations, upper or lower, where loading and unloading took place. Electricity was generally used for driving the cableway, with the energy being supplied by power-generating units consisting of a high pressure diesel engine and an electric generator. The Imperial and Royal High Command adopted the aerial cable transport on a wide scale for conveying weapons, munitions, gear, and wounded soldiers in mountain military operations.

The battery reached Dol in the afternoon, picked up the guns, ammunition, and the gear for the battle line, and waited for the protection of darkness. After 9 p.m. the front-line group—the gunners, the observers, telephone operators, medics, supply men, and all the packhorses with their heavy loads and drivers—left for the battle station on the mountain. "Barbara" was the mountain's code name; no one knew for certain its real name. On the steep path up the mountain slope the men came under Italian fire for the first time. The six rounds that greeted them unnerved the men but fortunately did no damage.

The position assigned to the battery was located on the side of the mountain facing the enemy below, a rather exposed and dangerous place, or so it seemed to the men. In Vienna and in Imst they had been told repeatedly that while "open" positions might have to be occupied on occasion, they were to be avoided since they could be quickly obliterated by hostile fire. As a rule, positions were to be concealed from direct view and from air observation behind a ridge or cover of trees, the elevation and direction necessary to hit the target to be determined by the battery observers, not by direct observation from the position.

In the darkness the men unloaded the parts of the four guns stored in the saddle bags of the horses, assembled them, and set the guns up in firing positions. The horses with their drivers were sent back to Dol. At daybreak, in order to estimate the range, they fired eight ranging rounds, two by each gun, bracketing and framing the targets to determine both the elevation at which the greatest possible number of shells would hit the target as well as the line for the lateral direction of the fire. The two ranging searches were carried out simultaneously. Then they fired several rounds for effect to test their reckoning.

After these preliminaries, they set up the observation post, dug protective trenches for the officers, men, and ammunition, built a dugout for the command post, set up telephone lines, and dug latrines. They had practiced these operations many times in Imst. In its battle position, the battery again became part of the First Artillery Regiment: though separated from each other, all three batteries of the

The Italian Campaign: The Isonzo Front

Third Reserve Battalion were now stationed in the same sector of the front, each independent but all under unified command.

On May 9 two officers came to inspect the battery, a major from the regiment in the morning and a colonel from the division in the afternoon. Apparently, according to the battery commander, Capt. Müller, both found everything in relatively good order and ready for battle ("...more or less," said Müller).

For the next two days the battery fired for effect at various enemy targets. But by then the Italian artillery had found the range of their new targets as well, so now both sides shot intermittently at each other. This was the battery's first taste of battle, and for this reason, the men concluded, their rations that day included a quarter liter of wine and an eighth liter of rum. Nonetheless, some men were trembling, some praying, and all were quite pale—or was it green? It gradually dawned upon them that the enemy was shooting at each and every one of them personally. What a discovery! "An oncoming shell would begin as a distant hum, that grew into an approaching buzz, that escalated into the sound of a reverberating gong, and then the earth exploded. The shock waves resonated in our very bones," Jan writes. Fear enveloped them like a dense fog. Crouching behind the protective shields of their cannons, they absorbed it; only shame kept them from running away. "Simply put," Jan remarked, "we did not feel good.... Everyone longed for the ordeal to be over with soon, and mercifully it was."

In the evening of May 10, a regimental order relayed by telephone to Capt. Müller instructed the battery to move that same night to a new position close to the small village of Avšje, where an Italian offensive was expected at any moment. The men did not know what to think. On the one hand, the two days of hard labor to set up the present position were wasted. On the other hand, the new position might be safer, less exposed to enemy fire. Just before departure, the men were issued gas masks. The level of their apprehension rose.

Battle in Earnest
Avšje, May 11 - 26
May 12: The Tenth Battle of the Isonzo begins.

It took the battery crew longer to dismantle their guns, pack them and the ammunition boxes on the horses, and leave, than it took to move to the new location, even in the darkness of a moonless night on a narrow, winding, mountain trail. The new position was situated on a steep ledge high above and overlooking the Isonzo River, which here had the effect of a no-man's-land dividing the two armies. In front of the battery and almost directly below them in the river valley and parallel to the river were several rows of infantry trenches, Austrian on the battery side of the river and Italian on the other side. Behind the battery extended the trenches of the Austrian infantry reserves. The Italian trenches were only about 800 meters across the river from the battery.

The new battle station was a well-established, strongly built position. The damage from previous bombardments was light. The men set up the guns in the existing gun placements. These were enclosed, fortified dugouts, buttressed and roofed with logs and provided with gun slits arranged in such a way that the guns would command, jointly, the whole perimeter of the battle sector below, thus overcoming the limitations of the terrain. Except for direct hits, the simple bunkers protected the guns and their crews from the incoming enemy artillery fire, both grenades and shrapnel. But the sound of their own gunfire in the enclosed space was deafening. To protect their eardrums from bursting while shooting, the men pried their mouths open by chewing on matchsticks or toothpicks. Sometimes nothing would help, and later two gunners would have to be evacuated with ruptured eardrums.

Once the guns were in shooting position, the battery began to fire, 80 rounds to start with, to make sure that all four guns established ranges pronto. At the same time the men worked quickly to repair and improve the dugouts and the trenches for the officers, for themselves, and for the ammunition supplies. Tired, hungry, and sleepy, they were nonetheless motivated by the fact that it was in their own interest to increase the overall safety of the place.

At first the Italian batteries fired only sporadically. It was rumored that they were preparing for a really big offensive. Italian observer planes were busily combing the skies, apparently photographing and reporting back to the Italian artillery command the exact locations of the Austrian forces and their dispositions along the whole front. There was also a tethered Italian observation balloon far enough away to be out of range but close and high enough to view the Austrian lines and to direct the enemy fire accordingly. At night Italian searchlights worked the Austrian positions systematically; the men of the battery learned quickly to become invisible by arresting all movement when the lights were on them.

On May 12, twenty-four hours after their arrival and exactly one hour after midnight, the Italian offensive started. This was the beginning of the Italian Tenth Battle of the Isonzo.

* * * *

The Italian Campaign: The Isonzo Front

In 1914 Italy had not been ready for war. When the government announced in August 1914 that Italy would remain neutral, Italians were very much relieved. In 1915, however, the situation had changed. Worried that staying out of the war would be much more costly than joining the "right" side; tempted by the Franco-British offer of rich spoils if Italy joined the Allies; and assuming, as did all the combatants on both sides, that the war would be short and victorious, Italy, this time with broad popular support, declared war in May, 1915, on her hereditary enemy, Austria.

The new Italian-Austrian front ran along the whole Austrian-Italian border, the entire length of the Alps from Switzerland in the west to the Slovenian plain bordering on the Adriatic Sea in the east (Map B). The Italians had launched their major offensives in 1915 and again in 1916 in the east, along and over the river Isonzo, hoping to capture the city of Trieste situated in the northeastern angle of the Adriatic. Trieste was the only salt-water port of the Habsburg Empire, but it was a coveted prize for the Italians, too: two-thirds of the population of Trieste were Italians. In the west, the Italians attacked the Austrians on the Trentino front in a region of high Alpine peaks, but in severe weather conditions and heavy fighting they were repulsed there just as they were on the Isonzo. But the Austrians lost out in 1916, too, when they launched a heavy offensive of their own on the Trentino front, in south Tyrol, hoping to break through the Italian forces, cut them off, and march from the mountains to the plain of Venice.

When Jan arrived in the Isonzo sector in May 1917, the Italian front was at a standstill. Both sides had tried and both had failed to overrun their adversaries. As was true elsewhere in World War I, the defense had the advantage over the offense most of the time.

For two years, in the nine Battles of the Isonzo, the Italians had doggedly attacked the Austrians across the river in ever increasing numbers and suffered ever larger losses for tiny gains here and there. Although it is true that the Italians had fewer heavy guns at their disposal than the Austrians and were constrained to fight in the open and uphill against the defenders, the terrain favored the Austrians, who were hidden in ramparts and deep dugouts on crests of the mountains and hills that dominated the east side of the Isonzo along most of the front. But the Austrians suffered heavy losses, too, in this day-to-day war of attrition, a fruitless, no-win, bloody see-saw.

* * * *

To begin this Tenth Battle of the Isonzo, Italian batteries opened fire simultaneously on the whole front. Shrapnel, grenades, and mortar shells of various types and calibers, short range as well as long range, incendiary and armor-piercing, and rounds and rounds of heavy machine gun fire rained on the Austrian troops—on the infantry, artillery, and on the reserve and supply lines. The noise was overwhelming. This was the "drumfire" they had all heard about, a gunfire so heavy and so continuous as to sound like the beating of thousands of huge drums, a thunderous barrage designed to demoralize the enemy, hamper his communication, and destroy his bunkers, dugouts, trenches, and the barbed wire entanglements protecting the trenches. In addition to frightening and killing as many of the enemy as possible, the attackers were instilling courage in their own infantry for the heavy fighting ahead.

The Austrian artillery, alert and ready, responded along the whole front promptly and with resolution, thus adding to the pandemonium. The give-and-take continued on both sides; the double drumfire maintained its ferocity without a break. In the evening a thunderstorm accompanied by heavy rain and strong winds added to the drama and the misery. The men were dazed by the intensity of the simultaneous attack on all their senses. Well-trained soldiers, they ceased to think and responded like automatons. Still, the battery's supply detail managed to travel that night to and from the supply line, bringing plenty of ammunition and two days' worth of rations as well: cold, unappetizing, watery soup with red cabbage and a small piece of meat (which the men called *"Drahtverhau,"* "wire garbage"), five cigarettes, and, as was apparently usual before an offensive, double rations of wine and rum. The seriousness of the enemy offensive was affirmed by yet another double ration of rum that was available to all those who asked for it. Everybody did, and they thought they felt better.

The bombardment continued, night and day. The gun crews of Jan's battery, soaked to the skin, painfully cold, and sleep-deprived, continued to fire around the clock. Some men in the reserve line went to the small village of Levpa to practice throwing hand grenades. Should the Italian infantry break through the Austrian lines, the plan was to pummel the Italians with hand grenades from the battery position. Returning to the battery from the exercise, the men brought with them a goodly supply of hand grenades for that purpose, hiding them in deep trenches.

Taking turns, the gun crews slept when they could. Everyone was beginning to get edgy. The losses along the front were mounting but as yet had not much affected the Austrian artillery. At the battery, only three men had been wounded severely enough to be sent back to the dressing station.

The heavy double barrage, Italian and Austrian, continued almost without pause. The supply people now had to concentrate solely on ammunition. For rations the battery sent its own detail to the supply line. The round trip, under constant enemy fire, took almost three hours. Those on ration detail were not only sorely missed at the guns, but they also lost out on their own rest. Inevitably, the food was late, cold, sometimes spoiled, and always meager. Supplying food to their own fighting men was the Austrian command's Achilles' heel. The Austrian troops were reduced to 30 grams (one ounce) of meat per day, while the Germans reportedly received a munificent daily ration of 180 grams (6 ounces).

In the evening of May 14, despite heavy Austrian shrapnel shelling, Italian sappers did manage to build two sturdy-looking pontoon bridges across the Isonzo at Doblar (Map III). That night wave after wave of Italian infantry attacked. At first the advance petered out due to the concentration of the Austrian bombardment and the barrage of heavy machine guns and accurate rifle fire. The sharp light provided by a profusion of illuminating flares and white star shells of high intensity swinging slowly down to earth helped the defenders to stand their ground. But then after several failed attempts, two Italian infantry battalions, despite heavy losses, managed to cross the Isonzo. Once there, however, instead of attacking the Austrian infantry positions, the Italians dug themselves in, in front of the Austrian trenches, to wait for reinforcements. In their shallow foxholes and shell craters, they were easy targets for the Austrian artillery.

At 5 p.m. the next day, May 15, the Austrian infantry counter-attacked. Under a barrage of enemy fire, the men had to turn back, but not before destroying one of the two bridges. The Italians mounted another attack, only to be repelled. The next morning the Austrian infantry counter-attacked again, this time chasing the few remaining Italians back across the Isonzo.

On May 16 the artillery fire slowed down on both sides: after four days and four nights the drumfire ceased. The exhaustion was universal. Still, in the evening, the desperate Italians attacked again and reinforced that attack the following morning, May 17. They managed to hold their position on the Austrian side of the river bank, but this time, pressing their advantage, they attacked the Austrian infantrymen in the trenches and battled it out with rifles, hand grenades, trench knives, sharpened trench spades, and bayonets. At the end of the relentless bloodbath, the Austrians managed to drive the attackers back across the Isonzo. By then, the craters on both banks of the river were filled with bodies. The men on both sides had to listen helplessly to the heart-breaking cries of their wounded and dying comrades.

After this battle, enemy observation planes appeared again and continued their activities during the day, while at night searchlights, parachute flares, and star rockets illuminated the barren landscape without pity. But for all practical purposes the situation had again stabilized into a standstill, no gain–no loss trench warfare. The Italian offensive had not succeeded. Would it ever succeed?

The next day, May 18, the status quo continued: the front was relatively quiet. Jan's battery was able to take care of its wounded (6) and dead (2) and to replenish its major needs—new men to replace the dead and wounded, more ammunition, and food. Jan was put in charge of ammunition procurement; his predecessor had been wounded and evacuated. His duty was to ensure that adequate quantities of shrapnel and grenade shells were safely stored in the battery *cavernas* (rock caves) for immediate use at all times, and to monitor the supply of ammunition at the arsenal depot. The ammunition was now delivered to the guns twice every night; in addition, the gunners kept a generous supply directly in the position. Jan made sure that the ammunition details carried back to the reserve line the empty shells and ammunition boxes that had accumulated in large piles all around the battery.

The following day, May 19, under the umbrella of heavy Italian cannon barrage the Italian infantry attacked once again, but the half-hearted effort spent itself and petered out before doing any damage. It was, it seemed, the tail end of the Italian offensive. From then on, except for occasional exchanges of gunfire, both the Italian and Austrian artilleries remained quiet.

Fighter planes, however, became active on both sides. Once, directly above the battery, two Austrian fighters attacked an Italian plane but failed to shoot it down. Another time, a whole squadron of Italian fighters challenged a squadron of Austrian planes for air supremacy over the battleground; the Austrian response was to disappear from the sky. Several battery gunners took carbine potshots at the Italian planes. One of the planes, pretending to be hit, fell to about sixty meters above the battery, only to level off, take photographs of the well-masked Austrian position, and fly away.

At night the battery gunners tried repeatedly to put out the troubling Italian searchlights located in front of the Italian artillery positions but well-hidden in hilly terrain in a forest of small trees. The problem was that the moment the searchlight crews saw the flashes of the Austrian guns, they switched off the lights, making any calculation of accuracy—of hits and misses—all but impossible. In the end, the gunners managed to hit one of the searchlights—by luck, not by skill.

In between, the men kept receiving their usual 48 hour rations of food, cigarettes, wine, rum, and occasionally even a piece of soap. The field post also delivered free printed postcards to the crews, seven per person, to be mailed to relatives and friends. The text, printed in the twelve languages of the Empire, was simple: "I am alive and well." The sender had only to add his signature and to address them.

One evening the order was "strict readiness" for all; another Italian attack was expected by the High Command. But nothing happened, and the men went back to improving their individual dugouts and trenches, repairing their boots, mending their uniforms, and doing the "small" laundry, their underwear and socks. Those who were not on duty slept well. Even the weather was good.

Unexpectedly, two colonels from the divisional command arrived independently to inspect and review the gun crews, one in the morning and one in the evening. They both praised the men for blocking the concerted enemy offensive. Their reward: each man received two small packets of tobacco from the first colonel, and two cigarettes apiece from the second. And for those veterans who had been in the front line for ten months or more, the colonels had a special prize: permission to apply for a bronze Medal of Valor. The men, wryly amused, muttered obscenities.

Sunday, May 26, the lull continued. The gun crews worked on improving the shelter cover on the ammunition bunker. Jan received a food package from Božena and shared the bounty: mazanec (a sweet, eggy, round-shaped raisin loaf traditional at Easter), koláče (filled sweet buns), a jar of drippings, dry sausage, cigarettes, and coffee. In the afternoon, not entirely unexpected, an order arrived for the battery to move "on the double" to a new position on the front, where presumably another Italian offensive was being mounted. The number of the regiment was officially changed from 1 to 201.

The dismantling of the four guns, packing them and the ammunition boxes in the saddle bags of the packhorses, and then reloading everything in the supply line below onto carts and wagons, were established routines by now. By 8 p.m. the men were ready. At 10 p.m., after dark, they set out.

"Slaughter"
Monte Ermada, May 31 - July 6
The Tenth Battle of the Isonzo ended June 8.

On May 26, the battery marched (and rode) the whole night via Škodniky, Levpa, and Kal nad Kanalom back to Špilenca, where the men loaded all their heavy equipment onto an aerial cableway. After a late breakfast they set off north on foot by way of Ravne and Santa Lucia/Most na Soči to Bača pri Modreju (Map III). Weary and wet—it had rained heavily most of the way—the men were ready to collapse. They were assigned to empty barracks to sleep on bare wooden platforms—after a hot dinner, for which they were grateful.

In the morning of May 28 the battery moved, still in heavy rain, to the Klavže railroad station at Baška grapa, the large war supply depot, where it rejoined the other two batteries of the regiment. Together they loaded their gear and animals onto a military freight train, boarded, and took off south via Ljubljana/Laibach to Prosecco/Prosenec/Prosek, northwest of the port city of Trieste and close to the Adriatic seacoast (Map II). There they unloaded their guns and ammunition from the train onto mules, which, unlike horses, were said to be able to carry heavy loads—even a gun barrel weighing 120 kg—on the steepest and narrowest of mountain passes. "The Austrian army has learned something," the men commented among themselves.

A separate unit once more, the battery rode and walked through cherry orchards laden with ripe, inviting fruit, which the men picked and enjoyed. The next stop was Aurisina/Nabrezina, the reserve and supply line, where they ate a hot meal and received a three-day supply of food. Afterwards, the front-line personnel with their mules and drivers waited for the cover of darkness to move up to their advance position on Monte Ermada/Grmada/Hermada, located on the rocky, barren Carso/Kras/Karst plateau some ten kilometers northwest, which overlooked the town of Monfalcone and guarded the road to Trieste (Map II). Later that evening, they set out for M. Ermada but daybreak caught them well before they reached their exposed destination. In turning back, they had to share the steep, narrow path with returning infantrymen, walking wounded as well as medics and their helpers, carrying loaded stretchers to the field hospital in Aurisina. The front-line was "a real slaughterhouse," the returnees reported.

Back in Aurisina, dazed from exhaustion, hungry, and unwashed since they left Baška grapa, the men collapsed. Six hours later they were awakened and fed. They washed themselves as well as they could; the more ambitious among them washed their laundry, too, but water was scarce. Jan marveled that a food package from home had found him there. At 8 p.m. they started out again for their position on M. Ermada. This time, after a tough and narrow ascent they reached their destination before dawn—and came under enemy fire immediately.

The Italians knew the location well, had established the range to perfection, and had much improved with practice. Jan's battery predecessors had apparently suffered such heavy losses here in a short time that they were forced to evacuate the position well before their replacements arrived. The gunnery area was full of debris, shell holes large and small, unexploded shells, and, in shocking disarray, even the broken bodies of dead artillery men still lying where they had been felled. "The sour smell of death hung heavy over the abandoned position," Jan writes. The men considered the odds of staying alive. Were they, too, here to be sacrificed? It was May 31, 1917, still the Tenth Battle of the Isonzo.

The battery was located below the top of M. Ermada on a small plateau rising sharply above the adjacent area and dominating a slope ending, ultimately, in a large valley below. There, again, the Austrian infantry trenches hugging the slope faced the Italian trenches farther down the valley. M. Ermada, an elevated natural fortress 323 meters high, was not only an outstanding artillery position but an excellent all-around observation point as well. To the battery's right was the city of Gorizia, a strongly fortified Austrian bridgehead which the Italians had taken in August 1916, and thus had established a bridgehead of their own on the Austrian side of the river. The Italians had pushed the Austrians slowly back in the center part of the Isonzo front, between the Banjška Plateau that Jan's regiment had just left and the Carso. On the battery's left was the Adriatic coast and the port city of Trieste, the Italian operational objective from the start of the war, which the Italians had not succeeded in taking as yet. Behind Gorizia in the north were the snow-covered peaks of the Julian Alps.

Above the battery's four guns and just behind the top of the hill were several barracks that had been built by the evacuated Austrian reserve infantry. There the men had rested briefly before moving to their position—and discovered, to their disgust, that the huts were heavily infested with lice! The battery commander left a hapless observer in the huts to direct the battery fire, but the men shunned that particular place from then on.

Behind and to the left of the battery was a deep, natural cave, which proved later to be a godsend. It was a good place to store reserve ammunition, but it was too far from the guns for the storage of the shells needed during a battle. For that purpose there was a large wooden ammunition box located in front of the battery on a ledge just large enough to hold it—there was no other suitable place on the small plateau. The danger was evident; a direct hit would blow the whole battery to smithereens. While the position itself was somewhat protected by overhanging rocks, bushes, broken trees and tree stumps on both sides, by the ledge in front, and by the curvature of the terrain, the enemy knew its location well, "too well," according to the men. Something would have to be done about that box and perhaps about the location of the battery as well.

The next day, June 1, the battery, under intermittent enemy shelling, continued to fire to find its several ranges. But the men, the NCOs, and the officers were all uneasy. It was clear that their position was precarious.

Having carefully scouted the adjacent areas during the day, the battery commander, Captain Müller, ordered the battery to move during the night all the guns and the ammunition some eighty meters to the right and below their position, where there happened to be a relatively small, rocky, flat shelf. In the open and completely exposed and unprotected, it was directly above and opposite enemy positions. The captain gambled that the enemy would be fooled by this maneuver; how could they believe that a sane commander would ever place his battery directly in harm's way?

The gunners moved to the new position and dug out shallow trenches for the four guns, the ammunition, the officers, and the crew. At midnight and under medium shelling, the supply detail from Aurisina found the new location and delivered both ammunition and food rations to the battery. A double ration of rum was included this time, confirming the expected continuation of the enemy's tenth offensive. Jan and his helpers distributed shells to individual guns and stored the rest in a trench behind the guns. The cave in the old position would still be used for ammunition overflow.

Early the next morning the enemy cannonade increased. In addition to the artillery barrage, the Austrian positions were bombarded by heavy Italian naval guns from ships in the Gulf of Trieste. Fortunately, the large caliber shells (up to 25 cm) and mortar bombs came in high above the battery and either exploded harmlessly on the mountain or somersaulted down without exploding.

The battery gunners were still finding their respective ranges and just beginning to fire for effect when at 3 p.m., June 3, the dreaded enemy drumfire began again along the whole front. The enemy offensive was on—a continuation of the same Tenth Battle of the Isonzo the men had undergone on the Avšje front. The firing became so intense that the battery commander ordered the crew to abandon the position temporarily and retreat into the cave. There was no alternative. The men responded quickly and rested in the cave until dark.

Twelve hours later, at 3 a.m. the following morning, June 4, the Italian infantry attacked along the whole front. The Austrian artillery responded with a heavy defensive barrage, a drumfire of its own. Jan's battery joined in and kept firing as rapidly as it could, using high explosive shells as well as shrapnel. When the guns became too hot, the gunners took turns letting one gun at a time cool off so that the shell would not explode before leaving the barrel, while the other three guns kept firing. Since there was no water to be had, the men routinely urinated on the gun barrels to cool them.

The Italian infantry, in spite of the rolling barrage of the Austrian artillery, gained ground in the no-man's-land but failed to overrun the Austrian trenches. Both the Austrian and Italian walking wounded and Italian POWs began arriving at the battery position. The busy gunners kept sending them to the rear. Unnoticed, a low-flying Italian airplane circled the battery and dropped three bombs on their position before the men had time to run for cover. Seeing the bombs falling, the men ran in all directions. Fortunately, the first bomb failed to explode, and the other two missed the position by 100 paces. Soon thereafter, the enemy drumfire slowed down again to intermittent fire.

Jan's battery had been under enemy observation ever since it arrived at this sector of the front. First it was spotted close to the top of M. Ermada where the men rested in the filthy reserve infantry barracks on the way to their front-line position. Then they were pinpointed at the position evacuated in a hurry by their predecessors. And finally they were detected at their present open location. (The Austrian intelligence confirmed the presence of French artillery; apparently, the French had sent about a dozen heavy gun batteries and the British some heavy artillery pieces, mainly six howitzers, to the Isonzo front.) The Italian and French gunners must have assumed that there was not just one but three distinct Austrian batteries, a full artillery regiment firing at them: they kept shelling all three places. The battery suffered one direct hit; luckily, only three men were wounded severely enough to be carried back to the field dressing station. Miraculously, the store of munitions was not touched. Jan's arm was scraped by a small piece of shrapnel, his first wound that drew blood. Since their arrival at M. Ermada the battery had fired 1,820 rounds in less than five days, or almost 400 rounds a day. Jan figured that thousands of tons of ammunition had been fired daily on these few kilometers of the front.

On June 5 at midnight the intermittent enemy fire changed to drumfire again, and at 4 a.m. the Italian infantry attacked anew. The Austrian artillery responded in kind, firing rolling barrages of great depth and receiving heavy shelling in return. This time the Italians achieved their goal: soon after daybreak they overran the Austrian trenches. The Austrian infantry was retreating in orderly fashion, but retreating nonetheless. Using mostly shrapnel, Jan's battery employed drumfire of their own in an effort to stop the advancing Italians. Just then, a large caliber direct hit killed one gunner, seriously wounding two more and less seriously four others, smashing one gun, and putting the other three guns out of commission. Immediately, the battery crew retreated to the cave.

The battle raged on. The cave was hit several times, too, but incurred little damage. The Austrian infantry suffered terrible losses. The most severely hit was a Czech regiment from Prague, which was almost completely wiped out. There was no break in the action. The wounded were coming up in droves from the battle below, Italian POWs as well as Austrians, walking or being supported or carried by others. They rested everywhere, outside the crowded cave as well as inside. They were begging for water, but there was none to be had. Those gunners who still had a little rum left gave it to the severely wounded, whom they permitted to remain in the packed cave. The walking wounded were sent, under enemy fire, to the rear.

During the previous night one of the new, heavy, Škoda-made howitzers, a Model 12, 30.5 cm caliber gun, was brought up the mountain on special motorized tractors that carried three separate sections of the howitzer. It was to be placed behind and to the right of the battery. But while the Austrians were laboriously assembling the large gun and setting it up, piece by piece, in firing position, they were observed early in the morning by an enemy plane. Soon thereafter the position came under such concentrated enemy artillery fire that the heavy gun was hastily dismantled again and evacuated to the rear without firing a single shot.

The barrage never stopped. The shelling became so intense and so accurate that the walking wounded could no longer make it safely from the trenches to the cave. They had no choice but to stay below with the dead and the dying, crying out and begging for help.

Later that same day, June 6, the fire power of the enemy slackened. The battery was ordered to move, under cover of darkness, up to the lice-infested huts, the place where they had rested the first night on M. Ermada. They moved all their gear and the equipment that was still usable or could be repaired, as well as the remaining munitions stored in the cave, to the new location. A new gun was delivered from the reserve line, and repairmen brought new parts and other gear for the three damaged guns. Ammunition and kitchen details arrived with their wares, and replacement details came as well. Even the field post arrived, with two food packages for Jan that had gone astray. All this was taking place under enemy fire, the shells whistling in the air.

This position seemed no better than the two previous spots—the huts were smashed, trees broken, and shell holes were everywhere. Half-heartedly, the men worked on the new location, dug trenches, set the guns in place, and transported the gear and ammunition. They were fed and had some sleep, so they felt better, but the shortage of drinking water was becoming acute. In any case, by the end of the day the guns were in the new position ready to fire. The regimental command telephoned to praise the men for their bravery under fire. This time no colonel appeared in person to deliver compliments and the welcome gift of a few cigarettes.

The following day and night, June 7 and 8, the enemy shelling let up. Jan's battery gunners fired several ranging rounds to bracket the targets and kept working on the trenches and shelters. At night food and ammunition arrived, and the next day the gun crew, using dynamite, began to excavate a cave adjacent to the new position. Enemy fire continued but seemed desultory. A thunderstorm drenched the men at the guns, but they were delighted to have the water, which they saved in empty shells and collected in shell holes draped with waterproof ground cloths.

On June 13 the food detail brought generous rations of rum and wine. The battery, on strict alert, kept shelling the enemy infantry with shrapnel and grenades, employing both a "closing fire" pattern to keep the enemy infantry in their trenches unable to attack, and intermittent "disturbing fire" to keep them under pressure and to hamper communications. The battery itself was under fire, both frontally as well as from the sea, again by large caliber guns and mortar shells. Fortunately, the mortar shells could be seen coming, and the men ran for cover before they landed. In a direct hit on the newly completed cave, the telephone operators working inside were half buried but otherwise unharmed.

And so it went, day after day. Finally, on June 22, three weeks after their arrival on M. Ermada, the Italian infantry began a new attack in several waves. There was heavy and bitter man-to-man fighting in the Austrian trenches, but the Austrians held and ultimately chased the Italians back. It seemed that the Italian offensive had lost its drive and determination. Rather than use the opportunity to counterattack, the Austrians, too, appeared to have lost steam. Exhaustion had set in on both sides.

The Tenth Battle of the Isonzo, the bloodiest single onslaught as yet on the Isonzo front (52,000 Austrians were later reported killed and wounded and 23,000 captured), seemed to be over. In fact, however, the men at the battery found out later, the Italian offensive had been over two weeks earlier, on June 8, but the battery did not know it. The Italians must not have known it either, because their artillery kept firing at the Austrians, the Italian infantry kept attacking the Austrian trenches, both sides were apparently on strict alert, and the rations of rum kept coming....

In the lull that followed, the men at the battery worked on the cave to extend it deeper into the rock. Closer to the cannons they carved out a smaller cave for the ammunition. And they kept firing at enemy targets of opportunity such as the changing of the guards and movements of the supply details and rotations in the reserve lines. But the intensity and resolution were gone on both sides. The men wondered if the state of strict alert would ever end.

The field post brought not only another precious food package for Jan (Božena had been sending them almost daily) but also a notice to all personnel from the High Command: Soldiers who purchased war bonds would be granted home leave, the length to be determined by the amount of money subscribed. Jan signed up right away. The modest amount he was able to put down, 300 crowns, was enough to grant him five days leave plus travel time, not much but a respite nonetheless. Unfortunately, all home leaves were canceled later the same day they were announced: army intelligence reported that a new enemy offensive was about to start.

And, indeed, the enemy artillery fire increased again, the Austrian artillery responded, and both sides kept going. One morning when Jan was briefly off duty, he left his dugout to go to the cave to write a letter to Božena. The moment he departed, a heavy grenade exploded almost directly in the spot he had just left. Jan wondered at his luck—or was it telepathy?

Jan did not feel well; he had suffered headaches and fever for several days but was not sick enough to be relieved from duty. Now almost daily someone left for the field hospital, and there were no replacements. By July 5 the battery was down to almost half of its original number. But the remaining gunners managed to fire the four guns "as usual," according to Jan. Finally, on July 6 the battery received word that it was to be relieved. They would not find out if the expected renewed Italian offensive took place (it did not), but they were too weary to care and glad to be gone.

At noon the reserve battery staff sergeant (*Feuerwerker*) arrived to relieve Jan, who briefed him and handed over the battery ammunition stores in the two caves. Jan and his men were now free to leave the position. That evening, after five brutal weeks at this sector of the front, what was left of the battery packed up and left without looking back. The reserve battery was already in place with the blessings of Jan's gunners.

Retreat Under Fire
Mount Liesl, July 11 - August 22
The Eleventh Battle of the Isonzo began August 18.

From the Monte Ermada position the battery made it back that night to Aurisina, where they rejoined the supply and reserve teams and again, as a complete battery unit—minus casualties—they rode and marched in the morning to the train station in Prosecco. Waiting for additional freight cars to be added to the next available train, they camped at the station for almost 24 hours. At 6:00 a.m. on Sunday, July 8, they left for Ljubljana, Podmelec, and their familiar destination, the Klavže railroad station and Baška grapa.

In Baška grapa they unloaded their guns, carts and wagons, animals, ammunition, and all their gear. What they enjoyed there most was the abundance of water. After five parched weeks on M. Ermada, they had water to drink, water to wash with, water to do their laundry, and, for the first time since they left Imst over two months ago, a clear mountain stream to bathe in. One tough gunner maintained that the dirtier the underwear, the fewer the lice. He, for one, would keep his underwear the way it was. There was something to it. They all had learned that in the foul conditions in which they lived, clean underwear, for some strange reason, appeared in fact to attract lice. Still, the majority of the men did their laundry diligently; it was such a luxury to be clean, however briefly. Even the brave holdout washed his undergarments when no one was looking, but he was found out! He never lived it down.

In the evening it started to rain. By the time the battery was ready to leave, at 10 p.m., a violent storm swept across the valley. In addition, on the way to the village of Ravne they came under enemy fire. The flashes of lightning helped them to see better on the narrow winding road, but the shell explosions were hard to distinguish from peals of thunder. The horse that Jan led by the bridle, although used to the sounds of battle, hid his head under Jan's arm. Jan was touched.

The poor, dumb animals suffered as much as the men, perhaps more. Ravne was a small settlement, just a few abandoned houses. Wet, cold, tired, and hungry, Jan found an empty barn, poured the water out of his boots, and threw himself on a pile of dry straw. Almost immediately he fell asleep.

Early in the morning the field kitchen handed out bread and hot coffee. There was a blazing fire to help dry off the wetness of the night before. The men loaded their equipment on the aerial cableway and marched to Špilenca over narrow mountain roads deeply rutted by shell holes full of mud. It was hard to navigate. Two horses broke their legs and had to be shot. The battery reached Špilenca by noon; a hot lunch awaited them, a pleasant surprise. They unloaded their gear from the cableway onto packhorses and prepared themselves for yet another inspection. A colonel arrived, spick and span and full of health. The men rarely saw anyone of his rank do anything other than inspect troops. For the men, inspections meant extra work, often useless and cosmetic labor such as cleaning and polishing, standing at attention sometimes for hours, and listening to boring speeches in a language some of them did not understand. But it also meant small rewards like cigarettes and tobacco, hot food, and rest.

On July 11 in the morning the battery left for the hamlet Dol near the village Kal nad Kanalom, their reserve line, and from there they proceeded to the front, at Mt. Liesl, undoubtedly another code name, which they reached in the afternoon. The shelling, both hostile and friendly, was light. From the departing battery crew they took over a position which looked much less dangerous to them than their last three positions on Monte Ermada had been. They assembled and placed their guns in the established trenches and, as usual, fired ranging rounds to bracket the targets. This time it took only four rounds per gun. Then they started to work to improve and fortify the station both for the storage of ammunition and shelter for the crew. They also began to excavate an additional cave in the rock larger than the existing one. Since the front was relatively quiet, they now worked for days and nights on the position's fortification. The battery commander, Capt. Müller, stayed true to the old Austrian army adage, "Soldiers must be kept busy at all times."

But the men had their lighter moments, too. Almost directly above them, several aerial dramas took place. On July 13 an Austrian fighter plane found an Italian fighter plane; both planes, flown skillfully by daring pilots, tried to shoot each other down. Their amazing acrobatics entertained the men for almost half an hour. Finally, the Italian fighter managed to maneuver behind the Austrian pilot and downed him. In appreciation the battery shouted and applauded,

The Italian Campaign: The Isonzo Front 43

drawing sharp words of rebuke from the duty officer, who reprimanded the men at length for their lack of patriotism: "On whose side are you, you scumbags?"

The frequent use of war planes by both sides in this sector of the Isonzo front was new to the men. They enjoyed watching the fighters in combat—on July 15 they saw for the first time pilots jumping from doomed planes with parachutes—but they feared the Italian Caproni "bombers" and the hovering observer planes. Both meant trouble to them or to their supply line. The gunners camouflaged their position as best they could with the branches of trees and shrubbery.

Food was getting scarce. Ever since they moved to this position, the food and cigarette rations were shrinking. If it were not for the occasional packages from home, the men would go hungry. Were they only imagining that they felt weak? When yet another colonel came for inspection, he rewarded the men with four cigarettes apiece, "the soldier's food" when food was in short supply. Cigarettes did diminish the pangs of hunger.

On July 16, a beautiful, sunny day, the artillery fire on both sides slackened to zero. During the lull at noon, Jan, who was not on duty, took off his shirt and lay down on a warm, flat rock behind the battery to enjoy the sunshine. It felt almost peaceful there. Gradually, however, he became aware of a gentle, barely audible rustling next to him. Slowly, he turned his head in the direction of the sound: a black snake over a meter long was coiled on a rock in the sun next to his right arm. Quietly and very slowly Jan rose to his feet and tiptoed toward his foxhole to retrieve his service revolver. When he came back, the snake was gone. "Well," thought Jan, "perhaps it wasn't a poisonous snake after all...."

Jan received additional responsibilities. On alternate days he served as "Corporal of the Day" although his rank of private remained the same. He was still in charge of the battery ammunition, making sure that the supply was always larger than the need. The ammunition supply depot at the reserve line as well as the delivery routes to the battery were under constant enemy observation, and fire alert applied. The men were poised to duck at a split second's notice. A sustained supply of ammunition, food, and spare parts was no longer reliable, and the losses of packhorses and men were slowly mounting. Jan was beginning to worry.

But there was good news, too. On July 17, together with three NCOs, Jan was awarded a silver medal second class for bravery under fire, "*Der Tapferkeit*." The medal carried with it a monthly stipend for life of 7.50 crowns. On July 28 after another inspection by still another colonel, Jan was promoted to the rank of Private First Class (*Vormeister*). Best of all, on August 3 he received a five-day home leave pass plus travel time, his first home leave since arriving at the front on May 6. This was the home leave he had been granted during the M. Ermada battle on June 24, a reward for soldiers who had bought war bonds, only to have it canceled the same day it was announced. At last it came through. Jan was ecstatic.

First Home Leave, August 7 – 17

On August 7 Jan and three other gunners who had received their home leave papers left that evening after dark. On the way to the supply line in Dol, they walked on a mountain road highlighted, more often than not, by enemy searchlights. When the beacons were on them, the gunners froze. The road was also under enemy fire; whenever the men saw enemy gunflashes, they threw themselves on the ground. In a small mountain village, Zavrh, where the men rested, three houses suddenly burst into flames, struck by incendiary shells. It was a long, nerve-wracking walk.

From Zavrh their pathway was safe again, and from Ravne they hitched a ride on a truck all the way to Podmelec and the Klavže train station, arriving at 1 a.m. on August 9. They slept on the floor of a flimsy supply shack and at 7 a.m. boarded the train for Vienna. It took them 25 hours and six station changes to get from the front to Vienna via Klagenfurt, Leoben, and Brück an der Mur. The Austrian train network in that part of the Empire proved less than adequate for the exigencies of a full-fledged defensive war. By now the men expected delays; they were used to them and would have been surprised had it been otherwise.

At 8 a.m. on August 10 at the South Station in Vienna, Jan made a beeline for the first barbershop he saw on the Gürtel, the wide boulevard circling the heart of the city. He needed a haircut and shave desperately. As luck would have it, the barbershop was empty. What must the barber have thought, seeing this unkempt, disreputable-looking soldier at the door in full field uniform? When he smelled the man's approach, the barber truly did not know what to do. As a patriot he could not make himself tell a front-line soldier to leave the shop and come back when he was clean. On the other hand, he rightly suspected that Jan must be infected with lice and other noxious pests. So he made a Solomon's decision: he asked Jan to sit down on a hard chair; he cut his hair and shaved him at arm's length, so that only his tools touched Jan. These he disinfected and washed thoroughly afterwards. Jan was grateful and tipped him generously.

On the Gürtel again, looking for a streetcar, Jan suddenly realized that the crowded Vienna trolleys were unlike the train cars "for military personnel only" he arrived on. He did not have the courage to take public transportation in the shape that he was in. Feeling sorry for himself, he walked home.

Božena was in the store waiting on customers. When she saw Jan, she dropped everything and ran to him, but he stopped her short, warning her to keep a distance. "When I'm clean we'll celebrate." He escaped to their one-room apartment behind the store, undressed completely, washed himself as much as he could, and changed into civilian clothes. Darting unseen into Božena's kitchen, he put all his dirty military clothes and his putrid underwear into a large boiler, filled it with water, and brought it to a boil to get rid of the lice and the ground-in dirt. In the neighborhood public steam baths he treated himself to the longest and hottest bath he could tolerate. By the time he walked home, he was ready at last to put his arms around Božena.

She was waiting for him in the apartment. She had closed the store for the rest of the afternoon for reasons of "family emergency." The welcome she gave Jan made up for everything: the long separation, his misery at the front, his loneliness for their baby daughter, whom Božena tried to visit at least once a month at her mother's in Bohemia. Božena could not believe her good fortune. She had not seen Jan since April in Imst, almost four months before. She had no idea that he was coming home. In fact, she had worried that she might never see him again. That this gaunt, pale, tired, unkempt soldier appearing suddenly behind her customers was Jan—she could not believe her eyes. She was overcome with relief and gratitude that he was there, alive, whole, and all for the price of a 300 crown war bond!

The first thing she wanted to do was cook his favorite meal, wiener schnitzel and potato salad, in her own kitchen, listening and talking to him just the way she used to, the two of them, away from other people. For four days they were inseparable. Jan helped Božena in the store, went over her account books and the food ration coupons, checked her supplies of food on the shelves and in the storeroom, and made himself as useful as he could. How good it felt to live like a human being again!

But not for long. On August 14, accompanied by Božena, who was in tears, Jan reported to the South Station Military Command and left Vienna for the front by the same train route he had come. From the Klavže railroad station Jan and a friend from the battery walked to Ravne by way of Baška grapa and S. Lucia. In Ravne they put their gear once again on the aerial cableway and walked to Špilenca, where they took another cablecar up the mountain and walked to Dol, site of the battery supply line. Resting there briefly, they made their way cautiously to the battery on Mt. Liesl. They reported back at nightfall on August 17 and fell asleep immediately, exhausted.

The Eleventh Battle of the Isonzo, August 18 – September 15

The position on Mt. Liesl was different from the one Jan had left ten days before. The four guns were now located in trenches on top of a protruding hill with a shallow hollow behind it. There were two wooden huts built on the slope of the hollow, protected by the hill and facing the rear. One housed the office and the officers' quarters, the other the telephone exchange and the enlisted men's billets. At a safe distance from the two huts was a large, wooden ammunition box. In this location, only the guns were exposed to enemy fire.

The artillery activity of the enemy was steadily increasing. The battery supply teams continued to travel back and forth under enemy fire, and their casualties, both in men and in horses, were becoming noticeable. A man in the supply team, scared out of his wits by the shells exploding all around him, hid behind a bushy outcropping and shot himself in the thigh. Unfortunately, he nicked an artery and bled profusely. Hearing his cries for help, his friends rushed to his side, stopped the bleeding as best they could, and called for a medic. Because of the unusual circumstances and the nature of the wound, a supply sergeant questioned the man closely. The poor soul, weak from loss of blood and in great pain, confessed. The sergeant had him carried to the field hospital in the rear. A week later the man was propped up in front of a firing squad and shot.

The morning after Jan's arrival, on August 18 the expected Italian offensive began, the Eleventh Battle of the Isonzo. At first the Italian artillery fired rapid volleys; then they switched to closing fire, thus preventing the Austrian artillery from firing shrapnel at the Italian infantry with any degree of effectiveness. Finally, they escalated the barrage to the dreaded drumfire along the whole front. The Austrian artillery responded in kind.

Jan's battery suffered losses; two men were killed and four were wounded. A medical NCO who came to evacuate the wounded was killed by a shrapnel shell fragment that made its way through the back of his steel helmet to his forehead just above his nose. And in spite of its protected location, the telephone exchange was hit by a mortar shell which, coming in at a high angle, flew over the guns and hit the hut directly. The explosion killed the telephone operators and destroyed the only telephone connection the battery had with its own observers as well as with the rear and the regimental command.

About 200 paces behind and above the battery, on a rocky hillside the Austrian infantry faced the enemy in shallow trenches dug into bare, stony ground. This was an unusual battle tactic; normally, the infantry was in front of the battery, not behind it. The men at the battery were not happy to be so exposed to a potential frontal enemy infantry attack.

Three enemy batteries were now firing at Jan's battery as well as at the infantry behind them. The battery gunners fired back as rapidly as they could, but in the approaching darkness they could no longer see the Italian infantry below them, nor could they hear any major movements there in the din of the battle. Was the infantry advancing? How close to the battery were they? Without telephone connection to the rear and to their own observers, they were without direction. To make matters worse, the Austrian infantry behind them, under unusually heavy enemy fire, began to retreat.

After nervous consultations and prolonged hesitation, the battery command—two young lieutenants who were left in charge while Captain Müller was recalled on official business to the rear—ordered retreat. They felt there was nothing else to do. The battery could be overrun at any moment, and the Austrian infantry, a scout now reported, had fled, all of them. Since there were neither horses nor men from the reserve line in Dol to carry the guns and ammunition back to the rear, the gun crews disabled the guns by removing their firing mechanisms. Then half of the crew was ordered to leave; the other half sought refuge in an old cave on the rear side of the hill well below the hollow and waited for developments. But the heavy enemy fire persisted and increased to closing fire to prevent further retreat. By 10 p.m. on August 20 the men in the cave were ordered to leave for Dol as well, after only three days of the unrelieved, fierce Italian offensive.

Later that night, the regimental command, eager to retrieve the guns if at all possible, sent two consecutive patrols back to the battery position to find out what was happening. Both patrols reported that, incredibly, the advancing enemy infantry had not yet reached the gun position. There was still a chance to save the guns. On regimental orders, the gun crews with packhorses and drivers and additional men returned to the position, dismantled the guns, loaded them on horses, together with the ammunition left in the large wooden box, and headed back to the rear—all under heavy enemy fire. The cost of this brave but questionable enterprise was two men and two horses killed, two men and several horses wounded, one gun severely damaged and another almost completely destroyed. The two lieutenants responsible for the unauthorized retreat from the position were ordered to report, under guard, to the regimental command without delay. They were replaced then and there by a second lieutenant.

The next day, on August 21, the battery was ordered to move from Dol to a new position. By 10 p.m. all was ready, but the battery was short of horses, carts, and men to transport all the gear in one move. Jan was ordered to remain in Dol to guard the remaining equipment. In departing, the new battery commander, Second Lieutenant Witteka, promised—"You have my word"—that he would be back with two wagons to pick up Jan and whatever was left behind. Jan wanted to believe him, but the enemy advance to Dol, now open and unprotected, was proceeding apace. Who would get to him first, the lieutenant or the Italians?

In the relative stillness of the night—the bombardment seemed far away for now—Jan waited. To be on the safe side, he put away both his carbine and his service revolver. He did not want the Italians to make a mistake. If he were to be taken prisoner, he wanted to be taken alive. At 2 a.m. on August 22 he heard sounds from the direction of the departed battery. It was the second lieutenant with two large horse-driven wagons and four men. Jan helped to load the gear and the munitions he was guarding onto the wagons, and, with the detail, took off to rejoin the battery.

The Italians Advance
Koren, August 23 – September 14
The Eleventh Battle of the Isonzo ended September 15.

On August 22 the detail caught up with the battery in Špilenca. From there, together with the First Battery, the Second Battery moved first to Baška grapa and then to the Slap ob Idrijci supply depot to await orders. In Slap Captain Müller returned from the rear and took over the command from Lieut. Witteka. The battery received two brand new cannons, new replacements (green recruits), horses, additional gun and wagon parts, supplies, and, most welcome, new boots for all. While the men were assembled in front of the supply barracks, an enemy plane dropped three bombs on them, but it flew too high and missed. That night they all went to the field movie theater.

On August 23 the battery was ordered to move on to the next battle station located just below the top of a nearby mountain, not far from the small village of Koren, the position's second line and supply station. On the way there, they rested in Ravne and in Špilenca and arrived in Koren at 5 a.m. the following morning under light enemy shelling—one man was wounded. From Koren it was a relatively short hike to the position. While assembling and mounting the guns in the covered trenches there, the men were shocked to discover, late that afternoon, that the enemy infantry had advanced since their arrival and in fact now occupied the road on which they had come, thus cutting off the battery from its supply line, without ammunition and defenseless! What now?

Since they had sent the packhorses back, under light enemy fire the men had no choice other than to dismantle the guns again and carry them, piece by piece, over the knoll behind the position in the direction of Koren. They were on their way when the ammunition detail, traveling by a roundabout route, reached them after all. The detail helped the gunners carry the guns back to the position, assemble them, and place them in the trenches again, ready to fire. The hungry and thirsty gunners—the detail had brought ammunition but no food or water—started to shoot without delay. They sent three casualties back with the detail. On the way back to the new reserve line in Žable, the detail itself lost three men, two wounded and one dead.

The gunners found their main target fast: it was the enemy infantry that had occupied the village of Dol almost immediately after Jan's departure. After some ten hours of concentrated shrapnel fire from all four guns, the battery managed to chase the Italian infantry back to another village, Široka Njiva. By doing so, however, it attracted heavy enemy fire both from cannons and heavy machine guns. In front of the battery the village of Kačja Draga was on fire. In the midst of the commotion, the ammunition supply detail brought meager food but no water. Again, the men had to urinate on the gun barrels to cool them.

On August 26 the enemy infantry began an attack on the Austrian positions from three sides. After hurried discussions among the officers and the NCOs, Captain Müller had the gun crews remove the protective steel shields from two of the four guns and move the guns to a ledge jutting out below the battery position and overlooking the slope immediately under, around, and opposite the ledge. The two gun crews responded quickly. The enemy infantrymen, positioned opposite the battery on a similar rocky slope and hiding behind rocks and boulders, were slowly but surely pushing the Austrian infantry down the slope, using mostly hand grenades.

The two gun crews started to shoot. Aiming the guns along the barrels as if they were rifles, the men fired grenades at the rocks, cliffs and boulders above and around the hidden infantrymen. The ruse worked! The fragments of rock were more effective than shrapnel. The Italian attack began to falter. Even without the Austrian infantry counterattack, the Italians started to retreat back to the top of the ledge.

After dark, having used up all their ammunition, the gun crews dismantled the two guns and quickly moved them back to the battery position, all the while under steady enemy machine gun and rifle fire. On the way, Jan's mule, which carried a 120 kg gun barrel, suddenly dropped, felled by a shot in its right front hoof. With the help of the crew, Jan raised the animal with its heavy load onto its feet. Luckily, the wounded mule resumed walking and carried the barrel all the way to the position. Jan sent the mule back to the reserve line, together with the casualties of the two-gun stratagem, one man wounded and one dying. A third man was left for dead in the two-gun position.

Upon their return that night, Captain Müller sent Jan back to check the ledge and to retrieve anything that had been left behind. Jan found a forgotten box of hand grenades. The wounded infantrymen who were able to walk were making their way to the dressing station. All around, Jan heard the moans and cries of others waiting for medics. The man left behind for dead on the ledge was, incredibly, still breathing, in spite of a shot clean through his head. Jan decided to carry him back. He abandoned the hand grenades and lifted the man onto his shoulders, but the man died before Jan reached his first rest stop. Jan returned for the hand grenades. On the path he stumbled across a Hungarian infantryman with a bad stomach wound crying out for help. Jan examined the open gash. It was obvious to Jan that the man was beyond hope, one more victim of war—"a primitive, stupid, cruel way to kill and destroy everything and solve nothing!" Jan writes, shaken. The man died in his arms.

The following day, August 27, the battle continued unabated. The two-gun position of the previous day had been annihilated by concentrated gunfire during the night. The aerial cableway which carried the ammunition to the reserve line in Žable was destroyed as well, but the ammunition detail from Žable made its way to the battery before daybreak. There were enough rounds for the four guns to sustain fire during the day, but not more. The battery was under light enemy shrapnel fire the whole day. After dark Jan and thirteen other men from the battery were sent for ammunition, supplies, and food to the supply station in Cvetrež. They could not use the narrow, winding dirt road to Cvetrež because in places it was held by the enemy. Visibility was almost zero. The men had to walk in single file, each man holding on to the shoulder of the man in front of him, through the dense, deciduous forest. It was a long, arduous walk, but nothing compared to the walk back that night, with packhorses and heavy loads. One man was wounded.

The battle continued. On August 28 the battery came under infantry fire again, both by machine guns and rifles. One man was killed and four were wounded, and three wounded horses had to be shot. By noon the following day the battery was out of ammunition. Except for those on duty, the men slept, a well-deserved respite. The supply detail arrived that night with ammunition as well as food and water, but the rations were small, and most of the food was spoiled. The men ate it anyway and suffered stomach cramps the next day. The horses were beginning to show signs of starvation.

On August 31 a severe thunderstorm erupted. There was no shelter from the heavy rain at the battery, and within minutes the men were drenched. To provide cover as well as drinking water, Jan attempted to hang a tarpaulin from a wire strung across several broken down trees. Working with the wire, Jan was struck by lightning—a relatively mild strike but enough for him to give up on the idea.

The Eleventh Italian Offensive continued. It had started on August 18 and had succeeded in chasing the battery as well as the infantry to the rear of Mt. Liesl in just three short days. The enemy infantry now tended to attack the Austrian infantry position early in the morning or late in the evening but without much success. Under heavy fire, the battery was located between the Austrian front-line infantry trenches below and in front of them, and the reserve infantry positions above and behind them. During the Italian attacks, the heavy machine guns of the reserve infantry fired at the enemy over the heads of the battery gunners, who were caught in the middle of the crossfire, too close for comfort. The numbers of the killed and wounded at the battery increased daily. The men—wet, cold, tired and hungry—were becoming dispirited.

There were more and more warplanes in the air, both Italian—joined by the French and British, the men guessed—and Austrian, although clearly the Italians had the edge. The enemy were the better pilots, especially those flying fighter planes. Jan's count one day was five Italian wins, three losses, and three draws.

And so it went, day after day and week after week. It seemed at times that September that the Italian eleventh grand offensive was weakening again. Each side fired fewer shells, mostly at suspicious targets only, using shrapnel, and there were fewer serious Italian infantry attacks. Other sectors of the front seemed livelier, though; the sector on the battery's left around Plave was noisier (Map III). At night only one gun of Jan's battery kept shooting. This was the "disturbing fire" intended to keep the enemy alert and awake. However, the Italians tended to respond by "assault fire," brief but fierce and rapid volleys, whose individual explosions were lost in the overall sustained din of the battle. The battery gunners, who by then could distinguish by sound whether the shells fired at them came from guns, howitzers, or mortars, as well as their caliber and the content of their explosives, were often at a loss during "assault fire."

They slept more now, some of them almost the whole night, in their dugouts under their tarpaulins, and Jan often sought the cover of thick shrubs and tree branches for warmth. Almost everyone was sick, some more than others—with low grade fevers, dysentery, nausea, disorientation, malnutrition—but no one was excused from duty. It rained, and a strong, cold wind blew for days. Field mail was non-existent, incoming or outgoing. The men felt abandoned and forgotten, except by the enemy.

On September 13, completely unexpected, a battery of the Twenty-fourth Artillery Regiment arrived from Kačja Draga to relieve Jan's battery. Finally! The rain eased up toward evening, the packhorses were brought in, and the next day, September 14, at 4 p.m. the battery was ready to depart.

The Eleventh Battle of the Isonzo, the greatest of the eleven Italian offensives, was almost over. Later, reading about the offensive in the Vienna newspapers during his leave, Jan learned that it included some 51 Italian divisions and over 5,000 guns attacking the Austrian positions between Tolmin/Tolmino in the north and the Adriatic Sea in the south. In the Gorizia sector of the front and on the Carso plateau, the Austrian defenders managed to push the Italian attackers back. But on the strategically important Banjška Plateau where Jan and his battery were located, in the first few days of heavy fighting the Italians crossed the Isonzo in force, drove the Austrians back almost 10 km on a broad front, and captured the whole western half of the plateau. But the heavy losses, said to amount to almost 150,000 killed and wounded, the want of adequate artillery support, the difficult terrain, the lack of supplies, and sheer exhaustion—all played a part in halting the Italian offensive. Thus, in two and a half years on the Isonzo the Italians had virtually spent all their resources in eleven fruitless offensives. At most, they had advanced 11 kilometers at a total cost of almost 600,000 men killed and wounded.

The men at the battery were relieved to leave this part of the front. They felt that one additional hard Italian thrust would have turned the Austrian retreat into a rout. The Austrians were dog-tired and perhaps not too far from quitting themselves, or so it seemed to the men. A visiting colonel from the Division told the men before their departure that the Austrian-held Tolmin bridgehead now dangerously imperiled the shaky Italian advance on the Banjška

Plateau. The colonel praised "the brave Imperial and Royal Austro-Hungarian defenders" and distributed cigarettes, five per man. He did not mention the Austrian total losses up to that time—almost 350,000 killed and wounded—nor the grievously weakened Austrian forces that remained on the Isonzo.

Victory at Caporetto
Kanalski Lom/Ravne, September 15 – November 6

It took the gunners three hours to reach Koren, the supply station, where they waited for the cover of darkness. Then they continued behind the front to Kanalski Lom/Lom de Canale and from there up to the new front line and their designated new post, a medium-sized hill facing west, another three-hour hike ahead. The night was cold, there was no shelter, and their winter blankets had not been delivered as yet. The men slept poorly.

In the morning the gunners went through the routine of arriving in a new position which had not been built up before. With the skill and determination of seasoned veterans, they assembled the guns, dug gun trenches, placed the guns carefully into position, and started to fire ranging rounds, bracketing the targets. Then they dug shelters for the ammunition and dugouts for the officers and for themselves. They received two new cannons to replace the two old ones; all four guns were now new. The ammunition supply they brought with them was unusually abundant, with a promise of more to come. The men, sensing that something was in the air, began to worry as usual.

The food rations, however, were as meager as ever. This time the new location was to their advantage. The fruit trees behind and below the battery glistened in the sun with apples and pears, many of them ripe and inviting. Within walking distance potatoes grew in small fields, and there was plenty of fresh, clean water for the first time in Jan's experience. What more could an Austrian soldier ask for?

There was more. In Ravne, a small, almost deserted village close by, the men requisitioned anything they could use for themselves, the battery, and the officers. They looked especially for lumber to build shelters and ammunition magazines and to improve their own slit trenches and dugouts as well as those of the officers, their "bedrooms," which frequent rains made wet and muddy; sometimes several centimeters of water remained on the bottom.

All this took place under relatively light enemy shelling while the battery responded in kind. The norm was at first 100 rounds per day per gun and fifty rounds at night. Just to be on the safe side, the twenty-four hour supply was 900 shells, a mix of grenades and shrapnel. (The supply on hand in the battery reserve line was 4,000 rounds, by regimental order.) After September 18, however, the norm was randomly doubled, then halved again, and then doubled again. There were a few quiet days and nights in between, but not many. During one of the night interludes the battery suffered a direct hit from a 15 cm. enemy howitzer about 50 paces from Jan's dugout. Two men were killed and eight were wounded. The gunners buried the dead; the medics bandaged the wounded and sent them back to the rear.

Something was definitely afoot. For the first time ever, the battery was issued sixty shells filled with poison gas, plus gas masks for those who did not have them, and a supply of carbines, side arms, and hand grenades, as well as new Austrian issue steel helmets for all hands. Up to that time only a few men at the battery had been wearing helmets, and those were German army issue; the new Austrian helmets were barely distinguishable from the old German ones. Simple postcards printed with the message "I am healthy and well" in the twelve official languages of the Empire were again distributed to the men, ten postcards per man this time, which had only to be addressed, signed and returned to the field post. Any other outgoing mail was forbidden. And the supply of ammunition at the battery was larger than ever before. A strong sense of foreboding filled the air; surely the long-awaited offensive was near.

Only food, cigarettes, and matches were scarce. Here the men could cope with hunger: fruit was available, and they boiled the potatoes they gathered in the fields and ate them with salt when they had it. But cigarettes, the soldiers' sustenance, were sorely missed. Jan started to smoke a pipe, but when matches were almost impossible to come by, he had to give that up, too.

As the rains became more frequent, the men spent much of their free time improving their dugouts. They deepened them, placed raised boards across the bottoms, dug drainage canals, and covered the dugouts with waterproof ground cloths. For a day or two these improvements helped; thereafter the dugouts were about as wet and muddy as before.

There were more airplanes, friendly as well as hostile, flying above the front. The military value of airplanes in support of ground troops was clearly recognized by now and was being implemented by both sides. Observation planes, "bombers," and fighter planes, often flying in formation, were a daily occurrence. The men at the battery watched the aircraft with fascination mixed with fear. They all agreed, however, that watching the deadly duels between hostile fighter planes that took place above and in front of them was sheer delight. It was like sitting in the balcony of a theater watching a spectacular show.

On September 28, Friday, a red German fighter plane confronted two Italian fighters. Everybody knew, of course, that the red plane was piloted by the famous ace and German war hero Baron Manfred von Richthofen. The first Italian fighter veered, dove, and took off in a hurry as soon as the pilot recognized the plane. The other stayed and began to maneuver for advantage but had no chance. Rapidly, the "Red Baron" managed to get above and behind the Italian fighter and, circling ever closer in graceful pirouettes, pushed the Italian pilot lower and lower until he was forced to land. The men—including the officers and the NCOs—cheered and applauded. (Only later did Jan find out that Manfred von Richthofen had not fought on the Italian front. Had it been his double, a *Doppelgänger*, flying a replica of the Baron's famous plane?)

Toward evening a tethered enemy observer balloon was shot down, one less problem to worry about. That night, under heavy enemy fire, when "the shrapnel bullets filled the air like swarms of buzzing flies," the battery was ordered to fire all of its sixty poison gas shells. Afterwards, the men talked quietly about the changing nature of the war, the acceleration of its dehumanizing aspects. They were appalled. To what end? Where would it stop? Surely the enemy would reciprocate.... Six houses in Kanalski Lom burned to the ground that night. The Italians must have used incendiary shells.

On September 30, a cold, rainy and windy day, the suspicions of the battery crew were confirmed: they received word that a German-Austrian offensive was about to start, perhaps in five days. The battery was ready in many respects, but the men themselves were not. Their anxiety about food and cigarettes had not diminished. The rations were smaller than ever, the fruit from the trees and the potatoes from the fields were almost gone, and packages from home were rare, due to the inefficiency of the field post—and also outright thievery, the men suspected.

The men had access to a German anti-aircraft battery that was stationed in the valley behind the battery. Jan had heard that the German army was poorly fed, but judging from the example of the German battery, whose crew was clearly well provided for and had almost always some spare food to sell or even give away, the German army rations seemed good and plentiful.

The Germans were friendly. They were paternal toward their Austrian comrades, whom they viewed as easy-going, relaxed, not very aggressive, and not particularly formidable in battle. They referred playfully to their Austrian cousins as "lace boot comrades" ("*Kameraden Schnurschuh*") because of their old-fashioned, laced-up boots, but they enjoyed talking to the Austrians, comparing experiences and making small presents of food and cigarettes. The men at Jan's battery were sorry for themselves. They were ashamed to beg food from the Germans. Jan had heard that while the official Austrian meat rations per day for front-line troops were 30 grams (one ounce), and the German rations six times more—the American army's rations were 24 times as much. He just could not believe it.

The mutual shelling continued. The battery received another consignment of poison gas shells—84 rounds. On October 4 the Regimental Command reported that the two lieutenants formerly with the battery were to stand trial before the Regimental Field Court-Martial in Bohinjska Bistrica/Beistritz for desertion under fire. They were accused of ordering the battery on August 20-21 to retreat from its position on Mount Liesl without an explicit order from the regimental command. The men remembered that terrible night well—the retreat of the Austrian infantry, which became a rout, every man for himself running to the rear and leaving the battery exposed to the concentrated attack of the Italian infantry. Without telephone contact and under heavy enemy fire, the lieutenants had no choice but to order the battery to retreat; there was no alternative.

What the lieutenants could not have known and what the Regimental Command had discovered subsequently, was that the Italians had never succeeded in overrunning the battery station. They stopped just below the position, probably exhausted, and stayed there. Jan never found out what happened to the two lieutenants. It was assumed that they were convicted of cowardice and dereliction of duty in the face of the enemy and probably shot. But there was no one in the battery who doubted that the lieutenants were completely innocent of the charge.

On October 5 Jan had a visitor, Franz Dubový, his good friend and future brother-in-law. He was returning from home leave in Vienna to his unit, a regimental slaughterhouse located in the regimental supply line, where he was a butcher. He brought Jan a welcome package from Božena containing a loaf of fresh bread, two pound cakes, and 300 cigarettes. To that bounty good friend Dubový added a large package of beef liver. Jan was grateful. He did not mention to Dubový that he had been in his dugout picking off louse number 114 from his undershirt when his friend arrived, and lost count....

Dubový also brought Jan the news from Vienna of the other Italian front, the Trentino, a region of high Alpine peaks, steep ridges, and sharp rocks. Jan already knew that the year before, in the summer of 1916, the Austrians had attacked the Italians, and it seemed for a while that they might break through into the Venetian plain and cut off the Italian Isonzo army. But the Italians, favored by the murderous topography whipped by storms, avalanches, and slides, managed to halt the Austrian offensive. What Jan did not know was that a year later it was the Italians who attacked the Austrians, but after two and a half weeks of heavy fighting, the attackers had to give up as well. The high mountain terrain was unforgiving in both cases, and the losses of both friend and foe were devastatingly high. Dubový claimed that in the entire history of mankind, no armies had ever before fought in such high altitudes. He was right, Jan found out later.

The weather was worsening. The rains became heavy, and the bora, a cold, powerful, violent wind from the northeast, now blew constantly. To avoid having to sleep in pools of water in their dugouts, the men again deepened them, placed several layers of boards on the bottom, and used wooden doors from bombed-out houses in the village as covers. But nothing seemed to help. The men used their mess kits to scoop out the water, which was sometimes as much as 10 centimeters deep. In the daytime whenever they were free, the men built small fires in the deserted houses and hovered around them to dry out and keep warm. It was a miserable existence.

To make matters worse, the Italian artillery shelled the battery at night, just to chase the men out of their dugouts into the rain, the gunners firmly believed. To get even, they fired back, to make certain that the Italian gunners were as miserable as they were.

The engagement continued, as did the bora and the rains. In the morning of October 7 the Italian artillery began to shell the Austrian positions with poison gas for the first time in Jan's experience. Was it possible that the Italians wanted to start an offensive of their own in order to beat the Germans and Austrians to the draw? The increasing noise of battle was now compounded by the echo effect of the hills and mountains around them. The gun crews had to resort to lip-reading at first. Once they donned gas masks, they communicated with their hands. The gale and the pounding rain continued without a break.

On October 8 the Italian infantry below them mounted an attack, and the Austrians counterattacked, but both efforts, relatively feeble, failed. Then a shell in one of the battery guns exploded in the barrel, and the fragments wounded two gunners. Jan poured iodine on the wounds of one man, dressed and bandaged them, and sent him to the rear. The other man's wounds were more extensive; after a medic gave him emergency first aid, the man had to be carried back to the field dressing station in the battery supply line. The trunk of a large nut tree that protected Jan's ammunition supply had neatly split in two in a direct hit.

The battle, the rains, and the bora continued. For the first time in Jan's memory the battery received beer, an allotment of fifty liters, which they could buy for 1.04 crowns a half liter. Each man was again issued ten free pre-printed field postcards, his military pay (Jan now carried 129.98 crowns in cash on his person), a winter blanket (finally!), nine "strike anywhere" sulphur matches, a packet of pipe tobacco to be divided among five men, and a packet of cigarette tobacco for twenty men. But there was no coffee, sugar, or salt. Warm food from the field kitchen reached them perhaps once every three or four days—usually a thin soup, a few dumplings, and minuscule pieces of meat. The men lived on bread and water, but there was never enough bread. Routinely, they made formal complaints, knowing full well that they were wasting their breath, but what else could they do? Prisoners in jails were fed better than they were.

Early one afternoon, off duty, Jan decided to hike to the officers' tailor shop in the reserve line, about an hour's walk. The tailors, a friendly bunch, let him use a hot iron. He proceeded to iron his "clean," just-washed laundry, especially the seams, to kill the multitudes of lice once and for all. It was a pleasure to listen to the music of popping lice! The tailors let Jan take a bath, and he changed his underwear. Free of lice, he walked back to the line in a buoyant mood. Needless to say, the next day the lice were back, but a different species this time, marked with red crosses and somewhat easier to detect, but just as troublesome and vexing as the familiar yellow ones.

On October 13 Franz Dubový came to have supper with Jan. This time he brought as gifts a loaf of bread, matches, and a blanket. It was rumored at the regiment, he told Jan, that in the upcoming Austrian-German offensive, Jan's battery, the Second Battery of the regiment, was to be attached to the regiment's Third Battery at the Tolmeiner Brückenkopf (Tolmin Bridgehead) on the Isonzo River, and that during this offensive all three batteries of the regiment, First, Second, and Third, were to advance together under German command as the First Mountain Field Artillery Regiment No. 201. Was this good news or bad news? Since they would function as "advancing artillery," the Germans might push them too hard. On the other hand, their food rations would undoubtedly improve. The two friends discussed the pros and cons far into the night.

There was no let-up in the weather or in the shelling. Unexpectedly, on October 17 after an unsatisfying meal of unsalted potato soup, the battery was ordered to pack up and leave immediately. No reason was given, but the men hoped that it meant much deserved rest and recreation in the rear. In heavy rain and deep mud they dismantled the guns, packed up everything as fast as they could, and were ready to leave—when in the last minute a new order came, countermanding the first one: "Stay, man the guns, and fire at will." Sick at heart, they complied, of course, every last man of them exhausted, wet, muddy, and worn down by hunger, wind, and cold. Was this an example of the fabled Austrian "*Schlamperei*" (slovenliness), or was it an unprecedented aberration on the part of the disciplined Germans? A week later they found out it was neither.

An order came to send the battery horses and their drivers right away to those batteries needing transportation. Miserable food rations arrived, as did the mail with two letters from Božena. The men were hungry but tried to forget it. Cigarettes helped but were scarce. The ammunition supply at the battery was now larger than ever before: on October 20 Jan counted 4,400 rounds, many of them filled with gas, and more was coming. The German-Austrian offensive was clearly imminent, but where were the rations of wine and rum?

On October 23 a "state of readiness," the heightened alert, was declared along the entire German-Austrian front. At precisely 2 a.m. the following morning, October 24, the German-Austrian forces burst out with a heavy cannonade, the drumfire, along the entire Isonzo front, with the enemy artillery responding. The offensive was on. The earth shook; the pandemonium of sound and sight was overwhelming, even for the seasoned veterans at the battery. Their guns became hot fast: by evening of the first day of the offensive they had fired 2,000 rounds! In unison with all the other artillery units along the front, they switched to "disturbing fire," designed to destroy the entangled barbed wire protecting the Italian trenches and hamper enemy communications along the front and in the rear, in preparation for an attack by the Austro-German infantry.

The following morning, October 25, the men at the battery could barely make out below them, through kaleidoscopic patterns of exploding earth and heavy clouds of acrid smoke, the Italian infantry retreating and their own infantry, bit by bit, in hand to hand combat, advancing slowly but savagely through the Italian trenches and then beyond. That day and the following night the battery crew, soaked to the skin, continued firing rolling barrages of great depth as well as counter battery fire.

Airplanes, both hostile and friendly, were busy along the whole front, keeping the anti-aircraft batteries at maximum alert. This time the Italians—and reportedly the few French and British—suffered most of the losses; several of their planes were forced to land on the Austrian side. Jan's battery suffered six casualties, but the Italian infantry was decidedly beginning to falter.

By the morning of October 26 the retreat of the Italian infantry looked like a rout. The German-Austrian forces were advancing rapidly now, beyond the Italian infantry reserves, beyond their artillery positions, and beyond their supply lines as well. By late afternoon there was not a gunshot to be heard at the battery, hostile or friendly. The battle of Karfreit/Caporetto was over. The rain was constant, but the men, knocked senseless by the intensity of the last sixty hours, slept wherever they happened to be, officers included.

The next two days were leisurely, with only a few men assigned to brief tasks. Jan suffered a minor flesh wound on his left thigh during the battle and was excused from duty; he rested and slept. Thanks to his frequent efforts to improve his "abode," his dugout was almost dry. He was even excused, on October 30 and 31, from the detail that carried the unused boxes of ammunition and empty shells back to the reserve line in Kanalski Lom.

By November 1 the battery position looked and felt like the rear, as if a magic wand had lifted the war and put it down in some other place. By then the Italian forces, retreating rapidly, had apparently reached the Tagliamento River and beyond. Free that afternoon, Jan and his friend Josef decided to take the risk and cross the now deserted Italian infantry trenches, artillery positions, and supply lines in the hope of finding something to eat, perhaps even a few potatoes in the abandoned fields. They were happily surprised. They found so many potatoes that they had a hard time dragging their full sacks back to the battery. Clearly, unlike the Austrians, the Italian soldiers had not had to forage for food. But there were dead bodies strewn everywhere, mountains of weapons of all sorts, dead horses and mules, live ammunition, burned-out houses, jagged tree stumps, craters, pockets of heavy smoke—a nightmarish scene of massacre, destruction, and utter desolation.

Jan and Josef's friends at the battery, properly impressed by the potatoes, followed in the footsteps of the two men as soon as they could. Jan also received a package of cigarettes from Božena and purchased from an enterprising medic a box of expensive candy, which he ate with gusto. Even the eternal rain ceased. All was well at the battery again, for the time being.

On November 4 the battery received orders to pack up and move to the rear to the depot at Slap ob Idrijci again and to await further orders there. The men, with assistance from the reserve line teams, dismantled the guns, packed them and the remaining ammunition, some sixty boxes, plus all the other equipment and the empty shells, on horses and mules and left the position at 6 a.m. on November 6.

Only during his next leave in Vienna two weeks later did Jan get a fuller picture of the Austro-German Isonzo offensive that he and his battery had just survived. His friend and neighbor Karl, a teacher, who had lost his right leg in the First Battle of the Isonzo in 1915, had friends in high places with whom he kept in touch. Soon after their retreat in Banjška Plateau in September, the Austrians had apparently asked the Germans for help; the Germans complied gladly and began to plan the whole operation. The result was a joint Austro-German assault of eight Austrian and seven German divisions under German command.

Jan remembered well the day the attack began, October 24, along the whole front, from Avšje on the Banjška Plateau to Monte Rombon, north of Bovec/Plezzo/Flitsch, a distance of some 40 kilometers. Not only was this a thinly held Italian front-line area, but the Italians, knowing that their gas masks were primitive and useless, panicked and ran. Jan remembered that his own battery had used mostly high explosive and gas shells during the rolling barrages of the drumfire. The German-Austrian infantry attack, assisted by thick mist and low-lying clouds, was overwhelming, sustained, and relentless along the whole front—and quick. In three days the Austro-German infantry ran through the center of the Italian defensive line, overran the entire Italian front, and retook the Banjška Plateau. By then the Italian front disintegrated; the Austro-German forces trapped most of the Italians in the Carnic Alps, broke into Friuli, and then marched into the Venetian plain. Their rapid advance was finally halted on November 7 on the Piave River, some 130 km west from the Isonzo, chiefly because they ran out of supplies and reserves. Karl said that the speed of the Austrian-German advance had outstripped the Austrian High Command's capacity to keep the troops supplied and in top fighting condition.

Both sides suffered heavy losses: the Italians, some 40,000 men killed and wounded, and the Austro-Germans, about 20,000 casualties. In addition, the Austro-Germans captured over 275,000 Italian POWs, clear evidence of the magnitude of their victory in this twelfth and last battle of the war on the Isonzo. The Caporetto disaster, as it became known, was now a major issue not only for the Italians but for the Allies as well.

Drills and More Drills
Slap ob Idrijci, November 6, 1917 – January 12, 1918

On the way to Slap the men saw many dead horses. Earlier passers-by had cut choice parts of the horseflesh, some of which was already rotting. The men now followed the example of their predecessors and took what they could salvage.

The battery rested in Špilenca and arrived in Slap before dark. The men slept well on bales of straw in a large barn, grateful for protection against the elements. The following day they repaired their *carrettos*, the wooden, horse-drawn two-wheelers on which they transported the guns and the ammunition, and cleaned the guns and the gear. In the process they discovered, to their surprise, that horses have lice, too, a species twice as large as the men's, so they scrubbed and cleaned the horses as well. They washed themselves and their underwear. The field kitchens provided hot water, as much as they wanted, a luxury beyond belief.

In Slap there were a few Slovene civilians who sold fruit—apples, pears, and plums, one kilo for three crowns—and sweet cider, one liter for 4.80 crowns. There was little else to buy, and many men suffered from dysentery. The latrines were in constant use. Jan, too, had intestinal problems—at which time twenty-three of the most deserving front-line veterans, Jan among them, were invited to apply for home leave, but only if they were in good health. All twenty-three men, most of them weak with "the runs," reported healthy and ready for home leave. Without a moment's hesitation the regimental doctor approved them all. On November 12, with home leave permits in their pockets, the lucky twenty-three left Slap before daybreak in order to reach Sv. Lucija/S. Lucia/Most na Soči, some 10 km northwest of Slap, before the expected arrival of the evening train. They wanted to make sure they would get on it.

Second Home Leave, November 12 – December 5

What a walk it was! Forewarned, none of the men had breakfasted that morning or eaten supper the evening before. Every fifty paces or so, groups would scatter and make a dash for the bushes, often before they could lower their pants. They arrived in Sv. Lucija exhausted but in plenty of time for the train, still determined not to touch food or drink. They washed and cleaned themselves as well as they could, lay down in the weak autumn sun in a meadow close to the station, and rested.

The train was overcrowded. After the successful Isonzo offensive, a total frontal breakthrough, the Austrian High Command granted generous leaves to as many deserving front-line veterans as it could spare, in Jan's case three full weeks plus travel time! The railroad cars were packed, and the air was foul with the rank odors of soiled clothing and unwashed bodies. Jan was glad to be one among many, especially since it was almost impossible to get to the toilet, which was never free anyway.

In Vienna there was another joyous homecoming. After thorough and heavy-duty bathing, washing, delousing, cleaning, and ironing, Jan became a dapper civilian again, physically almost relaxed and mentally as close to peace as he could be. He gloried in the timely disappearance of his dysentery. He and Božena spent every moment together, talking, laughing, eating, loving—between waiting on customers in the store, of course. They could not get enough of each other. Jan had not seen little Božena, now fourteen months old, since a year ago. His approaching departure was never mentioned, but it hung heavily over both of them, especially during the third week.

Since Jan's last, very brief leave barely four months before, Vienna had changed perceptibly. The gay city of 1914 was long gone, of course, but so was the sober Vienna of 1916. The food queues were noticeably longer, the shortages of fuel, clothing, shoes, and medicine more severe, the numbers of refugees from the east larger, the prices considerably higher, and the black market, bribery, and corruption much more widespread. Božena had written Jan of all this, of course, but now he could see for himself what the prolonged war was doing to this city of lights, now dimmed. There were more women working in munitions factories than men, church bells were being melted down for guns, newspaper accounts were checkered with white spaces where censors had altered the text, and children were being sent to gather firewood in the Vienna Woods. While the coffeehouses were still open for business, theaters and movie houses playing, and concert bills posted on every street corner, Vienna was decaying visibly. Jan was saddened to think of Božena so brave and alone in these dreary times.

Still, the leave restored him. He needed the rest and the loving human touch more than he knew. The one response that puzzled him was that he could not sleep! Staying for any length of time in a warm bed was painful. His bones, especially his joints, ached terribly. After many months of sleeping in the open, more often than not in harsh conditions, the softness and comfort of a clean bed and the weight of light goosedown comforter were more than Jan could bear. His shoulder joints hurt so much that, to relieve the pain, he had to get up and walk around with his arms outstretched and held high above his head. He was perplexed. He told Božena that he hoped the mysterious ailment might lead to a prolonged rest in a field hospital, a prospect he had often wished for at the front.

The parting was heartbreaking, as always. Would they see each other again? The unspoken question was present, unbidden, at every departure. They clung to each other and wept, each for the other.

Back in Slap, December 5, 1917 – January 12, 1918

By December 5, Jan was back in Slap. Miraculously, he was able to sleep again, night after night after night! A smart medic told Jan that the pain in his joints was an allergic reaction to the down covers in his feather bed, for certain. Jan believed him. He was back in thrall to the article of faith of the Austrian (or, perhaps, universal?) military, that even in the rear and resting, soldiers must never be idle. The drills, marches, lectures, schooling, mending, and cleaning went on. Grudgingly, the veterans submitted to the regimen, officers and NCOs as well. During Jan's leave Captain Müller had been promoted and left the battery. Lt. Kreibich, battle-seasoned and experienced, arrived to replace the captain as acting commander. The men took to him right away. The quiet understanding between him and the men on what was excessive attention to duty and what was too little worked out well.

On December 19 additional men from the regiment, some 113 total, left for Christmas leave. Jan was put in charge of a detail of 35 men to travel to the town of Celje, almost two days away by train via Ljubljana, to pick up 35 horses for the regiment. It would be a welcome break from the daily routine and a new experience, Jan thought. As always the train was full, and the men had to stand all the way. In Celje they marched to broken-down barracks, where they were meagerly fed and slept poorly, shivering with cold and wet to the skin. On December 25, Christmas Day, the horses, with harnesses and blankets, were ready for transport, but the detail had to wait several hours for four box cars to be added to the regular train. Even when finally they were under way, there were additional long delays to allow priority military and express trains to pass ahead of them en route to the front. The men, frozen and hungry, were sorry for themselves. What a rotten Christmas!

Back in Slap, two packages from Božena awaited Jan, one which had been long lost and the other hand-delivered by a friend, Schimunek, who had just returned from Vienna. There was at least a taste of Christmas in the goodies Božena had sent and in Schimunek's account of his visit with her.

The successful, German-led Austrian offensive now over, the magnitude of the victory within the context of a long and essentially static trench war on the Isonzo and the opportunity which it offered must have jostled the Austrian High Command out of its complacency. On January 5, 1918, all leaves were canceled, and a new battery commander arrived, Captain Ritter, to replace the acting commander, Lieut. Kreibich, and to prepare the battery for its departure to the new front nine days hence.

The new commander, a greenhorn to the front lines, replaced a lieutenant who was a combat veteran. Up to that time, the new captain had been posted in Vienna, "a real shirker," the men commented among themselves. To make up for his lack of experience in battle and to prove to one and all his mettle as a tough soldier, Capt. Ritter instituted a regimen of full-time drills across the board, with all the absurdities of correct saluting, precision marching, taxing exercises on the parade grounds, and, above all else, iron discipline—at inspections, musters, and drills, drills, drills. Lieut. Kreibich stood calmly by; the men, who knew him well, read the amusement and chagrin in the lieutenant's face and fully agreed with him. Happily, this nonsense would be over soon—sooner than they expected.

After a week of this organized lunacy, the battery received orders to leave Slap on January 12. All hands worked overtime, especially the blacksmiths, to repair guns, carts, wagons, kitchen gear, to shoe the horses, and to do the thousand tasks that needed to be done. Jan was sent as an orderly to Kneža, a village in the vicinity, to return some borrowed army manuals. It rained the whole day, and he was soaked. New replacements arrived to put the battery at full strength, a staff sergeant (*Feuerwerker*) and ten men, who had to be trained. New equipment was issued, tested, and distributed as needed. Somehow, as scheduled, on January 12 the battery was ready to move.

III
THE ITALIAN CAMPAIGN: THE PIAVE FRONT

The Magic Castle
From the Isonzo to the Piave, January 12 – February 6

On the first day, January 12, the battery marched to Tolmin via Bača pri Modreju and Modrej, a distance of some fifteen kilometers; the next day they marched to Staro Selo-Marony/Sella di Caporetto via Caporetto, some twenty kilometers northwest; the third day, in steady rain, south to Ponteacco, entering Italy for the first time; the fourth day in heavy fog southwest to Moimacco via Cividale di Friuli; and the fifth day via Udine west to Pasian, their first and well-deserved rest stop (Map IV). The battery stayed in Pasian for three days to clean up everything that was muddy from the unpaved roads full of deep potholes, to unharness the tired horses and let them graze, to get hot coffee and food more often than once a day (for two days they were without bread), and to rest their weary feet. They were in Italy! When the morning fog lifted, an expanse of sunny, beautiful and inviting flat land opened up in front of them. The civilians remaining here (many of the locals had fled with the retreating Italian army) sold them wine for 1.50 crowns a liter and exchanged milk and polenta for tobacco. The front seemed far, far away.

On January 20 the battery was on the road again. That day they marched to the small town of S. Lorenzo; the wine was cheaper here, one liter for only 1.20 crowns. The next day (very much like a warm spring day in Moravia, Jan thought) they crossed the Tagliamento River and, bypassing Casarza di Delizia, halted in S. Giovanni. Here there was no more food to be bartered: the advancing German army had already requisitioned everything in sight. The few remaining locals were ordered to turn over all edibles, including animals, to the Austrian military command.

The next day, January 23, the battery marched via Casarza and Pordenone to a small village nearby, where they rested again for a day. Everyone was worn out, and Jan had a stubborn fever that had persisted for almost a week. That night he slept in a loft in warm hay and felt better. The battery had been on the move since January 12, and there seemed to be no end to the marching. Their feet hurt. The success of the offensive had taken its toll on the weary men of the Second Battery.

On January 25 the men marched to Sacile and then to Colle Umberto, a small town southeast from Vittorio Veneto, that they reached late in the afternoon. Although the night was cold, Jan again slept well in a small barn in soft hay. The next day dawned sunny and almost warm. The mountains in the distance glistened with fresh snow, and the lowlands shone bright green. Some distance from their bivouac, atop a low hill, stood an imposing old castle. Drinking their morning coffee, the men noticed that there was much activity in the environs and on the castle grounds. Large crowds of soldiers seemed to be milling about. What was going on? The battery observers pulled out their binoculars and, to their amazement, saw men in various stages of disorder staggering and falling in all directions, seemingly drunk! Surely, this could not be. The battery was intrigued. The men who were not on duty volunteered on the spot to walk over, investigate, and report back. Jan was among them.

What they found was a soldier's dream. The crowds of men around the deserted castle were indeed drunk, some of them passed out. The battery scouts walked through the large gate into the castle courtyard to see for themselves the source of all that pleasure. In the spacious cellars of the castle stood butts, large barrels, and casks, some as large as small houses, full of delicious, aged wines, mostly red but white as well, and spirits, especially brandies and cognacs, of many kinds and vintages. Wine flowed freely from many of the open spigots. The cellar floors were knee-deep in wine. Just below the stairs to the cellars floated the body of a drowned infantryman. "There are worse ways to die," Jan thought to himself.

Electrified, the scouts ran back to the battery and told the incredulous men of their astonishing discovery. They collected as many pails and buckets as they could carry and ran back to the castle to fill them. First, they themselves needed to sample freely in order to select only the choicest wines from the many available. They barely made it back to the battery. Before dark that day, the entire battery—the men, the NCOs, and the officers, including the tough new battery commander, Capt. Ritter—were dead drunk.

The next morning, January 27, armed regimental guards were posted around the castle, and a thorough investigation began. But the officers, like the guards, were hung over, and around all of the field kitchens stood rows and rows of buckets filled with wine. The battery had to stay in Colle Umberto an extra day "to clean up and to give the horses a rest...."

On January 29, a pleasant, warm day, the march west continued via Vittorio Veneto to Follina. Here, the regimental supply people exchanged six tired battery horses for six fresh ones, and the officers of the battery consulted with the regimental command on the next field assignment. They came to the decision that in the future the three batteries of the regiment would once again operate jointly.

The men could sense that they were approaching the front, which from Follina was only three marching days away. On the road to Lentiai, a village in the mountains northwest of Follina on the east bank of the Piave River, their last full stop before their new position on the front line, the battery's first line—the guns, their crews, the packhorses with their drivers, plus the usual contingent of field observers, medics, and telephone operators—separated from the second line, comprised of supply and reserve personnel. The latter could not make it with their carts and wagons over the steep and narrow mountain paths ahead. Instead, they took a longer route around the mountain range, to rejoin the battery in Lentiai two days later (Map V).

On the way the gun crews and their packhorses stopped for the night in the small village of Pialder. The day was sunny and pleasant, but there was snow in the mountains, deep in places, and the night was freezing cold. The men, hungry and without rations, spied an old, tired cow that had lost its way; they killed it, butchered it, and cooked it then and there. They slept with full stomachs that night.

The next day the two lines of the battery met in Lentiai. With the remains of the beef, there was more than enough food for all that evening, for a change. The following morning Capt. Ritter, and his second in command, Lieut. Kreibich, went on ahead to have a look at the battery's designated front-line position. They encountered no problems.

In the evening of February 5 the battery left for the front. They marched the whole night, running into light artillery fire for the first time in a long while. The mountain road was full of ruts and potholes; even the horses tended to stumble. Milies, a tiny village high up in the mountains, their supply line and the last rest stop before their final destination, lay on the east bank of the Piave, almost 20 km south and down-river from Lentiai, in the vicinity of the Austrian military designation "Kota 981." They reached Milies in the morning, rested, and left for the front in the evening. Their designated station was the westernmost position of the battery up to that time, more than 100 kilometers from the Isonzo; it was situated on the top of the crooked mountain in front of them, an uphill hike of about three hours.

Buckling Under
Milies, February 7 – May 5

The mountain trail was steep and the night dark. It became clear, about half way to their destination, that the packhorses were not up to the task; with their heavy loads they were unable to negotiate the precipitous, winding, slippery, snow-covered path. The men stopped at an empty mountain hut, unloaded the guns and ammunition from the horses, and sent them back with their drivers. The men themselves sought shelter for the night in and around the hut under brush and trees.

In the morning of February 7, cold and miserable, they returned to the Milies supply line. The hike there and the hot coffee helped to revive them. Returning to the resting place of the night before with men from the supply line to help them, they shouldered the saddle bags with the gun parts and ammunition and carried them, laboriously, to the new site. Fortunately, the distance was short; even with the heavy loads, they reached their destination in a little more than three hours. It was also to their advantage that the route was on the side of the mountain hidden from the enemy, who did not know of the battery's existence as yet.

The battery crews had time to dig trenches and build protective covers for the guns, dugouts, and the officers' quarters without being distracted by the enemy artillery. Jan found several deserted mountain huts nearby, one-room shanties where shepherds had lived in the summer. The men used the doors and windows of the huts to build simple structures sheltering the officers' dugouts. Like some of his friends, Jan decided to sleep the first night in one of the shepherd huts. He found a small place in the loft which was protected, more or less, from the wind and snow blowing through the gaping windows and doorways. He put one blanket underneath him; then, believing that he would be warmer undressed than dressed, he took off his muddy and soaked boots and his uniform, lay down in a fetal position, and covered himself with the second blanket and his overcoat. With his knapsack under his head, he slept like a baby.

In the morning Jan found his boots frozen hard as stone, the water in his canteen frozen, and the canteen cracked and useless. He washed himself with snow, dressed, built a small fire, boiled snow in his mess kit, added chicory, and drank the hot brew with satisfaction. He was ready for the new day.

On February 8 and 9 the supply detail delivered boxes of ammunition twice each day but not much food. The men continued building dugouts for themselves and the NCOs. The enemy still had no idea that a new Austrian battery was facing them. At night on February 10 heavy caliber Italian cannons fired several rounds in the vicinity of the battery, but not at the battery itself. The men enjoyed the unexpected calm.

On February 11 Jan was promoted to commander of one of the battery's four guns. He was happy to be relieved from the responsibility of ammunition procurement for the battery; he often worried that he had no effective control over the availability of the ammunition, which depended on supplies in the rear and on the efficiency of the detail that brought them to the battery. He was pleased, too, that his gunnery skills were recognized.

The lull ended on February 13, when the battery started to shoot a few ranging rounds and a few rounds for effect, but the Italian response was mild and slow. The big news that day was that Russia, indeed, was about to conclude a separate peace treaty with the Central Powers—an interesting bit of information but far from vital to the well-being of the battery. What mattered most to the men that day was the weather, which was terrible and getting worse: freezing cold, sharp winds, and frequent snow storms—nearly two feet of fresh snow that day alone.

Another vital concern was the food. Not only was its delivery increasingly irregular, but the quality and quantity worsened every day. On good days, if they were lucky, the daily rations consisted of 450 grams of old, moldy bread, two herring to be divided among three men, 4-5 spoonfuls of watery soup, a hardtack, and a bit of dry polenta. For coffee they boiled water with chicory twice a day. The field kitchen ran out of salt again, and cigarettes and tobacco were rare. At least the incoming artillery shells were infrequent now, some days fewer than others.

On February 18 the men were subjected to surprise searches by field police looking for leaflets being dropped from Italian planes over the Austrian lines. In the leaflets Czech soldiers were encouraged to desert and come over to the Italian side, where they would be warmly welcomed, treated honorably, and could, if they wished, fight back with the Italians against their "Austrian oppressors." The men knew better than to keep such leaflets if they saw them. Everyone was searched routinely, but there was only a handful of Czechs in the whole Second Battery, a unit from Vienna. Among the gunners, Jan was the only Czech at that time, and for a Czech artillery man to desert was practically impossible. He would have had to cross the many infantry trenches, which here included the reserve infantry trenches as well, and then swim across the mighty Piave holding a white flag over his head! And how would Božena fare when news of his desertion reached the authorities in Vienna?

Compared to the Isonzo front, the battery sector here had been relatively quiet. There was intermittent mutual shelling on some days—one man at the battery was wounded in the chest by a grenade fragment and had to be carried back to the reserve line dressing station—but the action was limited. There were rumors of an upcoming Austrian offensive, confirmed, everyone thought, by a special issue of rum—but nothing came of it. The Italians kept four tethered observation balloons in the flat lands well beyond the Piave, which, on clear days, gave the men a reason to stay hidden and an excuse to rest from their daily chores, a break they appreciated.

One by one the battery horses were dying of starvation; there was almost no fodder left. Of the thirty-six horses assigned to the battery, twelve remained, and only six were healthy. The men would have dearly loved to keep a carcass for themselves, but the supply detail was ordered to deliver the dead horses to the regimental slaughterhouse. The men were distinctly weak from lack of food.

On February 27 while carrying ammunition to the battery, the supply detail found, in the hollow of a receding snow bank close to the trail, a frozen cow that must have perished there the previous fall. They butchered the carcass on the spot, kept the choicest pieces of meat, hid them in the snow to be picked up on their way back to the supply line, and informed the gunners of the location of the carcass. The gunners appeared right away, cut as much meat as they could from the heap of bones, brought it back to the position, divided it, and boiled it in their mess kits.

By coincidence, that same afternoon Jan's friend, Franz Dubový, now a sergeant, had just returned from Vienna and brought a package from Božena, a large, fresh apple strudel wrapped in a piece of newspaper that had stuck to the succulent pastry. Starved as he was, Jan devoured the whole thing, newspaper and all, to the amusement of Dubový, who, as butcher at the regimental slaughterhouse, seldom experienced hunger. Jan was not ashamed. Nothing had ever tasted as good as that papered strudel. By then the boiling beef was tender enough to eat, but it smelled so bad that Jan could not swallow it, even a small piece. He gave it to his grateful friends, who were eyeing it.

In his free time Jan worked on improving his dugout. He deepened and widened it and filled it with straw from one of the mountain huts. At one end he built a small, discreet fireplace, hidden from the outside but providing warmth inside. Firewood was increasingly hard to find, especially since everyone else was looking for it, too. All the men were foraging for pieces of lumber and other useful items to embellish their dugouts and trenches and make them comfortable. The freezing cold was like an unwelcome, angry guest that refused to leave. A thick, heavy layer of snow covered everything.

At noon on March 4 a regimental physician arrived to check on the men's health. He set up his expensive camera on a tripod, taking the time and trouble to adjust everything to perfection—and spent the time allotted to him taking artistic photographs of the guns shooting, the picturesque countryside below the battery position, and the splendid mountains overhead. Nodding amiably to one and all, he departed without even opening his medical bag. The men were just delighted. The doctor must have thought they looked healthy, despite their weakened state. It was Jan's twenty-eighth birthday.

A Battery Field Observer, March 10 – May 5

On March 10 Jan was promoted from commander of his gun to battery observer, a function that normally called for the rank of corporal or better, which Jan, a private first class (*Vormeister*), had not attained as yet. After dark he left for the battery observation post, which was located on a large mountain ledge about three kilometers away from the battery but only about 300 meters above it. Walking at night it took him almost an hour to get to the spot because the path was visible to Italian observers.

Jan was glad. The new job would exempt him from the daily routine at the battery, which was becoming increasingly onerous. The regimental command had just ordered the gunners to build three new reserve positions and air raid shelters behind the positions, but provided no building materials. The lumber from the mountain huts nearby was by then long gone. Also, serving as an observer would not only offer Jan a certain amount of personal latitude, but was also a task he had enjoyed doing a few times earlier, when sent out to scout an area.

At full capacity there were four men at the observation post: a designated officer deputy, two sergeants, and a corporal. But sometimes there were only three or even two observers present, when extra men were needed at the guns. The observers shared several pairs of good, strong field binoculars and a powerful telescope mounted on a sturdy tripod, with a viewing range, on a clear day, of up to almost fifty kilometers.

The observation post was located in the stone cellar of a mountain hut; next to it was a cowshed, where one of the sergeants and now Jan slept. A field telephone connected the observers with the battery. The enemy had not discovered the observation point as yet.

The next morning Jan began to learn the lay of the land in front of him with one of the sergeants as his instructor, a good one as it turned out. The detailed, topographical local maps issued by the German High Command were invaluable. In the valley below, dividing the two hostile armies from each other, flowed the Piave River. On the right beyond the Piave was the Monte Tomba range, and on the horizon beyond it the glaciers of the Swiss Alps. On the left was the Montello rise. Between Monte Tomba and Montello and extending to the river Brenta, a green and fertile valley glistened in the sun. To the left of Montello, a large, low plain extended all the way to Venice. The view was breathtaking.

Below the observation point, on the battery side of the river, lay the complex trenches of the Austrian infantry facing the Italian infantry in their trenches on the other side of the river, a situation similar to Avšje at the Isonzo. In both sets of trenches all was relatively quiet except for the sharpshooters on both sides, who, with telescopic lenses mounted on their marksmen rifles, were searching for and finding likely targets. Jan could hear these exchanges. But what intrigued him the most was an Italian heavy machine gun nest located somewhere on a hill to the right of the observation point. The lone gun controlled, masterfully, the main Austrian access road from the trenches to the rear. As yet the battery observers had not been able to pinpoint the exact location of the machine gun, not even at night. They guessed that the nozzle of the barrel was equipped with some kind of funnel shield so that the shot flashes were not visible. They surmised that the gunner, being as good as he was, must be French.

The four tethered enemy balloons Jan had watched from the battery position were located on the flat land behind a group of low hills between Monte Tomba and Montello. They arose daily in the morning fog and descended in the evening after dark. During the night both sides, mainly the Italians but the Austrians, too, shot up flares, cartridges which released stars that burned with brilliant intensity, some suspended from parachutes, illuminating brightly the darkness above the no-man's-land and the trenches. The best visibility over the whole area, Jan discovered, was early in the morning between 3 and 5 a.m., when the air was the clearest. The observers could then spot and report to the battery any movement of Italians altering their positions.

On March 21 the battery commander, Captain Ritter, reported ill and left for the regimental field hospital. His departure caused no stir since the veteran Lt. Kreibich was running the battery anyway. The following day a green second-in-command arrived, Second Lieutenant Zeigner, and all went on as before.

Directly in front of the observation post some eight kilometers away was a small village clustered around a church with a high steeple, from which Italian observers directed their artillery fire at the Austrian lines. The Austrian observers reported this finding to the battery, who directed their fire on the church steeple. The battery guns may have had the precision but not the range; the church tower remained intact.

The battery did, however, put out of commission one of the Italian observation balloons due to Jan's perseverance. The balloons appeared to emerge from behind a group of small hills out of battery range. The matter absorbed Jan; he began to concentrate his attention on the one balloon which seemed closer than the other three. Every evening he marked on his chart the spot where the balloon seemed to disappear in the darkness and every morning where it reappeared again. After several days Jan was certain: the balloon was not tethered behind the hills but in the village in front of them. He measured the distance; it was about ten kilometers, still too far for Jan's battery, which had a range of only seven kilometers, but there was a new battery located to their left with the most recent model Škoda 14/19 howitzers of ten centimeter caliber, that had a ten kilometer range.

On March 26 in the morning, with the permission of the commander of the observation post, Jan telephoned his discovery to the howitzer battery, but the duty sergeant did not believe him. Jan asked to talk to the battery commander, to whom he repeated his finding. The commander did not believe him either but promised to pass on the information to the regimental command, frustrating Jan. Late that afternoon, however, Jan saw that the new Škoda battery began to shell the balloon with shrapnel, one round after another. The balloon came down in a hurry, never to be seen again.

The front remained relatively quiet. Except for occasional fire fights at night between hostile patrols probing each other's positions and their respective states of alert, there were no infantry movements of any depth or size on either side of the Piave. The artilleries of the two armies shelled each other but without much conviction. The airplane activity did not seem to amount to much either; to the men at the battery, what they saw in the air seemed more like drills and exercises than the real thing.

The Italians, with their post-Caporetto English and French reinforcements—six French divisions and five British, it was rumored—were engaged in strengthening their defensive positions while apparently preparing for an offensive. The Austrians, on the other hand, now viewed their highly successful Caporetto offensive almost as a Pyrrhic victory, one that was perhaps achieved at too great a cost. With the invaluable help of the seven German divisions, they had chased the Italian army across the Friuli-Venezia Giulia area all the way to the Piave. Once there, however, they lost their momentum. The High Command was unable to supply the rapidly advancing forces with their vital needs—food, medicine, horses, warm clothing, equipment, spare parts and, in some cases, even men, weapons, and ammunition. The Austrian army was not sufficiently prepared to exploit its huge advance and to finish off the demoralized Italian army, just as Karl, Jan's neighbor in Vienna, had predicted. Nor were the Germans there to supply the needed push.

At the moment the two forces now facing each other on the Piave showed little energy, initiative, or enthusiasm. Possible offensives were expected, Italian at the end of March and Austrian at the end of April, but nothing in fact happened. There were a few half-hearted infantry attacks and counterattacks; in one case the Austrians moved several artillery pieces forward into the infantry trenches, and the men at the battery were issued rations of rum, but there was no follow-up. Neither side was ready for full engagement.

The weather was bad, for Jan the worst spring yet. If it did not snow, it hailed, and if it did not hail, it rained buckets. This was the storm season in the mountains, spectacular for those with roofs over their heads but miserable for those without. The frozen observer team huddled around a tiny fire, invisible to the enemy, who still did not know the location of the observation post. Jan and his teammates watched with envy the bright Italian sun shining down on the plains through rifts in the clouds. To make it worse, they, like their battery comrades, were ordered to turn in their second winter blankets to the regimental command, which offered no explanation. What could they have been thinking of, in this bitter cold...? The men were furious.

The lice seemed to thrive on the men's discomfort. There was no way to get rid of them. The new, clean, warm underwear which an orderly from the regiment had distributed to the battery two weeks earlier, attracted, as expected, more lice than the old, dirty underwear. Nevertheless, the men washed themselves as well as they could with hot water from the melted snow, but there was no soap to be had, for them or for their laundry. Mail delivery was sporadic, too. In fact, the battery regimental mail carrier, whose path to the battery was often under direct enemy fire, had set fire to the mail three times before being apprehended. What he did with packages from home one could only imagine. He was arrested, court-martialed, and sent to jail, too late to do any good.

But the most scandalous situation of all was the lack of food. While the officers were relatively well fed, or so the men believed, the rank and file were starving. The little bread or polenta they were now issued contained sawdust or even sand; there was little or no meat; for coffee they had chicory and little of that; and since food was distributed in bulk only once every two or three days with rations to be divided among three, four, or even five men, increasingly they had trouble with rats. Jan thought he had solved the problem: one evening he hung the small loaf of bread allotted for the next three days on a string tied to the ceiling above his pallet in the cowshed. In the morning the bread was indented with deep rat bites. Jan and his roommate finished the bread that day and did without the next day and the day after that. The tobacco situation was not yet desperate, but it was worsening, too, and precious matches were in short supply. Salt was only a memory. The men worried in earnest about losing strength.

More and more often now, the men were issued money, the inflated Austrian crowns, instead of food. But except for a very occasional black market can of meat or a frozen piece of horse meat or beef, there was nothing to buy and no one to buy it from.

When he was off duty, Jan often took walks behind the observation post in search of food and firewood. In deeper hollows he sometimes found young grass, which he gathered, carried back with him, and boiled in his mess kit; without salt it was hard to swallow, but it was hot and it was food of sorts.

One evening Jan found fresh animal tracks possibly made by a wolf known to be in the vicinity. Since he was not on duty that night, Jan asked one of the sergeants to take over for him so that he could watch for the animal. The sergeant, boasting of his own hunting prowess, refused. He wanted to shoot the wolf himself, and, indeed, a day later, about a kilometer from the post he spotted the wolf. Carefully, he stalked the animal, sneaked into shooting range, took aim, fired—and missed. Gone was the possibility of fresh meat. It was not easy for Jan to swallow his anger.

By May 5 the men were so weak they could walk only a few paces at a time. That morning the battery received orders to pack up, leave the position, and go back to regroup. The weakened observation team moved slowly down to the battery. The listless gunners followed the routines with difficulty and, together with the enervated supply people, set out for Milies. Fully loaded, they could hardly move on the steep trail, their knees buckling under them every few steps. The hike to the Milies supply line took almost a day instead of the usual few hours.

By then Lieut. Kreibich knew he had to act decisively. He telephoned the regiment and after a heated exchange received permission to kill a sick horse and feed the men forthwith. All who knew how, helped the cooks to butcher the carcass and cook the meat. There was no bread or vegetables or salt, but there was plenty of soup and meat. The men ate every scrap in short order; some, unused to a full stomach, became sick, but not critically. By midnight the whole battery, the front line as well as the reserve line, was revived and on its way. Those few who still could not march found space on the wagons or carts. There was plenty of good will all around.

Preparing for a Final Victory
From Milies to San Michele di Piave, May 5 – June 14

From Milies the battery marched to the Segusino supply line through large, beautiful, green forests under sporadic hostile fire. In Segusino, a small town south of Milies, several men had to be treated for acute malnutrition. Jan, reinstated as gun commander, was appointed the battery advance man on its way to S. Giovanni, their destination in the rear, some seventy kilometers east of Segusino as the crow flies. The battery was to rest there as well as train for its next front-line assignment on the Piave. Jan's task was to scout the best route and to secure nightly billets, lodgings suitable for the entire battery on its march east—first via Colderu to Trichiana; then via Belluno and Levego to Savassa; then via Vittorio Veneto to Baver, a small village south of Pianzano; and finally, to arrange transportation by train from Pianzano to Casarza d. Delizia and S. Giovanni (Map V).

This was an easy, week-long trip. Unlike the miserable, high altitude conditions at Milies, the May weather here was warm, the days sunny, and the nights pleasant and mild, a welcome change. The pace was relaxed. The daily marches started early but ended early, too, usually at mid-afternoon if not sooner. The food situation improved markedly. In Segusino Jan received two packages from home, hand-delivered by friend Dubový. One package contained a two kilo loaf of fresh, dark rye bread, which Jan devoured with black coffee in about twenty minutes while talking to Dubový, who was continually astonished by Jan's appetite. Bartering food along the road proved rewarding as well. In Trichiana and Savassa Jan exchanged cigarettes from Božena's second package for milk and polenta, but he did not have the courage to try the local garden snails offered as delicacies. Occasionally, the civilians took Austrian money, too.

In Savassa two of the battery packhorses became so sick that they could no longer walk. There was a field slaughterhouse in Savassa (happy coincidence), and the battery cooks served the meat from one of the horses for dinner that very night. Choice pieces of the other horse were sold or bartered by the slaughterhouse sergeants to the highest bidders. With daring but within reason, he argued to himself, Jan bought the liver, the heart with suet, and over a kilo of flank meat in exchange for his service revolver, a standard, ten-round M7 pistol, and ammunition. It was worth the risk, Jan told himself. He shared the liver with his friends; the heart with the suet he roasted, clandestinely, in a tomb that enclosed a small chapel in the cemetery close by. The tomb was old and crumbling; in the corner with jaws agape a skeleton stood watch. "Skeletons do not divulge secrets," thought Jan as he tended to his cooking. He saved over a kilo of precious fat from the suet.

In Baver, the battery's next stop, Jan chopped the flank meat, mixed it with some of the fat, and baked the ground meat in his mess kit. It was the best meal of the trip. Also in Baver, Jan was promoted to corporal, a rank whose duties he had been performing ever since he had become battery observer on the Milies front.

S. Giovanni, May 13 – June 3

Upon arrival in S. Giovanni on May 13, a beautiful spring day, the battery was billeted in and around a schoolhouse. The town was full of soldiers, mostly infantrymen, who were also there for rest and training. The battery's first order was to march three kilometers to a larger town south of S. Giovanni, S. Vito al Tagliamento, to a delousing station. They placed all their clothes, in separate bundles, into large metal ovens to bake the lice into oblivion while they themselves took hot showers. The bundles came back steaming hot, but the intrepid lice came back, too, alive and well.

After all this time in the field, Jan's uniform, like those of his comrades, showed signs of heavy wear and tear, especially the pants, boots, and gaiters. So he paid a tailor to make him a new pair of canvas pants and bought himself a pair of serviceable, used boots and leather gaiters. Many of the other men did the same. Imagine their surprise when two weeks later, before their departure for the front, the whole battery was issued brand new uniforms and boots! So now they had a welcome supply of scarce goods on hand for illicit barter. Also, on May 18 the regiment supplied the battery with new saddle bags for the guns, in the event they would need to be dismantled and carried by packhorses.

On May 19 the new training started. The battery was told that its next mission was to accompany the infantry and provide it with firepower, offensive as well as defensive, in "integrated forward battle engagements." The battery was to be part of the Thirteenth Group Division, a new major tactical unit. The men interpreted the order to mean that the battery would be posted in front of the infantry, not behind it. Indignant, the veterans at the battery remembered that dreadful night in August, 1917, at Mt. Liesl, during the Eleventh Battle of the Isonzo, when the battery, placed in front of the infantry, was forced into that terrible retreat! Their suspicions would be confirmed less than a month later on the Piave.

Operating jointly with the infantry, the battery practiced crossing the Tagliamento on pontoon bridges as well as on single pontoons, advancing and retreating with the infantry on both sides of the river. Then they practiced target shooting with live ammunition at relatively close ranges, firing over the heads of the infantry at mock-ups of tanks, trench mortars, flame throwers, and similar weapons that might threaten the infantry at close range.

On a beautiful sunny morning on May 21, the commander of the Imperial and Royal Sixth Army, Colonel General Archduke Joseph himself, arrived with his staff for inspection. (The Imperial and Royal Mountain Artillery Regiment No. 201 was part of the Ninth Infantry Division of the Second Corps of the Sixth Army.) His Excellency was especially interested in observing the battery in action against tanks, the highly praised new combat vehicles. The Group Commander ordered two mock-ups of tanks to be placed on rails behind a small hillside. The plan was to move the tanks back and forth while two guns of Jan's battery advanced quietly and, without being observed, shot and destroyed the tanks. Jan's gun—he was still the commander—was selected as one of the guns. The battery commander was to be present only as an observer.

The two guns advanced according to plan, followed at a short distance by the Archduke and his entourage. In what Jan considered a safe shooting range behind a burned out farmhouse, the two crews placed their guns into firing positions. About to pick up a shell below him in a shallow indentation, one of Jan's gunners lost his balance. Standing next to him, Jan tried to steady the man, but nervous at being so closely observed, pushed the gunner in the wrong direction. The man fell practically at the feet of the Archduke, who turned to Jan and shouted at him, threatening him with court martial for abusing his men. Steaming in his fury, he ordered Lt. Kreibich to punish Jan severely for his transgression.

In the aftermath of the scene, the two gun crews, ready and still in firing range, started to shell the two moving tank targets. The battery commander watched silently. On the third shot Jan's gun hit one of the tanks; the second tank disappeared from view behind bushes on a small, flat hill out of range. The men wanted to advance and move the guns into range once more, but the Archduke had had enough. Jan and his crew expected the distinguished inspector to congratulate them on the lucky shot, but he strode off. On the way back, Lieutenant Kreibich winked at Jan with a smile, that being the extent of the "severe punishment" he was due to receive.

On May 27 the battery, accompanied by several infantry companies, crossed the Tagliamento on pontoons and practiced integrated attacks and counterattacks on the beachhead. In one of the mock maneuvers, Jan and twenty-six men from the battery captured a lieutenant who was commanding one of the "enemy" infantry companies. Simple gunners taking an officer prisoner was a feat unheard of. Their reward, which the men agreed was miserly but better than nothing, was six cigarettes per man.

The weather in the S. Giovanni region was glorious. On their marches to the Tagliamento the men admired the large, cultivated expanse of mulberry trees on whose leaves silkworms fed. Apparently as early as the Middle Ages the region was famous for its production of fine silk.

Food and tobacco were now more than adequate—Jan sold some of his bread at ten crowns per loaf and 100 cigarettes for eight crowns. The quality of the barter was also favorable, the cheapest Austrian cigarettes being traded for fresh milk and good red wine. The men were rested, some even bored; but there was a field movie theater in S. Vito, which the men delighted in visiting as often as they could.

The silver medal second class *"Der Tapferkeit"* ("For Bravery") that Jan had been awarded in July, 1917, caught up with him here almost a year later, and he was formally decorated at an awards ceremony. At the same ceremony Jan received another medal, the *"Karltruppen Kreuz: Princeps et Patria: Vitam et Sanguinem"* ("The Cross of Emperor Karl's Troops: Prince and Country: Life and Blood"), which was awarded to all battle-tested veterans.

Finally, new replacement arrived fresh from basic training, recruits from the most recent Imperial draft: boys seventeen and eighteen years old. Lieutenant Kreibich sent six of them back forthwith. If these boys were the best new soldiers that Austria-Hungary could muster, the men thought, the war could not last much longer. Also, the battery crew was paid in Italian lire for the first time. Jan received 22 lire in pay and 7 lire 87 centesimi as the monthly stipend for the silver medal, not much money considering that a loaf of bread cost 11 lire. He mailed all his Austrian money to Božena. The Austrian crowns were just about worthless here; no one wanted them.

On June 2, the Thirteenth Group Division, of which Jan's battery was now an integral part, was poised for departure on the morrow. The long-awaited Austrian offensive on the Piave was thirteen days away.

S. Giovanni to S. Michele di Piave, June 3 – 14

They left S. Giovanni in rain on June 3 at 8 p.m. and marched west on the main highway through Pordenone to Fontana Fredda (some six and a half hours), their first rest stop; then through Sacile to S. Fior di Sopra (four and a half hours), their second stop; and then to the suburbs of Conegliano (eight hours), where they stayed for almost two days and slept in tents in the rain. A Thirteenth Group Division captain was scheduled to inspect and review the troops there the following day, so the general cleaning and polishing routine went into effect again. After the inspection, in the evening of June 8, in the rain and under the watchful eyes of Italian observer planes, the battery left for their final destination, S. Michele di Piave (four hours), the new reserve and supply line of the group as well as the battery (Map V).

The march from S. Giovanni in the intermittent rain was long, the food rations again small—the men bartered cigarettes for polenta—and the officers of the Group Division came down harder on the men of the battery than did their own artillery command. What did infantry officers know of the needs of an artillery battery and its highly skilled crew? Next to nothing, the men grumbled, offended at the rough treatment.

In S. Michele Lieut. Kreibich saw to it that the front-line segment of the battery lost no time in preparing themselves for the upcoming Austrian offensive. They practiced "crossing the river" at night and in the rain again and again. They listened to lectures on the new or updated weapons such as tanks and the new types of poison gas. Again and again they made certain that all their equipment was in readiness and in good working order. At the last moment, in the morning of June 13 Jan was promoted to the rank of sergeant (*Zugsführer*).

Late that evening in heavy rain, the front-line sector of the battery marched with their gun and ammunition carts toward the first trench on the bank of the Piave facing the enemy. The Austrian infantry was behind them, not in front of them, just as the men had predicted when they tried to figure out the meaning of "integrated forward engagement" when they had first received their orders. Before long the restless enemy searchlights spotted the marching column. When the lights were on them, the men and the horses froze, or tried to; when the lights moved on to other targets, they continued on their way, an ingrained response by now in those who were veterans.

In the dark the enemy began firing their heavy guns on the marching column; the explosions were close but caused no damage. When the battery reached the deep, wide trench the sappers had excavated for them the night before in the face of the river bank, the men placed the assembled guns as deep and as close to the river as they could without getting wet. To fire them, all they needed to do was dig holes in front of each gun barrel, a relatively easy task in the bank's wet clay. The battery position was virtually invisible to Italian observers on the other side of the Piave.

That night the drivers with their horses and empty carts returned to S. Michele. In the morning before daybreak, tired and dirty but their work completed, the gunners returned, too, all of them, to sleep and rest the whole day, June 14.

The Battle of the Piave
Montello, June 15 – 23

In the evening of June 14 the front-line men at Jan's battery received their emergency battle rations for two days: a quarter liter of slivovitz, half liter of beer, half kilo of bread, two cans of meat, several pieces of hardtack, and coffee for breakfast. At 10 p.m., wearing their steel helmets and taking with them only their rifles, sidearms, gas masks, and knapsacks, they departed for their new position, leaving their backpacks, greatcoats, and blanket rolls behind in S. Michele. On the way, they passed the infantry dug in deep and, the men observed with dismay, far from the river. Between the infantry and the battery and overlooking the river was a low-lying, elongated, wooded mound. The battery position was located on the river bank opposite Montello, the long, mole-shaped hill rising on the other side of the Piave. The battery's mission during the first stage of the offensive was to protect the Austrian sappers building pontoon bridges across the river, and then to support the Austrian infantry's attack on the Italian bridgehead.

On June 15 at precisely 3 a.m. the Austrian artillery bombardment opened up (including, reportedly, tear gas shells to neutralize hidden Italian artillery) on the entire Piave front, or so it seemed, from the Adriatic Sea to the Alps, with the exception of Jan's battery, who had orders to wait. Only about two hours later (clearly, the Austrian offensive came as a surprise), did the enemy respond with a heavy defensive artillery barrage which incorporated the French and English batteries that had reportedly joined the Italian defense. By 5 a.m. thousands and thousands of shells flew over Jan's position from both directions—concussion grenades, grenade-shrapnel, shrapnel, mortars, and bombs of all calibers. Light and heavy machine guns and trench mortars from both sides joined the fray. The din was overwhelming. Huddled in their deep shelter, the gunners were stiff with fear. Safely dug in, they still felt exposed and vulnerable in the eye of this storm of steel. This was much worse than anything they had experienced at the Isonzo. They were caught in the middle of one of the greatest battles of the war, and they could do nothing but sit, wait, and pray. They realized that the enemy had no inkling of their position; otherwise, they would not have lasted a minute.

The veterans among the gunners, terrified, could still manage to maintain their composure; but the 17- and 18-year old replacements, "cannon fodder," were a different matter. Nearly all of them had to be physically restrained from jumping up from the trench and running. They wept, wet their pants, cried for their mothers, and disintegrated completely. Two boys did manage, somehow, to escape from the trench and make a dash for the road parallel to the river. Some seventy paces behind the trench they were mowed down like weeds by enemy fire.

With daylight came enemy planes that bombed the infantry trenches, the reserves in the rear, the gun position, and the supply depots. Visibility, however, was deteriorating fast due to the heavy smoke emanating from the multitude of guns banging away, the fires that had started up everywhere, the smoke shells, and the fog and mist that covered the entire battlefield and curled up through the hills, bushes, and trees. The sun had disappeared. The acrid stench and tang of cordite filled the air.

Exactly as planned, at 5:45 a.m. the sappers began to build two pontoon bridges across the river, which here was about 700 meters wide, up to three meters deep, and interspersed with many small islands and gravel bars. The movement of the sappers provided the signal for Jan's battery to open fire to protect the bridge builders from enemy artillery and infantry barrage. The gunners dug small openings in front of each gun barrel and started firing as rapidly as they could. Before long Jan was almost deaf. Seventy-five minutes later, at 7 a.m., when the bridges were ready and in place (the gunners could not believe their eyes), the Austrian infantry, which in the meantime had moved to the river, began to swarm over the bridges to the Italian side. By then many of the enemy trench mortars and machine guns had been silenced. Once most of the Austrian infantry had made the crossing, which was the second signal for Jan's battery, the gunners stopped firing at the Italian infantry trenches and started to shell the artillery positions. When the Austrian infantry, after heavy man-to-man fighting, had secured the Italian trenches and had the enemy on the run, the last signal for the battery, the gunners stopped firing—the gun barrels were dangerously hot by then—dismantled the guns, and packed them and the remaining ammunition on the carts that were already waiting with their horses and drivers on the road behind the riverbank. The whole unit then crossed the river safely on one of the two pontoon bridges.

Unbelievably, this whole operation, which had started at 3 a.m. that morning, went like clockwork. The Italian armed forces—the remains of the Second Army decimated at Caporetto and all of the Third Army, which had fallen back behind the Piave where they were supposed to reconstitute—were clearly not reconstituted as yet. The British and French apparently had their problems, too. Some element of surprise may have helped the Austrians, as did the poor visibility. Perhaps, after all, it was possible that the Austrians could break through into the rich agricultural area of the Veneto! The veterans of the battery were hopeful but not convinced.

On the other side of the river the going was tough. The dirt road leading to the top of Montello was full of shell holes; there were dead and wounded men everywhere, mostly Italians, medics and stretcher bearers as well, dead and dying horses, broken equipment of all sorts, gun and mortar shells, and prisoners of war already under guard, either waiting to be picked up or passing to the rear. In order to be able to make the climb to the top of the hill, the battery needed help with the carts. The men commandeered several POWs to assist them. One was obviously reluctant; when told that he was a chaplain, Jan let him go. Upon Lieut. Kreibich's suggestion, Jan also dismissed two Italian officers; rank had its privileges, even on the battlefield.

By early afternoon when the battery finally did reach the topmost part of the hill, it came, unexpectedly, under heavy enemy artillery fire from the plain behind Montello. Short of ammunition and heavy machine guns and surrounded by a reduced 25th Infantry regiment—a segment of the Thirteenth Group Division of which Jan's battery was a part—the battery retreated below the top of the hill again, changing its battle position three times before nightfall. By then the Austrian forces had advanced over three kilometers and secured part of the northern end of Montello. During the night in heavy rain, the ammunition detail from S. Michele managed to find the battery. Dead tired, everyone slept on the ground right where they were, in shallow trenches. Miraculously, they suffered only four casualties. June 15 was a day they would long remember.

On June 16 in daylight the men were able to orient themselves better. The Montello hill was over eleven kilometers long, broadening to about six and half kilometers at its widest and rising from the river and the plain behind Montello to almost 300 meters. It was covered with pine woods interspersed with vineyards and small, cultivated fields, and the top of the hill was indented with depressions, clefts, and narrow ravines that were useful for protected artillery positions, Austrian or Italian. The terrain offered good cover for whoever had the advantageous position and ready-made obstacles for those attacking them. The northern slopes fell steeply to the river bank.

In the morning the battery shelled the enemy infantry that was active just below Montello, west and south of the hill, as well as a vigorous heavy machine gun nest to their right. In turn, they themselves came under the fire of a battery manned by excellent gunners, probably French; Jan's battery had to dig themselves deeper into the ground. The men had by now learned that in the heat of battle a shell hole, a trench, a dugout, or even a ditch was their friend, the deeper the better. They were used to cohabiting the earth, working in it, eating in it, sleeping in it, whether dry, wet, or muddy; they became one with the earth and wore it on their boots, clothes, and even on their hands and faces. And when they were thirsty, they drank the rain water left standing in shell holes and craters in the ground.

The battery men who had become separated and lost in the confusion on the way up the Montello hill were now showing up, bringing news of what was happening below. They told the men at the battery that south of Montello the Austrians had established several small bridgeheads on the west side of the Piave; that on the last stretch of the river before it entered the Adriatic, the Austrians apparently had been able to make a quick crossing, and the Italian line collapsed. The greatest success on the Piave that first day, June 15, apparently was the establishment of this last bridgehead, eight kilometers wide and almost half a kilometer deep.

The men who turned up were sorely needed. The battery suffered three more casualties that morning. One of them, a sergeant who commanded the third gun, had gone with Jan to look for a new, safer position for the battery. On the way, under light fire, the sergeant was eating hardtack while talking to Jan. Suddenly, Jan heard a soft tap; the sergeant had been hit in his right elbow by a rifle or machine gun bullet. A passing medic put a dressing on the wound and sent the sergeant to the field hospital across the Piave. By reason of this injury, the sergeant would now have a rest in the hospital, a medical home leave, and perhaps even a discharge from the army. "A lucky wound," Jan could not help thinking as he continued on his way alone.

Passing a hedge of small trees, he spotted two Hungarian Honved infantrymen hiding in thick bushes behind the trees. What in the world were they doing there? Intrigued, Jan came closer. He could not hear the soldiers, but he saw their excited gestures. Fascinated, he observed one infantryman aim his rifle carefully at the other man's thigh and shoot him through a half loaf of bread— making sure that a ring of black gunpowder, the telltale sign of a self-inflicted wound, would not appear on the flesh. Painstakingly, the first man dressed the resulting wound. In turn, the wounded infantryman, being very careful to avoid bones and veins, shot the first man the same way in the calf.

Jan walked away quietly, deeply affected by what he had just seen. He knew that he himself could not do anything like that, but the temptation was palpable. To be sent back to the rear from this lunatic war zone, where everybody was shooting at everybody else without any humane concern or rhyme or reason.... At that moment, alone, sorry for himself and for the human condition, he could not resist.

When he came to a clump of small evergreens heavily shelled by enemy light machine guns as a suspected Austrian observation post, which it was not, Jan lowered himself into a shell hole in front of the trees, lay on his back, stuck up both legs above the rim of the crater, and waited. The machine guns were firing at the trees in short, steady bursts. Jan kept his legs exposed to the sustained gunfire for almost thirty minutes, "hoping to be able to see for myself the quiet, clean, peaceful field hospital in the rear." Nothing happened. Jan's emotional, spur-of-the-moment impulse to tempt fate passed. Feeling silly, he rose to his feet. Once again, carefully trying to dodge bullets, he continued walking.

When Jan returned to the battery to report on the several possible positions he had found, two of the four guns had left to assist an infantry battalion in an attack on the other side of the hill. The remaining two guns, which included Jan's gun, and their infantry contingent were under relentless shelling by heavy machine guns, one of which seemed to be firing from the hillside opposite. With the permission of the battery commander—Lieut. Kreibich had stayed with the two remaining guns—Jan and his men moved their gun from the relative safety of the protective trench into the open, to a road facing the hillside directly; they began firing on the area where Jan thought the machine gun was hidden in the bushes. But the machine gunner opposite kept on firing; in fact, he was so good that Jan's men were forced to move the gun back in a hurry to its original position.

Just then they were subject to an enfilade by an enemy battery in a gully below them. The men responded in kind with the same rapid, raking, direct frontal fire. Suddenly, the sky filled with a large number of British planes, perhaps thirty, scoring hits on many targets including the ferry pontoons. One of the pontoon bridges, hit directly, broke in two and smashed into another bridge down-river, disabling it temporarily.

The battery, reunited later that day, suffered two scary near-misses that evening by as-yet-unidentified, high-explosive, large caliber shells, some new type of mortar the men thought. The shells were filled with picric acid, the type, reportedly, that the French used. The explosions were terrifying, and the craters so huge that "a small house could be hidden in each of them." Fortunately, the shells, being large, were as slow as freight trains. When fired they could be heard and seen coming and with luck could be avoided. Later that night an infantry lieutenant stopped by, openly weeping, on his way back to the rear. His whole platoon had been wiped out in a narrow cleft at the top of Montello by a direct hit of one of the picric acid shells. The lieutenant was the lone survivor.

At 2 a.m. on June 17, the tired and hungry men—they had been living on their emergency battle rations; no food had reached them since June 14—surrounded by what was left of their infantry contingent, lay down to sleep in their trenches. At 3 a.m. the cry "Gas!" jerked them out of their slumber just long enough to don gas masks and go back to sleep. Awakened at 4 a.m. by shouts of "All clear," the men took off their gas masks, went back to their guns and, in the rain, started to shoot again.

The fire of Austrian large caliber guns from behind the Piave fell short of the targeted enemy position on Montello, and the shells began exploding all around the battery. Hurriedly, the gunners shot red warning distress flares into the air, which, after a while, did alert the Austrian artillery to move their barrage farther over. The men were justifiably upset to find themselves the target of both friend and foe. What was going on? Was it a simple mistake, or were the gun barrels of the Austrian artillery so worn out by then, the bores of the barrels so much out of tolerance that they shot uncertainly and scattered the shells so widely they fell on their own troops?

The battery had three new casualties. The rain continued. At noon under increasing enemy fire, the battery changed its position again, this time moving to the right slope of Montello, and kept firing. The expanse of sunny plain below them dotted with large and small villages, fields, and woods presented a beautiful, panoramic view, which the men had no time to enjoy.

In the evening a heavy machine gun from one of the villages began firing persistently at the infantry contingent in front of the battery. Lieut. Kreibich was tempted to move one gun into the open and try to silence the machine gun. He talked to Jan, his most experienced gun commander, to assess the risk of such a move. Jan was game, although it was getting dark and they did not know the exact location of the offending machine gun. The Italian infantry, fearing penetration by curious Austrian patrols and possible night attacks, lit up the night with white illumination flares, which burned long with high intensity. The light of the flares exposed three large, substantially built houses. The machine gun may have been firing from one of them. Jan and his crew moved their gun from the protected position of the battery onto a clearing above it and waited for the next flare. When it came, Lieut. Kreibich gave Jan the bearings, and Jan gave the gunners the aim. They fired several rounds, but the machine gun kept shooting. After a few more tries, the lieutenant lost interest in the exercise and went to his dugout.

Jan stayed and watched. He suspected the two-story house on the left with three windows on the second floor to be the gunner's hiding place. Concentrating his attention on the windows, he waited for the next flare to take his bearings. It took him three additional flares and three more rounds to bracket the target. His next shot hit the first window. The "rat-a-tat" of the machine gun did not miss a beat. The second shot hit the middle window. The machine gun fire persisted. The third shot, landing squarely in the third window, drew silence. A long silence. Jan had the gun returned to its previous position. He, his gunners, and the battery infantry contingent could now sleep in peace. At least for the time being.

On June 18 the heavy rain started early. By then everyone considered the river impassable. At dawn the battery gunners, ever tired, wet, and hungry, began firing at the targets of opportunity. Their opposite numbers did the same, and since the battery was known to be one of the few Austrian artillery units (two mountain batteries and four "accompanying" batteries) to have crossed the river in the Montello sector, the enemy fire concentrated on them was heavy. The gunners were obliged to move the guns again into what they hoped to be a more protected position. From there, they were also firing into an Italian connecting trench directly below them. When, after their first direct hit, they saw medics and orderlies in white coats milling about in the trench, they ceased firing, resuming only after the white coats left.

Then the inevitable happened: the Italians scored a direct shrapnel hit on one of the battery's guns. Seven men were killed, among them the battery's second in command, Second Lieut. Zeigner, and gunner Schimunek, Jan's good friend; three others were wounded. Four wounded horses had to be shot. Clearly, the mission of the enemy was now the annihilation of Jan's battery. Later that afternoon five more men were killed and three more wounded. The casualties on Montello were mounting rapidly. No replacements arrived—of men, horses, or equipment.

The battery now seemed to be under fire from all directions. There were no places left to hide. The men were enveloped by bursts of incendiary shells, by heavy shells which screamed overhead like express trains, by machine gun bullets whizzing by, by flying rock as dangerous as shells, and even by flame thrower blasts aimed at the forward infantry in front of them but landing all around the battery. The stench of high explosives, the acrid fumes of shells bursting close by, the cries of the wounded and the shouts for stretcher bearers—inundated the men of the battery. The battle for Montello that had started out so bravely appeared to be in peril.

At 2 a.m. on June 19, under fire and in heavy rain, Lieut. Kreibich and Jan went to scout out still another, safer position for the reduced, three-gun battery. The men had received neither food nor cigarettes since June 14, and they had not slept more than ten hours in the last four days. They worried about losing strength and not being up to the task. Thick mud covered everything—men, horses, carts, guns, ammunition. There were gaping shell holes and craters everywhere, and Italian as well as Austrian bodies lay all around, sometimes on top of one another, as did the corpses of fallen horses. The muddy ground was littered with broken wagons, carts, and all kinds of gear and weapons including artillery pieces, some of them new Italian cannons that had been spiked and disabled by retreating gunners.

There was no protected position to be found anywhere nearby, but Lieut. Kreibich held to his conviction that any new position was preferable to the present one, for a while anyway, until the enemy spotted them again. And certainly such a move was needed, however brief, for the men's morale. So the battery moved again and built new covers and trenches some 300 meters to the right of the old position.

Kreibich was right. The change gave the men new hope. As a bonus the lieutenant ordered the battery to hold its fire for the time being.

At noon wave after wave of enemy planes bombarded the Austrian positions on both sides of the river. Where were the Austrian planes? At 2 p.m. came the enemy infantry attack. The battery (what was left of it) opened fire, as did the enemy artillery, several batteries at once, fiercely. Jan's battery gunners had to abandon their guns fast and duck into their trenches and dugouts. Fortunately for them, their group infantry repelled the Italian infantry attack and by 6 p.m. chased the Italians back. At 7 p.m. the food ration detail arrived, together with the ammunition detail. Led by a reserve gunnery staff sergeant, who supposedly knew where he was going, the two details reportedly had spent three days on Montello looking for the battery. Except for the bread, cans of meat, and tobacco, all the food was spoiled. Still, it was devoured without complaint, supplemented by mulberries that were plentiful on the hill.

On the entire Piave front, from the mountains to the sea, the Montello hill seemed to have assumed a key strategic position. Its capture was vital to the Austrians, but determined counterattacks by reserve Italian divisions brought the Austrian offensive to a halt. The Austrians attempted to cross south of the Piave at the island of Papadopoli, and farther down the river close to the Adriatic an Austrian bridgehead still threatened the Italian rear. But the Austrian High Command made the mistake of not following up on the original successful advance. The men at the battery considered it strange that Montello, where the Austrians held a strategic advantage, was not exploited for in-depth penetration of the Italian defenses. Why were there no fresh reserves moving in to supply muscle to the successful Austrian assault? Were the men on Montello being sacrificed for some unknown strategy? Where were the biggest guns of the Austrian artillery? Where were the airplanes?

That evening it was rumored that the Austrian High Command, desperately short of everything, had ordered the withdrawal of all troops from Montello to the other side of the Piave. The Austrian offensive was apparently over.

The Italians quickly realized that the Austrians had lost the momentum. On June 20 their counterattacks multiplied on the ground and in the air, during the day and at night. They now had the initiative. The Austrians never did manage to capture all of Montello, to gain full possession of this highly defensible position on the river, and now they were to suffer the consequences. British planes again smashed one of the new Austrian pontoon bridges across the Piave below Montello that had been restored during the night. But like the Austrians, the Italians, too, failed to follow up in force their very successful counterattacks.

The battery kept changing its position. The men fired and were fired upon. They suffered another direct hit. This time five men were killed and five others wounded. Also, the battery's Thirteenth Group Commander, Lieut. Sobocki, a Pole, was reportedly wounded. The men, who by now were accustomed to thinking along these lines, assumed that since the lieutenant had been wounded in his bivouac when the battery was not being fired upon, his orderly, also a Pole, must have inserted a grenade splinter in a revolver bullet and shot the lieutenant in his thigh, the favored target, through a loaf of bread, of course. In any case, the lieutenant was evacuated with his orderly. Montello was his first and probably his last battle.

The food and ammunition details made it up the hill again at 2 a.m. on June 21. Normally it would have taken three hours to get from S. Michele to the battery on Montello. Now, across the one remaining pontoon bridge, crowded and under enemy closing fire, it took the detail over ten hours. But there was rum, one-fourth liter per person, and tobacco. Was it because of their heavy losses that there were ample seconds on everything? The rain poured down. The enemy kept firing large caliber shells. The planes were hard at work, too. The gunners sat in the protective dugouts and trenches next to their guns, wet and miserable on the outside but, thanks to the rum, fuzzy and warm within. They changed their position once again.

On June 22 scuttlebutt had it that the battery might move back across the Piave to the dugout on the riverbank that it had occupied before the offensive, in order to cover the retreat of the infantry from Montello. The men found the rumor believable. Their own casualties were critical, and the enemy was becoming increasingly bold. The battery had exhausted all possible defensive alternatives. The Austrian offensive was petering out fast.

Indeed, that afternoon the battery was ordered to send two guns with all their equipment back across the river to man the old trenches on the river bank; their mission was to protect the orderly Austrian retreat. Jan was put in charge. By 10 p.m. the detail was ready, lined up, and waiting on the road for the horses. At that moment a large (perhaps 21 cm) mortar shell landed in the middle of the road just in front of the column. The tremendous explosion wounded six men. Miraculously, no one was killed. The air pressure created by the violent concussion had lifted Jan off the ground and hurled him across the road. Lying prone on his back, disoriented, smelling his singed mustache and eyebrows while small and large stones rained upon him, he was visited again by the welcoming vision of a soft, warm, dry, clean bed in the peace and quiet of a field hospital. Was he wounded? Jan sat up and systematically went over every part of his body. Nothing. He was in pain, yes, but nothing was broken or out of place. Not even a deep scratch!

The battery and infantry medics attended to the wounded, and Jan and his detail took off. The road to the river, well known to the enemy, was routinely shelled. Even the horses were apprehensive. But not Jan. Not any more. After what he had experienced on the front since May 1917, first on the Isonzo and now on the Piave, corroborated by this last direct hit, Jan knew he was invulnerable. He did not need to fear any more. He did not need to dodge bullets. His fate was to survive the war unharmed. He was sure of it.

The two-gun detail arrived at the river at daybreak on June 23. There was a crush at the bridgehead—it seemed that half the Austrian army was trying to retreat across the Piave on the one remaining pontoon bridge that was more or less intact. Traffic was one-way and interminably slow. Coming to Montello from the opposite direction was by pontoon boats only. The bridge, under fire by enemy artillery and mostly British planes flying overhead, was only weakly protected by Austrian artillery and heavy machine guns. The Austrian sappers were bravely attending to bridge repairs around the clock—they even built extra foot bridges—but many of the retreating soldiers, rather than wait under fire for their turn on the bridgehead, tried to swim across the river, singly or on horses. After the continuous, heavy rains, the mighty Piave was overflowing its banks and inundating its many small islands, a violent, dark-brown torrent, swift, turbulent, deep, and wide. Crossing it was treacherous. Very few men made it across by swimming, but not a single horse: the heavy undercurrent turned horses upside down like toys, their legs thrashing helplessly in the air. At a wide bend downriver, the dead bodies of men and horses stacked up like driftwood. No one in the detail had ever seen anything like it.

Aware of the battery's assignment, the field police directing the traffic at the bridgehead let Jan's detail cross the bridge ahead of all the others for reasons of urgent priority. That decision drew angry protests, shouting, catcalls, and dangerous pushing and shoving from the long line of waiting, frightened infantrymen. Meanwhile, behind them the enemy infantry continued to advance.

When Jan's men reached the other side of the river, what they encountered was worse than the battlefield they had just left. The staging area from where the Austrian infantry and later the reserves had advanced to cross the Piave had become a butchery. The men could not believe the utter devastation. Maimed bodies of men and animals, torn limbs hanging from tree stumps, crushed skulls, bloody open bellies with entrails spilling out—the sheer enormity of the gore was horrifying and the heavy smell of death sickening. An inferno encompassed them. The men found it almost impossible, among the carnage of bodies and limbs, to find a path for their carts to get through to the position on the river bank that the battery had left only eight days before—a bloody eternity.

They placed the two guns in the old trench deep in the river bank, wolfed down the bread, coffee, and cans of meat which the two supply men waiting for them had brought with the ammunition, and started to fire forthwith at the Italian infantry attacking the Austrian bridgehead on the other side of the river. They kept at it the whole day. Their orders were to send the two guns with their crews after dark to the supply line in the small village of Ramera, and for Jan and Rudolf, the commanders of the guns, to return to the one-gun battery that had been left behind on Montello.

Most reluctantly, the two men went back to the bridgehead through heavy closing fire. The pontoon bridges were so badly damaged by then that they were for all intents and purposes out of commission. The sappers were now transporting men and equipment back and forth across the river on pontoon boats. Going against the traffic, Jan and Rudolf had no problems hitching a ride back across the river. But when they reached the battery position on Montello, nothing was there, just scorched earth where the battery had been. The gun was gone, nowhere to be found. The people they met seemed dazed and confused. No one around seemed to remember the battery. The two men searched everywhere, up and down, back and forth, but there was no sign of the gun or its crew. Tired and frustrated, Jan and his partner gave up, returned to the river, waited—a long time—for a boat ride, and walked back to Ramera via Castello di Collalto (Map V). The battery was not there. Exhausted, they went to S. Michele. Nothing. Perhaps the battery was somewhere alongside the Piave, so they went back to the bridgehead to wait. Discouraged and dog-tired, they collapsed on the side of the road and fell asleep immediately. It had been a long, excruciating day.

IV
RETREAT AND CAPTIVITY

Killing Time
From the Piave to San Giovanni, June 24 – October 28

S. Lucia di Piave to Francenigo, June 24 –29

In the morning of June 24 after breakfasting on mulberries from the trees nearby, the commanders of the two guns, Jan and Rudolf, questioned some of the infantry field police passing by and finally determined that their battery supply line had moved to S. Lucia di Piave, a tiny village not far from Ramera. Indeed, they did find there not only their supply line but also the missing one-gun battery, or what was left of it. Lieutenant Kreibich told them that, all in all, in eight days of fighting on Montello the battery had lost 58 men—dead, wounded, and missing in action—over half the battery's original strength. The total casualties of the aborted Austrian offensive in the Montello sector were reportedly close to 15,000 men.

After the trauma of the preceding ten days, the gunners gladly exchanged their steel helmets for field caps again. Jan's backpack was returned to him—empty. Everything he owned had been stolen, including his greatcoat and blanket roll. He had hoped, naively, to find in the backpack the rations that had not reached him during the offensive, chiefly bread and tobacco, but no such luck. Like many others Jan suffered from dysentery and felt listless. They all needed some solid food, and here they hoped they would get it.

At a regimental inspection in the late morning of June 25, a visiting colonel praised the men for their bravery under fire and promised rest and recognition—but no cigarettes appeared. In the afternoon Lieut. Kreibich ordered Jan to take over as the new battery crew commander and duty officer, and, in the absence of the battery officers who were wounded on Montello and not yet replaced, Jan was also to serve as temporary (very temporary) second in command of the battery. He was to inform the men that those deserving recognition would be rewarded soon. With home leaves?

Kreibich respected Jan, trusted his judgment, and valued his advice. "I do not mean to boast," Jan writes, "but the lieutenant likes me, and I must say I like him, too." The two men developed not only a good working relationship in and out of battle, but also a degree of camaraderie unusual for a battery commander and one of his sergeants, within the stratified, class-conscious, and ethnically differentiated Austrian Imperial Army. Whether the lieutenant invited Jan to address him on a first-name basis, the foolproof test of friendship, Jan does not say. Probably not.

On June 26, together with two other sergeants representing the first and third batteries of the regiment, Jan, a scout again, left for the town of Sacile to secure billets in the rear for the regiment. The three sergeants walked via the town of Conegliano to the train station in Pianzano; from there they traveled by train to Sacile; and from Sacile, on a tip, they went on foot south to Francenigo, a small town (Map V). By early afternoon they found what appeared to them to be adequate quarters for the regiment in former Italian army barracks, two schools, and several half-deserted public buildings. They telephoned the good news to the regimental command.

The regiment was far too large and unwieldy to travel by train, so the men marched and rode on the main road to Pianzano and from Pianzano to the town of Orsago, where the road forked directly for Francenigo; the regiment arrived at 5 a.m. the following morning. The three scouts helped with the distribution and accommodation of the various regimental units in the several barracks and buildings, and directed the horses to the stables. That done, the whole regiment gratefully slept.

On June 28 the regiment rested. The men bathed, went through the delousing process, shaved, washed their laundry, cleaned and mended their uniforms, had their hair cut, beards and mustaches trimmed, and even took time to look around their surroundings. To his delight Jan discovered in the vicinity of the town real fig trees. He had heard of figs but had never seen or eaten one. He learned how to distinguish the ripe figs and eat them directly off the tree, as he had done in his youth with Moravian apples and pears. A ripening fig was green, at first, like a pear, but later when it turned blue, it was ready to eat. At first Jan did not like the taste, which seemed too bland, or the texture, which was grainy; but after eating several he began to appreciate them. They were a rich, filling, and satisfying fruit, and they were free. Bread and figs made a fine meal.

Jan sent his cannon with other damaged guns to Sacile for repair or replacement together with a request for two new guns for the battery. The food rations had improved, both in quality and quantity. And best of all, the hoped-for home leaves came through, to start immediately. The names of 45 "deserving" officers, NCOs, and enlisted men were posted on the regimental bulletin boards. Jan spotted his name quickly. The leave was for 28 days—four weeks!—plus generous travel time. Jan could hardly believe his good fortune.

On June 29, late in the afternoon, all 45 men reported to the regimental command. A captain made a speech congratulating the men and admonishing them to behave at home like the sterling, disciplined soldiers that they had proven themselves to be at the front. The men received their pay and took off for the train station in Sacile. They reached the station at 6 p.m. that evening, only to learn that the next train did not leave until 5 a.m. the next morning, June 30. They were not surprised.

Third Home Leave and Vedronza (Tarcento), June 30 – August 8

Home! "Peace and quiet, rest, food, sleep, and nothing biting." And Božena! Lovely Božena cooked Jan's favorite dishes. Although the food shortage was severe, Božena's store yielded much that Jan had been dreaming of. After a steady diet of field rations—meager and skimpy at the best of times—almost anything his wife put on the table was sumptuous, plentiful, and delicious. He helped Božena with the store, the books, and the ration cards. Sundays they went for long walks in the Vienna Woods or the several parks of the city. They planned to visit Božena's parents and little Božena, who was almost two, in Bohemia, but train tickets were available only on the basis of strict military priority. They attended two operettas and two outdoor concerts, venues which the government promoted as morale boosters in depressed wartime Vienna. They visited relatives and friends. Jan received a note from the regimental clerk that the regimental command was awarding medals to the men of the regiment: one gold, 23 silver first class, 49 silver second class, and 63 bronze. In a handwritten postscript, the clerk congratulated Jan on having been awarded the silver medal first class *"Fortitudini"* ("For Valour"), which included a stipend of 25 crowns per month for life.

Jan could not help but notice that conditions in Vienna had worsened dramatically since his last home leave just six months before. The deterioration of life in the capital was shocking. Jan had expected some decline in living conditions, of course; everyone knew that the war was not going well. Rumors that the war was lost and that defeat was now inevitable had been circulating in the battery as well. But the near collapse of the home front made that outcome chillingly believable. It was not just the long queues, the angry crowds, the poverty, and the misery. It was the sheer desperation in the tired faces of the people and the rumors that a revolution by armed Red Guards might break out at any moment that worried Jan. What would happen to Božena, alone, young, and vulnerable, trapped in the center of this potential time bomb?

The approaching end of the leave spoiled the couple's happiness, as always. Božena was braver than Jan was, at least on the surface. On August 2 the cherished month at home was over. The unspoken question that had dominated every leave-taking was the same: Was this the last time...? Their sense of helplessness was greater than ever.

Jan left Vienna for Francenigo via Tarcento, a town about 16 km north of Udine, from where he continued on foot to a small township, Vedronza, located about seven kilometers northeast from Tarcento on a stream called Torre (Map V). His brother-in-law, Alois, an infantry sergeant and electrician by trade, was stationed there in charge of a small hydroelectric power station. The two had not seen each other since December 1916. It was a memorable visit. They fished for trout in the clear waters of the mountain stream. The four small trout they caught they fried with sliced potatoes and served with fresh peas. Sweet crepes, Alois's specialty, finished off the meal, and there was plenty of good Italian white wine. What a treat! They even took several pictures of themselves with Alois's camera. They reveled—and yet felt sorry for themselves. What lay ahead of them in this unholy war?

Late that night, on unsteady legs, Jan returned to the train station in Tarcento and after an hour or two was on his way back to the regiment in Francenigo.

Drills, S. Giovanni, August 8 – September 22

The regiment, however, was no longer in Francenigo, and neither the local military command nor the field gendarmerie knew where they had moved to. But the field post officials knew, of course. The regiment had moved to the nearby town of S. Giovanni. Jan went there right away, found the regiment and the battery, and reported back on time on August 8. The next day he resumed his responsibilities of battery crew commander and duty officer.

What followed from August 9 to October 27 was the standard military procedure of keeping the troops busy and occupied at all times, especially in the rear. This rule was applied by the book, as always: two and a half months of drills, exercises, training, forced marches, maneuvers, parades, inspections, cleaning, washing, scrubbing, repairing, and mending. Mandatory Sunday marches to Catholic field services were reintroduced, especially when visiting dignitaries were present to say a few inspiring words to the assembled troops. One such Sunday was August 18, when Emperor Charles I was honored at a high mass in Budoia, a town north of S. Giovanni.

The specifics of the daily routine included cannon exercises; drills with carbines; instructions on using field telephones; drills with gas masks in special, airtight gas chambers; bayonet drills; and gunnery target practice. In addition there were details to do special jobs like cutting grass and drying it for the horses; gathering firewood for the field kitchens (even the green branches from certain trees resembling acacias burned beautifully, Jan noticed); gathering ripe corn in the fields (when roasted, corn on the cob was delicious); and, of course, peeling potatoes.

In preparation for a repeat of combined and integrated field maneuvers of the artillery with the infantry, on September 4 Jan went with Lieut. Kreibich to search for a suitable area. They found just the right location, somewhat hilly, with a few woods and low-lying barriers such as small, deserted villages. Kreibich ordered the guns to be moved there from S. Giovanni without delay. The battery started to fire at various targets even before the rest of the regiment and the infantry arrived. Once assembled, they practiced for several days shooting live ammunition, both shrapnel and grenades, over the heads of advancing as well as retreating infantry, at all kinds of "moving" targets including mock-up tanks. The new (since July) Commander of the Imperial and Royal Sixth Army, Colonel General Prince Aloys Schoenburg-Hartenstein, came with his staff to observe the maneuvers. Afterwards, at inspection, he praised the gunners for their "skill, perseverance, and initiative." No cigarettes. But on September 13, completely unexpectedly, Jan was issued a special six-day (plus travel) home leave permit. Again! So soon! Jan was delighted.

But then he had time to reflect. Here they were in S. Giovanni, in the rear, half way between the Piave and the Tagliamento rivers, after the bloody victory at Caporetto and an equally bloody defeat at the Piave, resting and training for over eleven weeks now, in addition to the week at home coming up, and after that perhaps even more time here. To what purpose? To wait for supplies, probably exhausted a long time ago, and for reinforcements, boys too young and men too old to fight in yet another gory Austrian offensive? Or were they waiting for the next punishing but inconclusive Italian offensive, only to continue the bloody see-saw in this hopeless war that had started four long years ago? With mixed emotions Jan put together the things he needed for the trip home.

Fourth Home Leave, September 15 – 22

Jan lost no time. On the morning of September 15 he was in Vienna. As always, Božena was taken by surprise. Immediately, she closed the store again for several hours and took care of Jan. Thanks to her ministrations, in 24 hours Jan was a civilian again—clean, fed, rested and happy to be home. His euphoria was short-lived, however,

After talking to his friend and neighbor Karl, who was following the progress of the war closely, some of Jan's suspicions about the war's outcome were confirmed. From his "friends in high places"

Karl learned the full picture of the Piave offensive. Over a cup of ersatz coffee in a nearby coffee house, he told Jan of two other Austrian-initiated encounters on the Italian front in June: a minor diversionary assault at Tomale Pass, west of Trentino, which failed; and a major two-flank pincer movement, the hoped-for knockout blow, in Trentino towards Verona and on the Piave towards Padua, in which Jan had just played a part. These two flanks of the pincer engagement, totaling some 58 Austrian divisions, lacked sufficient strength to carry out a successful offensive in depth in either place. Although simultaneous, they were entirely separate. The Trentino attack gained limited ground, was halted, and then was thrown back—it was over in 24 hours. The Piave assault forced a wide crossing of the river at three separate points, almost 100,000 Austrian soldiers penetrating over 4.5 kilometers into enemy territory, but the advance could not be sustained.

Unable to provide food, medicine, ammunition, spare parts, fuel, horses, airplanes, locomotives, and fresh reinforcements in the fourth year of a debilitating war, and having lost the sustenance of seven German divisions, who were transferred to the Western front, the Austrian High Command faced Italian armed forces reinforced by French and British divisions with no serious shortages of anything. In the Montello fiasco, the heavy rains had swelled the Piave to such power and swiftness everywhere that only a few of the Austrian bridges had held, and the few remaining fighting units on the western side of the river were without ammunition and food and close to exhaustion. The Austrian retreat across the Piave was a rout. Some 106,000 Austrian soldiers were killed and wounded in this joint Trentino and Piave offensive, and about 25,000 were missing in action or taken prisoner. Thanks to the Germans, Caporetto was the first, last, and only Austrian victory on the Italian front. Karl concluded that the planned knockout blow to Italy in the Trentino and on the Piave had turned out to be the knockout blow to the Dual Monarchy.

As Karl spoke it became clear to Jan that what he and his friends at the battery had quietly talked about ever since the debacle at the Piave was true: the war could not last much longer, and Austria-Hungary was about to collapse. What Jan saw in the angry faces of people waiting in lines in front of stores with bare shelves and in the overall turbulent atmosphere of Vienna, upset him more than what he had seen in the city just six short weeks before. In a few days he would return to Italy, leaving Božena to face what might become an ugly, explosive, and even revolutionary situation. He asked friends and neighbors to keep an eye on his young wife, and left Vienna once again distraught, frustrated in not being able to protect Božena himself.

More Drills and Waiting, S. Giovanni, September 23 – October 28

At midnight on September 23 Jan was back in S. Giovanni. The keep-busy activities of the battery and regiment remained essentially the same as before his leave—and, in fact, continued so for the next five weeks. But the overall conditions were becoming noticeably worse: the food rations were smaller and poorer in quality; the horses were fed corn straw and dry leaves; men walked around in old, torn, ragged uniforms which could no longer be mended or patched; and those without underwear finally did receive some, but it was used and dirty. The men's pay, again in Austrian crowns, included the monthly supplements for medals—in Jan's case, 7.50 crowns for the silver medal second class and 25 crowns for the silver medal first class—but was worthless because the Italian civilians would no longer accept Austrian money. The men could barter, especially with cigarettes if they had any, but they could not buy anything. To make matters worse, the money they were permitted to mail home was limited to no more than 100 crowns per month, a sum which by then did not buy much at home either. Nor were they permitted to mail packages home any longer. (The few German soldiers who were still around had no such restrictions as to what they could send to Germany, either money or packages.)

Food was in short supply. The regimental practice of requisitioning food from the civilian population in exchange for official, written receipts was now practiced as a rule rather than exception. Jan was ordered to requisition three fat cows at a nearby farm. Accompanied by three men, he wrote a formal receipt for the cows payable in the future in lire and presented it to the farmer, who angrily tore the receipt into small bits and threw them in Jan's face. What else could the man do? Requisitioning, the soldiers agreed, was a form of thievery, practiced from time immemorial by occupying armies and carried out by—what else?—force. Force was the law. There were no written receipts for fruit plucked off trees, the vegetables gathered from fields, the stray chickens and turkeys shot upon discovery, or the rabbits removed from hutches.

With October came the rains. The battery participated in an extended gunnery school in Budoia. Jan sent 100 crowns to Božena and received a food package from her, one of the few that had not been lost or stolen. Rumors were rampant: that on September 26 Bulgaria, an ally of Austria, sued for a separate armistice and an unconditional cessation of hostilities; that on October 3

Emperor Charles I, together with the governments of Germany and Turkey, offered to accept U.S. President Woodrow Wilson's Fourteen Points as a basis for peace negotiations with the Allied Powers; and that during all-regimental maneuvers near Sacile, conducted jointly with several units of infantry, artillery, and mortar companies and several wings of fighter and bomber planes—all using live ammunition—a large number of infantrymen had been killed and wounded. In the now widely-shared unease about the conduct of the war, rumors like these tended to fuel the increasing concern among the men that the war was lost and that their leaders, the powerful Austro-Hungarian military clique, did not care whether the troops continued to serve as cannon fodder for the leaders' selfish ambitions or were sacrificed as prisoners of war.

Retreat
San Giovanni to Grions, October 28 – November 4

On October 27 the battery was ordered to get ready to move again and on October 28 began what in fact became a week of confused but fairly orderly retreat. Jan was the battery scout once more; he left S. Giovanni early in the morning, arrived at Vigonovo, the next destination of the battery, and without much trouble secured accommodations for the battery in the town schoolhouse (Map V). That evening, however, he was relieved from his duties of battery scout and was assigned as battery orderly to the Thirteenth Group Division. In that capacity he learned that the Italian offensive, after four months of procrastination, had restarted and was successful: on October 24 the Italians, supported by the French and the British, had apparently broken through Austrian defenses, crossed the Piave, gained a large bridgehead, and continued their advance eastward toward Vittorio Veneto. Indeed, that night Jan heard for the first time in a while the thud of Italian heavy cannon fire coming from the west.

On October 29 the battery was ordered to face and counter the Italian advance. They rode and marched nine hours back southwest toward Vittorio Veneto to the town of Vistorta. After a two-hour rest, the men moved to a fork in the road overlooking both the Vittorio Veneto and the Conegliano roads, assembled the guns, readied them, set up an observation post on top of a nearby hill, and fired a few rounds westward at the advancing Italian infantry, over the heads of the masses of Austrian troops retreating in four separate columns on the highway. From the weary, hungry, and parched soldiers trudging down the road, the men of the battery gathered alarming pieces of information—were they rumors?—that in several areas the front-line Austrian infantry, sick and tired of war, was giving up and surrendering *en masse*; that the Austrian High Command had sent an urgent dispatch to the Italian High Command asking for an immediate cease-fire; and that the commander-in-chief of the Austrian front had already left, secretly, for Vienna on a special train, the last one available. The retreating men were cursing the "incompetent" Emperor, his "high-living" court, and the "coterie of elite officers" who had "betrayed" those who fought in the front ranks of the war.

In the afternoon, without firing another shot, the battery received orders to pack up their guns and together with the other two batteries of the regiment join the retreating columns. They rode and marched the whole night with the multitude, but took a side road southeast as soon as they could. They rested all of the next day, October 30, in the town of Maron, southeast of Francenigo. Out of food, they requisitioned four cows, a sheep, even a donkey, and the men shot chickens and turkeys wherever they found them.

The regiment was ready to leave Maron in the early evening of October 30, but the regimental command postponed the departure. Apparently the Italians that day had reached not only Vittorio Veneto but Sacile as well, less than ten kilometers away. The battery might be needed to counter the Italian advance. The evening was cold and rainy, and the men built fires, outdoors as well as indoors. They gathered in groups to talk, to listen, to argue, to try to understand what was happening and, most important of all, to try to guess what would happen to them. What were the practical consequences of losing a war? What effect would it have on the combatants, on the people at home, on the Empire? The questions were many, the answers few.

Later that evening officers from the regimental command had the whole regiment fall in, this time in groups formed (for the first time ever) according to the men's respective nationalities. The officers described the current state of the war—terrible but not completely hopeless—and then proceeded to shock their audience to its very core. The officers asked the men to reveal their opinions by voting! It must be the end of the war for sure—and of the Empire. "How many of you are for the Emperor?" Sixty flabbergasted men raised their right hands. "How many are for a republic?" Eighty-six were. "And how many are in favor of establishing your own national state?" Almost forty Czechs showed their hands, as did most other soldiers of various ethnic or national backgrounds. The fact was that the men—including many of the German-speaking Austrians and the

Hungarians—knew little about the actual social, economic, and political conditions in their respective national homelands, and what they knew was not good. Finally, the officers dismissed the men, who were now more confused than ever. What did the vote mean? Why was it taken? What was the motive of the officers taking it? The men talked far into the night.

On October 31 the regiment moved past Pordenone east towards Cordenons. Enemy tanks were reported to be approaching on the Sacile-Pordenone highway. The three batteries assumed firing positions on the side of the road again and waited. They saw many fires and thick columns of smoke and heard the sounds of heavy guns down the road, but no tanks appeared; only the retreating infantry continued filling the highway. After a while the batteries moved once more and took battle positions farther east, near the Tagliamento. Once more they waited, ready to fire, but again no tanks.

At 2 a.m. the next morning a general alarm was sounded. Apparently, Hungarian infantrymen were deserting the front-line in alarming numbers and were defecting to the rear, to return to Hungary in order to protect their national territory. (Rumor had it that Kaiser Charles I had converted the Empire into a loose federation of states, of which Hungary was one.) Their hasty departure created a large gap in the more or less orderly retreat of the Austrian front.

Hurriedly, the three batteries packed up their guns and continued to fall back eastward with the main body of the infantry, which they were supposed to protect, to the Tagliamento, the next Austrian line of defense. When the batteries approached the bridge over the river, they ran into an impasse. The four columns lined up to cross the narrow bridge of Ponte di Delizia blocked the road for several kilometers. Three low-flying enemy planes tried to bomb the jammed road and the bridge but were repelled by concentrated Austrian machine gun fire. The men had not seen Austrian planes in the air since they left S. Giovanni.

As the retreating Austrian army made its way bit by bit across the bridge, the batteries moved with it. Once across the Tagliamento, the batteries assumed a battle position on the river bank near the town of Redenzicco, the temporary headquarters of their regiment, a little over five kilometers north of the highway, and, poised for action, waited again. Nothing happened. Before long the exhausted men posted guards and went to sleep. Later that night the first cavalry units of the advancing Italian army reached the Tagliamento, as did several British companies.

Early in the morning of November 3, Jan, now the orderly from the battery to the brigade, reported to Brigade Command Post No. 86

in Grions, a town about two kilometers from Redenzicco. There he received orders to go back to the battery and monitor the battery telephone. After 7 a.m. a telephone dispatch from the Austrian Army Headquarters informed the brigade, which in turn informed Jan at the battery, that all hostilities on the Italian front—on land, in the air, and at sea—were to cease and terminate as of that moment. Austria had, indeed, sued for armistice, which Italy granted. Representatives of the two belligerents had apparently signed the armistice agreement on that very day, November 3.

Why, then, did the Italians continue their offensive? Had no one told them that the war was over? Austrian "parliamentarians," noncoms mounted on horses and on motorcycles, rode toward the advancing Italian troops and waved white flags, but without much success. Jan stayed at the telephone. No one seemed to know what to do. (Jan found out later that the armistice was to have been implemented to take effect 24 hours from the time of signature. But no one had bothered to inform the Austrian troops, and the Allies took advantage of the Austrian confusion.)

That evening Jan was summoned back to Grions to relieve a sick telephone operator. That night he slept next to the telephone. When he awoke the next morning, November 4, he and all the others around him as far as he could see—officers, NCOs and men—were Italian prisoners of war. For them the war was over.

Prisoner of War
Grions to Camponogara, November 4 – 20

On November 4, 1918, disarmed and free to move about, Jan walked from Grions back to the battery in Redenzicco. On the way he saw an Austrian general, under guard but looking comfortable, being driven to the Italian rear. He also met a heavily armed Italian patrol that paid no attention to him. Jan's battery, disarmed and under Italian guard, was getting ready to move back to the Tagliamento beachhead with all their supplies on horse-driven carts and wagons but minus their guns, ammunition, and weapons. The bridge was gone, probably dynamited by Austrian rear-guard patrols. A large crowd of disarmed Austrians, under the watch of a few relaxed Italian guards, were camping in the fields in front of the destroyed bridge.

Everyone ate well that night. Much of the remaining Austrian food supplies, mostly flour and rice and also, to the delight of all, tobacco, coffee, and alcohol, were distributed to the supply wagons and field kitchens belonging to each unit. The night was cold, but there was enough firewood. Before long the fields all around the bridgehead were dotted with many small fires, bringing to mind a painting Jan had once seen in the Kunsthistorisches Museum in Vienna, depicting the great army of Napoleon camping at night on its retreat from Moscow.

That night Jan learned more about how the Italians managed to advance so rapidly and so successfully on the entire front after their victory at Vittorio Veneto. As he understood it, the Austrian troops on the right flank, under determined Italian infantry attack, abandoned their positions—they had deserted and run. Without resistance the Italians were able to advance, break through the Austrian reserve lines, cross the Tagliamento, thus outflanking the Austrian center, and attack the retreating troops from the rear. The defenders on the right flank who broke and ran, Jan guessed, included the Hungarian infantry going home.

On November 5 the whole battery—officers as well as men—met and decided to divide all the remaining food, coffee, cigarettes, tobacco, and spirits equally among all the men. Later that day Italian troops came into the camp, separated the officers from the men, and took the officers away. They inspected not only the wagons and carts but also the pockets of POWs and removed the men's watches, rings, medals, money, cigarettes, and badges. The prisoners were upset to be thus violated by fellow soldiers, albeit the enemy, who behaved like common thieves, stealing for personal gain. Still, as POWs, how else could they expect to be treated?

On November 6 the men were taken, under guard, to wade across the river. The Tagliamento, mercifully shallow at that time of year, was cold and the river bed muddy, but the crossing itself was neither dangerous nor difficult, even for the wagons. On the other side of the river, along the way Italian civilians lined the roads and taunted the men, spat at them, and struck at them with their fists whenever they could. One of the guards, an officer, snatched from Jan his nickel sergeants' whistle to keep as a souvenir. The new POWs did not know that they were starting a long, increasingly painful, three-week march southwest to Padova, some 200 km away as the crow flies.

On the morning of November 7 the columns of POWs halted at the main square of Pordenone (Map VI). The Italian guards were dismissed, and British soldiers took over. Apparently, the Italian infantry was needed as the army of occupation in the Austrian far rear, in Trieste and in Slovenia. The Austrian troops there were desperately trying to avoid capture and were said to be leaving for Austria by any means available, even on foot. Large numbers of those traveling on the roofs of railroad cars, unable to get inside because the trains were jammed full, were said to have been decapitated in the many tunnels along the way. The camp was full of rumors like this.

Jan and his friends tried to sleep in their supply wagons and carts, both to protect their diminishing food supplies and to stay a little warmer, but there was not enough space for all of them, so some slept sitting up, wrapped in their blankets. The British guards were kinder to the prisoners than the Italians, a natural happenstance, the men concluded, since the Austrian army had not invaded England. The British protected their charges against abuse and theft, even against predatory fellow prisoners.

However, it happened that a British soldier did body-search Jan, who was returning from the latrine to his wagon in the middle of the night. Jan carried his gold wedding ring and his field watch in a small bag hidden in the crotch of his underpants and his paper money in his boots. (Because it had no monetary value, he did not hide his notebook, the fifth such notebook since he began writing his diary in November, 1917.) The guard missed Jan's valuables but did find Jan's nickel-plated cigarette case with the "good" cigarettes from home, "Sports," (for bartering Jan used the "bad" cigarettes, "Hungarians," from rations), and took it from him. Half an hour later the guard came back and returned the case to Jan, cigarettes untouched, with apologies.

In the evening of the next day, the columns of POWs stopped in the fields close to the Pordenone-Conegliano highway near Orsago. According to the most recent gossip, a free, independent republic was being proclaimed in the Czech lands and Slovakia. Jan could not believe it. And Emperor Charles I, deposed by the German Austrians, had supposedly fled to Hungary. Later that evening, standing around their field kitchen drinking coffee, the men of the battery were accosted by a horde of starved Austrian infantrymen who attacked the supply wagons and fought the men for the very cups of coffee they were drinking. The English guards had a hard time chasing the intruders away and were able to restore a semblance of order only by shooting in the air. One of the battery NCOs who spoke a little English was able to convey to the guards who these men were and what they wanted, and thus helped to prevent a punitive beating of the intruders. When the men of the battery found out that the infantrymen had not eaten for three days, they shared their supper with them.

The next day, November 8, the long, grey, dusty columns of Austrian POWs continued their march via Vazzola back towards the

Piave. Time and again they were overtaken by Italian military trucks transporting released Italian POWs from the Isonzo front back to the Italian rear. They jeered the Austrian POWs, called them names, cursed them, spat at them, threatened them with their fists and, when they could, struck them.

The Austrians took it all in. Should they feel angry or guilty? Jan thought about it. In the war they and the released Italian POWs were just like spokes in a wheel—fixed in place, indispensable to the wheel, but helpless to do anything more than to be propelled back and forth in the direction their drivers took them. They were "enemies" because they were ordered to be enemies. Now they were no longer soldiers but men traveling in opposite directions. The war was over.

The countryside they marched through now, the Piave battleground, was devastated, stripped bare of trees, bushes, and other vegetation. There were only water-filled craters, shell holes, and all kinds of rusting battlefield debris. In the middle of the eerie landscape, not far from S. Michele di Piave, their supply line during the Piave battle less than five months ago, a large area was cordoned off with barbed wire and guarded by a number of elevated machine gun emplacements. Jan's group of about 1,000 POWs, mostly artillerymen, were separated from a much larger infantry contingent and were herded, with their wagons, into a small section of the compound. Here, the more tolerant British guards were replaced once again by their rougher Italian counterparts.

The guards issued food rations to the POWs, one can of meat and three pieces of hardtack for three men. The portions were meager, but the men still had a little food left, mostly rice and coffee, in their supply wagons, which they guarded day and night. Also, since they had no idea what would happen to them as a group, the men of the battery voted, unanimously, to open the official battery strongbox (the top sergeant had the key) and to divide the battery cash—some 2,700 lire—equally among the current 125 members of the battery. Each man received the princely sum of 21.60 lire, which, on the Italian market, would buy almost 27 loaves of bread, or one and a half kilo of coffee, or twelve bars of soap, or almost sixteen spools of thread. After hiding their money, the battery men slept in their wagons again, sitting up. The night was cold and the dew heavy.

On November 10, after a day and a half of rest near S. Michele, the march continued across the Piave to Varago. They saw thousands and thousands of Austrian infantry POWs marching southwest to their respective POW compounds. In separate columns officers marched alongside the men, a sight so unusual that everyone took notice of it. At noon the battery went south to Biagio di Callalta, a POW sorting station. On entering the town they heard martial music. They were told that the German emperor, Wilhelm II, had abdicated and fled to the Netherlands, and that a republic was proclaimed in Germany.

In Biagio di Callalta the men received their second meal in six days, one can of meat and three hardtack for three men. The food situation was worsening. Also, the Italian guards looked for officers said to be hiding among the men and took away the few that they found. Why would officers want to hide? It was general knowledge that officers were treated much better than enlisted men. No one knew the answer.

On November 11 the commander of the POW camp in Biagio requisitioned the space in the battery wagons for camp supplies and for the increasing number of sick POWs. The men of the battery still had a little of their old food supply left, perhaps one or two small meals of rice per man, which they now distributed. They still had a little coffee, so they made a weak brew on small fires fed by kindling from the acacia trees. The dwindling food supply was troubling. There were 3,000 POWs in the compound, reportedly two-thirds more than could be provided for by the camp administration.

On November 13 the POWs sent a deputation to the camp commander, asking for increased food rations and also for blankets and tarpaulins; the nights were becoming increasingly cold and wet, and the ground was muddy. Addressing the entire camp from a small podium, in good German (he was said to be from Trento) the commander explained that the overwhelming numbers of POWs had taken the administration completely by surprise. The Italian High Command had not expected such a sudden and total collapse of the Austrian forces. The commander promised to do his best; he permitted the killing of a sick horse for food right away, which produced 900 portions, and that night Jan and many others slept upon thick, new canvas blankets that they wrapped around themselves.

That day the battery was broken up and divided: the supply and reserve men, with their horse-driven carts and wagons, remained in Biagio di Callalta while the gunners moved on alone. Was this a bad omen, they wondered? The battery top sergeant, a shrewd, ambitious sort from Vienna, decided to join the supply line. He removed the yellow ribbons from his collar and sewed on new silver ones. Now, with the officers gone, he was the top-ranking NCO. Jan wondered if perhaps he knew something that the rest of the men did not.

The gunners, together with some 1,000 other POWs, left Biagio di Callalta for a new camp located on the road to Treviso. Marching through many villages, the POWs tried to buy bread and milk from the mostly hostile civilians and to barter their few remaining possessions for food. Jan managed to trade a harmonica, which he had purchased early in captivity from a POW infantry officer, for bread and polenta.

In the camp built to accommodate 2,000 men but now crammed with almost 15,000 POWs, the men were divided into 100-men platoons and fed, minimally as always. Since they were not given any water to drink, they quenched their thirst, not for the first time, from the water remaining in ditches. When a POW delegation complained to the camp commander, he told them what they had heard before: that the Italian POW command had expected to house and feed some 200,000 Austrian POWs, not the one million they now had. (Jan found out later that the actual number of Austrian POWs at that time amounted to about 400,000 men.) "You were betrayed and sold out by your government," the camp commander told them. He was sorry, he said, that he could not increase their rations, offer them drinking water, or give them warm, dry places to sleep. Following the example of others, Jan boiled ditch water with grass, called it "tea," and drank it. He survived the cold nights under a tarpaulin from the Biagio camp, grateful to be protected against the rain and the ice-cold wind. That night six POWs died.

The next day, November 15, it was snowing. Six thousand, four hundred POWs left that morning for other camps, Jan and his group among them. On the road, different groups and units split off from the main column in different directions to different camps. The last unit, 800 prisoners that included Jan's group, marched eleven hours— cold, wet, and hungry—through Treviso to a camp at Noale, about twenty kilometers southwest of Treviso. On the way, civilians not only spat at them and jeered, but, when they could, beat them with sticks. The NCOs with stars on their collars were targeted for especially heavy blows. Here the villagers could encounter the enemy face to face and vent their anger safely: the hated Austrians who had initiated and prolonged the dreadful war, who had killed and maimed their loved ones, who had stolen from them and were responsible for the suffering and misery the civilians had endured for so long.... Helpless to defend themselves, the POWs were beginning to feel guilty.

For the last part of their long march, most men took off their boots; they preferred the pain of walking barefoot to the pain of leather chafing their raw, bloody feet. On the second half of their march to Noale, their guards were Serbian POWs who had volunteered to join the Italian army. (Normally, the guards from the camp the POWs had just left accompanied them half way to the next camp; at that point, guards from the camp ahead took over.) The Serbs were tough on the prisoners. Jan decided to speak to the commander of the Serbian guards in Czech, to tell him that there were many national minorities among the Austrian POWs, some of the same Slavic origin as the Serbs. This intervention seemed to help. The Serbs became friendlier. That day, November 16, marked the second anniversary of Jan's induction into the Austrian army.

In the Noale camp the wet and cold POWs slept on frozen ground. Many of them were afraid of freezing to death in their sleep. Dead tired, they collapsed, but soon, frozen, they would get up and walk around to warm themselves; then lie down again, rise up again—and in this way the night passed. In the morning 4,000 men left the camp. The rest, Jan's group included, was then subjected to a careful and detailed body search. The Serbian guards confiscated almost all of their remaining personal effects and belongings—pocket knives, razors, scissors, shears, hair clippers, cigarette cases, candles, matches, flashlights, maps, anything and everything. Jan's hiding places in his crotch and boots remained undiscovered. The food here was the worst ever in captivity: the canned meat was spoiled and the bread completely moldy. The prisoners devoured whatever was given to them.

The morning of November 17 was freezing; hoarfrost covered the ground, the tarps, and the men. The POWs left the Noale camp at 9 a.m., marching south in endless columns bound for a camp near Camponogara, by way of Salzano, Mirano, and Mira. Soon it started to snow again. The road was muddy and the march relentless. Half of the prisoners kept their boots on; the other half walked barefoot as before. Several men collapsed. Jan worried that he, too, might fall. His strength was ebbing. The huge camp just before Camponogara yielded rest for the weary, half-dead POWs but not much more. Jan could not sleep; he suffered not only from the cold but also from rheumatic pains in the joints of his arms and legs. And, for some reason, the lice tormented him to a degree he seldom felt before.

The guards who brought the prisoners to the Camponogara camp were Italian bicyclists—infantrymen who rode bicycles. The guards who took the prisoners from the Camponogara camp on November 28, traveling south to a camp near Pontelongo by way of Arzarello, were cavalrymen with lances. They looked like medieval knights ready to joust. The men were flabbergasted. On November 19, under the guard of former POWs of Russian and Serbian nationality, the prisoners reached the next camp, located in a large field, where they were divided again, this time into groups formed according to the national and/or ethnic origin of each individual. Jan was separated into a group of Czechs and also of Slovaks.

On November 20 the prisoners were marched to still another camp. There was no kindling to heat the water gathered from roadside ditches for "herbal tea," as the men called it. Jan had not washed, shaved, or done any laundry since being taken prisoner three weeks before; his uniform, socks, and underwear were filthy and tattered. The civilians in this area were not permitted to sell food to the prisoners, and the prisoners were rapidly losing what little strength they still had. In this camp five men, unable to stand upright, fell into the latrine and drowned. The camp was so packed that at night men walked on bodies to get to the latrine.

November 22, 1918, dawned a much different day. All men who asked for it received a tarp; each nationality group received water buckets, at least two to a group, so that now they could wash themselves (water was plentiful here); and the food rations were a little larger and of better quality. At 3 p.m. that day the guards gathered together all the Czechs and Slovaks. They were addressed by a fellow Czech dressed in an Italian captain's uniform. What was going on?

The captain introduced himself as an officer of the Czechoslovak Legion in Italy. He told the men that upon the capitulation of Austria-Hungary on October 28, 1918, a new, independent, free and sovereign state had been created, Czechoslovakia. Their new homeland was composed of the Czech lands of Bohemia and Moravia, and also Slovakia and Subcarpathian Ruthenia. According to the captain, already in April 1918, at a Congress in Rome to which representatives of all the subject peoples of Austria-Hungary were invited, the Italian authorities had agreed to enroll volunteer Czech and Slovak POWs into a Czechoslovak Legion in Italy, and that battle-tried veterans were needed to help the Legion drive out the Hungarian armed forces still occupying (formerly Hungarian) Slovakia and Subcarpathian Ruthenia, and also to oust the Polish armed forces from Silesia in northern Moravia. The captain asked his rapt audience to consider seriously his call for volunteers to enroll in the newly created Czechoslovak Legion; he would be back in a day or two to elicit responses. He then distributed special presents from the Legion, three-men tents for all. The prisoners would still have to sleep on the frozen ground, but they would be dry, protected from the rain and wind, and much warmer, thanks to the Czechoslovak state, their new homeland!

The men gathered around the captain. They were full of questions. Some of them had heard vague rumors about the Legion. Jan remembered the leaflets Italian planes had dropped, inviting

Czechs to come over to the Italian side and to fight back against their "Austrian oppressors." But this was different. This Czech captain in Italian uniform was flesh and blood. And the astonishing information he had just imparted was mind-boggling. Would he please do them the honor of staying on a little longer? There was so much to learn and talk about. In addition to the Czechoslovak Legion in Italy, they wanted to know about the other Czechoslovak legions that the captain had mentioned, about their new country, and about Professor Masaryk, its purported leader whom some of them had heard about, as well as the other leaders that had surfaced in their absence.

The captain gladly complied. A recruiting officer, he was not only well-informed but also warm, easy-going, and open. A member of Sokol, the all-Czech patriotic organization dedicated to physical fitness, he put them all at ease right away by asking them to address him as "Brother Captain." Pleased, they did, and hung on his every word. Jan took notes, as did several of his new friends. Later he augmented them.

About the Czechoslovak Legions

Tomáš Garrigue Masaryk, the new president of Czechoslovakia, had been a lecturer in philosophy at the University of Vienna, professor of philosophy at Charles University in Prague, member of Sokol national gymnastic association, and deputy in the Vienna parliament (*Reichsrat*) for the small Czech political party "Realists," which he founded. In addition, he was a prolific author, tireless activist, a man of great moral courage, born defender of just causes, and an inspired Czech patriot. He left Austria after the outbreak of the war in 1914 to launch an information and education campaign in the West aimed at the liberation of Czechs and Slovaks from Habsburg domination. Before the war Masaryk had stood firmly against the use of violence for any reason, however justified. Once abroad and with the war in progress, however, he changed his mind.

Soon after the outbreak of the war, the Czechs and Slovaks who either lived abroad, became Allied prisoners of war, or defected to the enemy at the front, volunteered to join the Allied armed forces—French, Russian, Italian—to fight against the hated Austrian monarchy. But rather than participate as individuals within the separate Allied forces, many asked to form their own Czech and Slovak units that would fight side by side with the Allied forces. This kind of separate but integral organizational structure might advance dramatically the Allied understanding of the Czech and Slovak cause and might help to secure Allied support for an independent Czechoslovakia.

Under Masaryk's leadership, the Czech and Slovak volunteers accomplished their goal. In October 1915, Masaryk, with the help of his many friends abroad, founded the Czech Foreign Committee, broadened two months later into the Czechoslovak National Council, which established its own press offices in Geneva, Paris, London, and Rome, contributed articles to Allied newspapers and periodicals, and published its own magazine, *New Europe*. At the same time, the Council began to lobby Allied governments not only to enroll Czech and Slovak volunteers into separate Czechoslovak military units within the Allied armed forces, but also to accept in principle the notion that these Czech and Slovak units were integral parts of the Czechoslovak Army, a member of the armed forces of the Allied Powers.

And, indeed, the Allied governments eventually did agree to accept this proposal. In fact, even before the end of the war the Allies recognized the Council as the legitimate representative of the Czech and Slovak people in Austria-Hungary and viewed it as the provisional government of a future, liberated Czechoslovakia. In this way, the Czechoslovak Legions, at first in France and Russia and later in Italy, came into being, ultimately almost 100,000 men strong.

France

In 1914 over 3,000 Czechs—men, women, and children—lived in France, mostly in Paris. With the outbreak of the war about 300 of them volunteered for the French Foreign Legion, where the French government created for them an all-Czech infantry unit named the "Compagnie Nazdar." By October 1914, after the battle on the Marne, the unit was sent to the front. Before long, perhaps 100 Czech "stragglers," volunteers from Great Britain, some of whom entered France illegally (no Czech volunteers were permitted to enlist in the British army), arrived to sign up with the French armed forces—as did about 400 volunteers from Romania, almost 4,000 from Serbia, about 1,200 from Russia, almost 850 from Italy, and, finally, some 2,500 Czech and Slovak volunteers from the United States. As a consequence, by May 1918, the Czechoslovak volunteer group in France had grown into the Czechoslovak Infantry Brigade—the Czechoslovak Legion in France—of almost 7,000 men. They fought side by side with the French armed forces on the Western Front.

Russia

At the outbreak of the war, some 70,000 Czechs and Slovaks were settled in Russia. Already in August, 1914, the Tsarist government permitted the organization of a Czech volunteer detachment of scouts, the "Česká družina" (Czech Company), to engage in reconnaissance at the front with the purpose of demoralizing the Austrian troops and encouraging Czechs and Slovaks to defect to the Russian side. Those who did swelled the numbers of Czech and Slovak volunteers to 5,800 men—a Czechoslovak infantry brigade—by the end of 1916. By the end of 1917 the Czechoslovak Legion in Russia included a Czechoslovak Army Corps composed of two infantry divisions of four regiments each, an artillery brigade, and two reserve infantry regiments, a total of 32,000 men.

However, the Bolshevik revolution in November, 1917 intervened and changed the direction of the Czechoslovak Legion. After the new Bolshevik government signed separate peace treaties with the Central Powers, the Peace Treaties of Brest-Litovsk of February and March 1918, it became increasingly hostile toward the Czechoslovak Legion, by then a heavily armed foreign body of 50,000 men, which refused to join the Red Army.

In view of this unexpected development, on behalf of the Czechoslovak National Council Masaryk ordered the Legion: (1) to remain neutral in the Bolshevik revolution as well as in the subsequent civil war; (2) to retreat east, across Siberia, all the way to the port of Vladivostok on the Pacific Ocean; and (3) from there to proceed in Allied ships to France to fight the Germans on the Western Front.

The captain paused in his account. As far as he knew, the Legion had not landed in France as yet.

He was right, Jan learned later. The Legionnaires did not make it back from Russia in time to finish the war in France. They were deterred by an increasingly bellicose Red Army and had to fight their way east slowly, step by step, in many tough, persistent, and cumulative battles. The main reason behind the long delay was Allied politics. Influential circles in Paris and London pressed their governments to use the Legion, by then an Allied armed force, to support the army of Admiral Aleksander Kolchak, the commander of the "Whites," the Russian forces fighting the Bolsheviks in Siberia. And, indeed, the Legion afforded Kolchak vital though temporary relief. Later in 1919 the "Reds" did defeat the "Whites" and executed Kolchak. The Allied war in Russia was over. The first Legionnaire ship did not leave Vladivostok until January 15, 1920, bound for Europe but much too late to be of any help to the French. By

September 1920, the remainder of the Legion, some 56,000 men, had left Vladivostok as well, evacuated mostly in the holds of Allied transport ships.

Italy

Very few Czechs and Slovaks had settled in Italy before the war, and those who were living there were perceived by the Italians to be either hostile Austrians or close relations of the South Slavs, no great friends of the Italians. But with the belated entry of Italy in the war and its initial powerful military campaigns against Austria, the Italian front became the major Austrian battleground. As a consequence, the number of Czech POWs, defectors, and deserters from the Austrian trenches grew rapidly. Their open hostility to Austria and their eagerness to join the Italian armed forces and fight alongside the Italian troops were favorably noted by the Italian public.

But it was the shocking Italian defeat at Caporetto in the fall of 1917 which brought the matter of the Czech and Slovak volunteers dramatically to a head. By then thousands of Czechs and Slovaks had volunteered to join the Italians at the front. The spokesmen who negotiated on their behalf with the Italian government were two young members of the Paris-based Council, Eduard Beneš and Milan R. Štefánik.

Beneš, a doctor of law from the University of Dijon, lectured at the Prague commercial academy and taught at Charles University. A member of Masaryk's Czech party "Realists" and a skillful negotiator and hard-working organizer, Beneš came to Paris in the fall of 1915 and became the Czechoslovak National Council's general secretary. Milan R. Štefánik, a naturalized French citizen from Slovakia, was an astronomer, construction engineer, meteorologist, fighter pilot, French army general, and recipient of the medal of the Legion of Honor. A talented, eloquent, and persuasive protagonist of the Czechoslovak cause and founding member of the Council, Štefánik became the Council's vice president. The two men, Beneš and Štefánik, helped Masaryk to organize the Czech and Slovak volunteers, negotiated with the Allied governments concerned, and kept in touch with the Czech and Slovak leaders at home. In Italy they bargained long and hard.

Unlike the Italian public, the Italian government remained hostile to the idea of a separate Legion until the beginning of 1918. Give weapons to Austrian POWs? Take major risks for doubtful gain? The negotiations were polite and friendly but interminable and generally unproductive. But Caporetto did help to change the official Italian point of view. The Italian government finally relented. On

April 21, 1918, a generous agreement was signed between the government of Italy and the Czechoslovak National Council. The Czechoslovak Legion in Italy was created, trained, and sent to the front. It fought on the Piave front and on the Lago di Garda–Adige perimeter. A Czechoslovak division together with 51 Italian divisions, three British divisions, two French divisions, and a United States infantry regiment, fought with distinction in the battle of Vittorio Veneto, the final and decisive Allied assault that knocked Austria out of the war for good on November 3-4, just two weeks before. The Sixth Czechoslovak Division grew to an army corps of almost 18,000 men, composed of two rifle brigades with three regiments each, and with its own artillery and technical services.

The Czech and Slovak POWs who listened to the captain that night eagerly absorbed all that he had to say. Deeply impressed, they were ready to sign up and join the Czechoslovak Legion in Italy one and all, then and there.

V
CZECHOSLOVAK LEGIONNAIRE

The Czechoslovak Legion in Italy
Legnaro, Saonara, Padova, Vicenza,
November 24 – December 27

Indeed, on Sunday, November 24, a recruiting team led by the "Brother Captain" arrived, and the battered Czech and Slovak prisoners lined up to volunteer, all 701 of them. Whatever their motives—and they ranged all the way from the most patriotic to the most self-serving—the men wanted to do the right thing for their new country as well as for themselves. They considered themselves extraordinarily lucky.

The selection criteria were relaxed—many prisoners were sick or weak from malnutrition. Those whose families lived in Austria proper or in Hungary worried about what would happen to their loved ones. Some men volunteered under fictitious names. By late afternoon they were all processed and, with a few exceptions, enrolled. They were to be transferred to the same type of service they had been assigned to in the Austrian army, in the same capacity, and were to be given the same military rank. They were to become part of a battle-ready division composed of three regiments and nine battalions, with the mission of denying Poland its claim on Těšín Silesia on the border of northern Moravia, and of helping to liberate their new state, Czechoslovakia, from the Hungarian occupation forces in Slovakia and Subcarpathian Ruthenia.

They received two blankets each, enough straw for a mattress, almost double food rations (still not quite enough, but the future looked promising), and, best of all, their guards vanished. The prisoners were free to move around.

Like everyone else, Jan was overwhelmed by his good fortune. He could hardly believe the sudden, dramatic, and sweeping change in his fate. From a wretched member of a despised, defeated army, he was elevated, almost by magic, to the honorable position of valued soldier in the army of his own free country, a sovereign state, a respected member of the Allied Powers! This abrupt, profound, personal metamorphosis was hard for Jan and for all the of the new recruits to fathom.

Their elation, however, was tempered by a sense of unease. Ever since their initial capture by the Italians—some of the men had been POWs for more than two years—the prisoners had had no communication with their families, who probably had no idea what happened to them. If mentioned at all, the POWs were included in the "missing in action" statistics. Should the ever-diligent Austrian police find out that the POWs had changed sides and defected to the enemy—an act of treason punishable by death and, more to the point, leading to the immediate arrest of the relatives of the traitors—what would happen to their closest family members?

Jan worried about Božena. He had not heard from her nor she from him since October. Should it become known that he had defected, she might be in serious trouble. Jan pondered the possibility and weighed its gravity. Knowing something of the Austrian police, officious but bumbling, and imagining the present confusion in Vienna, he finally considered the cause for which he volunteered more than worth the risk. So with clear conscience and with love in his heart for his wife and his little daughter, he entered the ranks of the Legion.

The following day, infantry, cavalry, and artillery units were formed from the mostly Czech POWs. Artillerymen were especially needed—skilled and experienced gunners, wagon and cart drivers, telephone operators, medics, cooks, field observers, ammunition and provision supply men, and various clerks. Jan was appointed artillery sergeant in charge of the battery gun crew, just as before. He and twenty other volunteer artillerymen were sent north to a sorting camp near the town of Legnaro to start building up the battery to full strength. The civilians along the road were perplexed to see Austrian prisoners marching in Italy without guards.

In the Legnaro camp Jan was put in charge of the field kitchen's food supply for the new battery unit—a dream assignment for a starved POW. For the next five days Jan drove a wagon drawn by two strong horses to an army supply depot located in a small village nearby to pick up meat, groceries, and fresh vegetables for the field kitchen. The new kitchen staff, delighted with the quality and quantity of the provisions, were inspired and proudly served Czech dishes to the newly formed battery crew. Jan made sure that the amounts were sufficient for breakfast, lunch, and dinner. Everyone ate his fill. The food was plentiful, wholesome, and delicious.

The cook-butchers admired the sizes of the sides of beef. The smallest side weighed 125 kg as compared to 90 kg of the average Austrian beef. Jan was told that the frozen carcasses were imported from Argentina. The men were impressed. They could imagine handsome cattle grazing on lush pampas grasses in meadows halfway around the world.

November 27 was another important day. The men were taken to a delousing station, a set of barracks where they underwent the extraordinary and final transformation from Austrian POWs to members of the Czechoslovak Legion in Italy. In the first room they threw away their shabby, tattered uniforms, remnants of boots, and lice-infested underwear. In the second room, under hot showers and with plenty of soap, they washed away the three weeks' worth of dirt, lice, and misery of captivity. And in the third room Legion barbers gave them haircuts, shaved their facial and body hair to get rid of the lice, and issued them brand new Italian uniforms, new boots, and new winter underwear. "We are human again," writes Jan.

On November 28 a cursory medical checkup completed the physical transformation. The men were invited to exchange their Austrian money, if any, for Italian lire, the rate being five Austrian crowns for one Italian lire. Jan was astonished, after all the thievery and body searches to which they all had been subjected, at how much money the prisoners, including himself, had been able to hide during the captivity. (He later discovered that the rate of exchange on the Italian open market was even more generous than the military rate: 5 crowns to 1.75 lire.) The official money exchange was followed by the distribution of tobacco rations—cigarettes, cigars, and pipe tobacco—in generous amounts but inferior in quality to Austrian tobacco. Lunch was an excellent, nourishing beef soup with plenty of rice. The heaps of white Italian bread that appeared on the tables made the meal, in Jan's view, "a feast."

On November 30 Jan was among the seventy cannoneers who left the Legnaro camp for the town of Saonara, a distance of about seven kilometers. There they formed the nucleus of a new Second and Third Battery, which received from an Italian crew four heavy howitzers that the Italian High Command had assigned to the Legion's First Battery. The cannons had relatively short barrels and were used for firing shells at high angles of elevation to reach targets behind cover or in trenches. The 15 cm caliber Model 14 Škoda field guns captured by the Italians were almost six times as heavy as the 7.5 caliber Mountain Type 15 Škoda guns Jan and his men were used to: these howitzers weighed almost 3,000 kg each. In fact, it took Jan and the new legionnaires over three weeks to familiarize themselves fully with the new, complex weapons.

By December 2 the men were ready to return to Legnaro with the four new guns. Each howitzer consisted of two carriages: one, a two-wheel mount upon which the gun was affixed, and the other, a two-wheel carriage which pulled the gun and was in turn drawn by three pairs of handsome, stout horses ("English-bred draft animals," writes Jan, who had only heard of such breeds.) Each pair of horses was controlled by a rider, and a six-man crew rode on the gun carriages. Horse-drawn wagons loaded with ammunition, supplies, and a fully equipped field kitchen followed the howitzers; the rest of the battery detail marched behind the wagons.

Back in the Legnaro camp 65 new men were attached to the battery, now over 135 men strong, and three new officers—a captain battery commander, a first lieutenant, and a second lieutenant. Riding horses were provided for the officers and for each gun commander. Jan, now on horseback, was to command the second gun of the new Second Battery once they received the guns. The men were given new insignia indicating that they were soldiers of the Czechoslovak Legion in Italy as well as badges indicating rank and service, to sew on their uniforms.

The entire regiment now participated in lectures and seminars, this time in Czech. Hands-on exercises and drills of all kinds started in earnest to whip the men into shape quickly in their new roles and functions. They all ate well, slept well, were clean (they all marched to the Saonara public baths twice a week) and shaved, and dressed smartly. They received their monthly military pay from the Italian government—5.10 lire as POWs, 25 lire as legionnaires, with additional amounts for NCOs and officers, plus occasional monetary gifts from the new Czechoslovak government. Their tobacco rations were adequate, and they could shop freely in the local stores, where a liter of wine cost two lire and a loaf of the whitest, softest bread imaginable, .80 lire. In the midst of this plenty Jan suffered from a cough and stomach flu, but he did not pay much attention to either of these minor annoyances.

On December 8 all the elements of the Czechoslovak Legion in Italy—infantry, artillery and cavalry, now some 19,000 men—marched and rode from all directions to the city of Padova, a distance of about 15 km from Legnaro, for the swearing-in ceremony. Of the three howitzer batteries, only the first was truly complete and ready for battle; the other two batteries, just as spick and span, polished, and attractive, were short of guns and personnel. Nonetheless, they marched proudly with the rest.

At the impressive parade they were welcomed by General Boriani, the senior-most officer of the Legion, who introduced the Legion's Commander in Chief, General Luigi Piccione. After formally inspecting the assembled troops, the general in turn introduced a high official of the new Czechoslovak government, whom Jan and the men at the howitzer regiment mistakenly assumed to be Dr. Eduard Beneš. (President Masaryk was scheduled to appear at the ceremony but was delayed in Paris.) Only later did the men learn that the Czechoslovak official was not Dr. Beneš but Dr. Leo Borský, a diplomatic representative of the Czechoslovak Republic in Rome.

In any case, against all regulations the new Legionnaires greeted Dr. Borský's brief but moving speech with loud cheers and thunderous applause. General Scipioni, representing General Armand Diaz, the Chief of Staff of the Italian Armed Forces, stood at the podium to welcome King Vittorio Emanuele III, who greeted the troops warmly in the name of Italy. Finally, the Legionnaires swore allegiance to the Czechoslovak Republic, received the new colors of the Czechoslovak Army Corps in Italy, and at the express wish of the king sang the first stanza of the new Czechoslovak national anthem, which they had learned and practiced for the occasion. Upon their return to Legnaro, each man was awarded a special bonus of 5 lire and an additional portion of meat for dinner. It was a day to remember.

The training and drills continued. The three batteries worked together as a regiment so that all the gunners could familiarize themselves fully with the four howitzers. It was warm for December; the occasional snow tended to disappear quickly. The battery accountant, an Italian sergeant, informed the battery commander that he would not go to Czechoslovakia with the battery. He was leery of the cold winters there.

On the morning of December 15 the gunners of the Second and Third Battery went on horseback by way of Padova to Vicenza to pick up the additional eight howitzers. Because of heavy fog it took them the whole day to reach Vicenza. The howitzers were the same Austrian 15 cm Škoda Type 14 model with a range of 8.5 km that the men were familiar with. In heavy rain, with the welcome assistance of Italian artillerymen, the two batteries were able to move the guns to Legnaro in the afternoon of December 17. By now Jan knew he had a fever. Back in his quarters he heated a bottle of red wine to boiling, drank it down in one swoop, and went to bed to sweat out the fever. He slept deeply and well. When he awoke he was as good as new.

The drills continued. Now all three batteries composing the Seventh Artillery Regiment had their own guns. On December 21, in addition to their pay, the men received a Christmas bonus of 25 lire and a special gift from the Czechoslovak Republic of an additional 25 lire. Jan went shopping. As presents for his wife he bought a kilo of green coffee beans for 12 lire, four cakes of fragrant soap for 12 lire, and twenty spools of thread for 26 lire. To celebrate his third Christmas away from home, he bought himself a liter of wine, two herring, half a kilo of figs, and three oranges. He and his gunner friends had a warm, relaxed Christmas dinner together—more than enough to eat, more than enough to drink, and yet...their hearts ached for their loved ones living in uncertain conditions in these uncertain times. What would the next year, 1919, hold in store for each one of them?

On December 26 half of the Second Battery with two of their four howitzers plus a fully equipped ammunition supply wagon was ordered to report to the Padova railroad station. There they learned that half of their regiment, that is, half of the Second Battery and the complete First Battery, with all their equipment and supplies, were about to leave for Czechoslovakia. The regimental commander, an Italian colonel, ordered the two-gun crew to return to Legnaro without delay (in a truck, much to their surprise), pick up the rest of their gear, men, horses, and wagons, and report back to the station *subito*. The second half of the Second Battery plus the Third battery of the regiment, with all their guns and gear, were to follow the next day, also en route to Czechoslovakia.

The Czechoslovak Legion in Czechoslovakia
Těšín Silesia and Southwestern Slovakia,
December 27, 1918 – November, 1919

On December 27 the special freight train carrying half of the howitzer regiment—six guns, ammunition, all the horses, fully stocked wagons, equipment, food, and ample fodder for the horses—left Padova for Czechoslovakia. The actual destination was the town of Trenčín in Slovakia, via Treviso, Casarza, and Pontebba/Pontafel, through which both trains would be passing into Austria (Map VII). That train, as well as the second special train carrying the second half of the regiment, which left Padua on December 28, was accompanied by several heavy machine gun crews, whose stated mission was to protect the trains against possible armed assaults when crossing Austria. The men were also fully armed, and guards were posted in all the boxcars. (In the Armistice agreement the Austrians granted the Allied armed forces the right of free passage through Austria as well as the right to use Austrian railroads for that purpose, but the Italian command was not taking any chances.)

But no incidents occurred. To the legionnaires, who were on the lookout for trouble, the Austrian people they saw appeared dispirited and dejected. To be on the safe side, the trains turned north at St. Pölten to avoid Vienna, where the streets were reported to be full of violence and considerable civic unrest, perhaps even a revolution. The two trains entered the territory of liberated Czechoslovakia via Gmünd on December 29 and 30, respectively.

Jan had very much hoped that his train would go through Vienna and that he would be able, somehow, to get in touch with Božena. Once he found out that they would bypass Vienna, Jan tried to reach Božena by telegraph, telephone, and even by mail, but was frustrated at every turn. Except for St. Pölten, the train stops were short, and leaving the train was forbidden. In St. Pölten the station telephone and telegraph office, besieged by too many legionnaires ("those traitors..."), simply closed for the day. Jan did not know that, in fact, the letter he had written in Padova just before their departure and mailed in Austria with a proper Austrian stamp did reach Božena, who was shocked beyond belief. By the time Jan arrived in Trenčín, Božena was getting ready to be there herself, by way of her parents' place in Bohemia where little Božena had been staying. The young mother had made frequent visits to her little daughter, so the Austrian officials would not be suspicious and question her travel.

At the first stop in the new Czechoslovakia, the legionnaires were greeted by a small but excited crowd of local citizens. Representatives of Sokol and the noisy oom-pah-pah of a small local band greeted and saluted the first Czechoslovak armed forces on their own native soil. The legionnaires were moved. They were home! Together, they joined the crowd in singing the national anthem. It was an emotional moment.

On December 30 Jan's half-regiment changed trains at the next station, Veselí-Mezimostí. The legionnaires unloaded their guns, horses, and wagons from the Italian train, which returned to Padova, and loaded them all onto a special Czechoslovak freight train waiting to take them directly to Trenčín (Map VIII).

During the changeover, another small, spontaneous demonstration of welcome took place, with music provided by the Railroad Workers Union. There were speeches and singing.... "After 300 years of Habsburg rule, we are free again...." Every man on that train, hoping for the best, used the precious minutes of the stopover to try to reach a loved one. Jan sent a letter to Božena's parents in Bohemia, giving them the news and asking them to relay his message to Božena in Vienna. From what he could see of the end-of-the-war disruption, he did not really trust the reliability of the Czechoslovak postal service. He also sent a telegram, but he was aware that the small village of Bratčice, where his in-laws lived, was some distance from the town of Čáslav, the closest telegraph station, which was out of order most of the time anyway.

On New Year's Eve, the legionnaire train stopped at midnight in Jihlava, a town close to the Bohemian-Moravian border. In spite of the cold and mist, the streets around the station were teeming with celebrants singing, shouting, dancing, embracing, young and old alike. There were festive garlands, tricolors, banners and flags everywhere. The public signs that were printed in German were covered up or crossed out and rewritten in Czech. Smiling Red Cross nurses and volunteers served the legionnaires coffee and cakes. "You could eat and drink as much as you wanted—and lovely young girls hugged and kissed us...."

The legionnaires were reluctant to leave Jihlava, but similar scenes of robust welcome and hospitality awaited them in Třebíč, some 30 kilometers east of Jihlava, and in Brno, the capital of Moravia. It was a heady journey.

Trenčín, Slovakia, January 1 – 28, 1919

Late at night on January 1 Jan's train arrived in Trenčín, a picturesque old town in western Slovakia situated halfway between the two disputed areas in the new Czechoslovak state: the Hungarian border with Slovakia and the Polish border with Těšín Silesia in Moravia. On January 2 the second half of the regiment arrived as well. The Czechoslovak Army Corps from Italy—Heavy Field Howitzers' Group 1, Batteries 1, 2, and 3—was in place. The legionnaires were billeted in empty barracks that had been abandoned by the Hungarian army. They made themselves at home, took showers in a local bathhouse, did their washing, assembled and cleaned their guns and other equipment, and were ready, on January 7, for an inspection and review by their Commander in Chief, General Piccione.

After the ceremonial festivities, polished and handsome they went out to mingle in the life of the town. Trenčín, a former commercial center on the beautiful, white-water river Váh, was an attractive and friendly place. First they changed their lire into crowns, one lira for 2.50 crowns. However, with the exception of slivovitz, the local firewater, there was little for the legionnaires to buy, and the prices seemed high. The break-up of the Austro-Hungarian Empire had left visible scars on Trenčín, too.

* * * *

Slovakia, a country of over three million people, had been part of the Kingdom of Hungary for almost a millennium, from the 10th century until the end of 1918. Hungary was first known as Magyarorszag, Land of the Magyars, and contained territories under the Crown of St. Stephen that included Slovakia. The Slovak people, of Slav origin, were related to but distinct from their western neighbors, the Czechs, who were more than twice as numerous as the

Slovaks. (The two were originally united in the 9th century in the Great Moravian Empire, last ruled by the sons of the wise King Svatopluk.) The vast majority of the Slovak population were peasants; the landlord class and most of the small urban population were either Magyar or Magyarized Slovaks.

In the second half of the 19th century the Hungarian monarchy pressed Magyarization on the Slovaks harder than ever before—much harder than the Habsburg government pressed Germanization on the Czechs—and with success. Nevertheless, a small Slovak National Party held a few seats in the Budapest parliament. On June 30, 1918, Tomáš Garrigue Masaryk, the then president of the Czechoslovak National Council in Paris, and Slovak émigrés living in the United States agreed in Pittsburgh that the Slovaks should join forces with the Czechs and press the Allies for recognition of a free and independent common state of Czechs and Slovaks to be known as Czechoslovakia, which would be carved out of Austria-Hungary after the war. The Paris Peace Conference sanctioned the union and drew the new borders separating Slovakia from Hungary.

The new state's first small volunteer army units, composed largely of former Austrian soldiers, mostly Czechs but also Slovaks, arrived in western Slovakia close to the Czech border in early November 1918 (the new Czechoslovak Republic was proclaimed in Prague on October 28, 1918). They expected the Hungarian forces to withdraw behind the designated boundary line, allowing the incoming forces to occupy the now free territory of Slovakia. The Hungarian forces, however, strong, fully equipped with plenty of artillery and even, it was rumored, armored trains, were not at all ready to leave. Instead, they chased out of Slovakia the bewildered would-be occupants, who were unprepared for serious military action.

Subsequently, the Slovak leaders tried to negotiate directly with the Hungarian government, but to no avail. In fact, their initiative angered the Allies, who considered the Slovak-Hungarian dispute, like the Hungarian border hassles with its other neighbors, their own exclusive responsibility. On December 18, 1918, the Allies ordered the reluctant Hungarian government to move its armed forces behind the Allied-drawn demarcation line forthwith. The Hungarians, after some hesitation, complied. By the end of January 1919, most though not all of the Hungarian forces were out of Slovakia, from Bratislava in the west to Košice in the east. By early February the Slovak government moved to Bratislava, and the chastened Czechoslovak troops began to occupy the country. But now they included a new, strong backbone, the Czechoslovak legions from France and Italy, troops which were well-trained, well-equipped, experienced, disciplined and motivated.

* * * *

In the evening of January 7, the legionnaires in Trenčín were returning, singly and in groups, to the barracks for supper. Approaching the barracks with his friends, Jan saw a strangely familiar figure sitting on the bench before the main entry. God in heaven! It was Božena, in a fashionable hat and warm coat, a travel bag and a suitcase at her feet! They ran to each other and fell into each other's arms, to the noisy amusement (and envy) of the soldiers passing by. Jan still could not believe that Božena knew where he was and had found out how to get there. They had so much to talk about.

Without delay Jan found Božena a hotel room on the main town square, where they also had dinner. The compassionate battery commander issued Jan a two-day family leave pass. Their reunion was blissful.

They had so much to be thankful for, but there were worries, too. Božena had heard rumors, second- and third-hand and as yet unconfirmed, that Jan might have been identified as a member of the Legion, and should that prove to be the case, her presence in Vienna could be viewed as undesirable—by certain neighbors, some customers, and perhaps even the police. The two discussed the problem at length. What should they do? Ultimately, they had to agree: the only solution was for Božena to pack up and leave Vienna for good, whatever the cost, after almost nine years. She would join her little daughter in Bohemia and live with her parents until Jan was demobilized, hopefully soon.

In the meantime, however, urgent steps would have to be taken for Božena to emigrate safely from war-torn Vienna. They would have to sell their business—fortunately, established food stores were in demand in food-deprived Vienna. They would have to pack their furniture and household goods and ship them to Bratčice, secure official permits of all kinds, and pay bribes. Myriad other issues would have to be attended to, coped with, and settled. Clearly, Jan's presence in Vienna was essential. Did he dare to go? Jan considered the matter from all angles, and the Czechoslovak Legion's legal officer confirmed that he should go. The war was over, Austria was under the control of the victorious Allies, and the Czechoslovak government had provisional diplomatic representation in Vienna to protect its many citizens in Austria. Jan decided to make the visit as a civilian, fast and simple, without provoking attention or feeling intimidated. He hoped his good luck would hold.

The next day Jan applied for a six-day family emergency leave pass to go with Božena to Vienna. On the urgent recommendation of the battery commander, the regimental headquarters granted the request. In the evening of January 9 Jan and Božena left Trenčín.

They detoured first to Bratčice, for Jan to see his small daughter, now two years old. He marveled that the helpless infant he had last seen in 1916 had become this beautiful, dark-haired toddler who hid behind the long, full skirts of her grandmother, shyly peering out at him. He longed to pick her up and hold her close but did not want to frighten her. He knew it would take time for both of them to become acquainted. He visited briefly with his in-laws and changed into civilian clothes. The following day the young couple left for Vienna, Jan with his old Austrian identity card and other documents in his pocket, which Božena had thoughtfully brought with her to Trenčín.

In Vienna, at a provisional Czechoslovak diplomatic office, a young clerk recommended that Jan and Božena reserve space for their furniture and other belongings in a special emigrant train organized by that office and scheduled to leave Vienna for Bohemia soon. At that time, many Czech and Slovak families would be moving permanently from Austria to Czechoslovakia, and this train made it possible for them to take their possessions with them. Unfortunately, even before Jan and Božena could begin to follow up on that good suggestion, the border between Austria and Czechoslovakia closed temporarily. With the exception of visitors returning to the country from which they came, no people or goods were permitted to cross the border until further notice. Jan returned to Slovakia on January 16, but the emigrant train was delayed almost six weeks, until February 27, before it was permitted to depart from Vienna and cross the border.

Thus, Božena had to arrange the moving and do most of the packing by herself. Her neighbors and some of her customers helped; they were truly sorry to see Božena and Jan go, but they understood. The world was changing, for better or worse. But there were others who let Božena know, in no uncertain terms, what they thought of her and her treacherous kind. Her last six weeks in Vienna were the longest in her young life. She was then 24 years old.

Těšín Silesia, January 31 – March 15

When Jan returned to Trenčín, for the next ten days the battery practiced various offensive and defensive exercises and maneuvers, alone, with infantry, and with the other two batteries of the regiment. On January 26 the regiment was ordered to report to Těšín, a town over 200 kilometers north of Trenčín on the Polish border (Map VIII). The Polish armed forces were reportedly standing ready for a hostile take-over of Těšín-Silesia, an iron and coal-rich district on the Moravian border that was part of a larger province formerly divided between Germany (Schlesien), Poland (Slask), and Czech Austria (Slezsko). On November 1, 1918, the Polish armed forces had occupied the city of Těšín, the center of the region. On January 23 the commander of the Czechoslovak forces in the area issued an ultimatum to the Poles to evacuate the city "in two hours." When the Poles refused, as expected, the Czechoslovak forces advanced on Těšín and chased the Poles out. The war was on.

Riding on the howitzer carriages, in wagons, and on horses, it took the regiment three days to get from Trenčín to the war zone. In Těšín, on January 31 the regiment was divided again into two separate segments of six howitzers each, one segment moving about 10 kilometers north of Těšín to the town of Karviná and Jan's segment staying close to Těšín, depositing the reserve and supply lines on a large farm not far from town. The guns took a battle position in the wooded end of a small valley in front of a lively brook. Once in place, Jan and the gunners fired a few ranging shots at what they assumed were the Polish positions and waited. Nothing happened. No Polish response materialized. The crew of the six howitzers waited three more days. Then, on February 4, they were ordered to move even closer to the Polish positions, to a place near the town of Skočov southeast of Karviná. Again, there was no reaction.

What Jan and his friends did not know was that by January 31, when they arrived in Těšín, the war with Poland was in fact over. Later, the Czechoslovak-Polish conflict was known on both sides of the border as "a seven day war" or "a tempest in a teacup." Apparently, neither side expected serious resistance to its own "just claim" to the disputed territory, and no heavy fighting took place, just a series of lackadaisical—and sometimes one-sided—skirmishes. Both governments viewed the conflict more as a police action than a war, conducted more for the effect it would have on their respective publics than as serious military expeditions. Both claimed victory. Still, the Czechoslovak forces did manage to push the Poles back and to occupy the larger part of the disputed area, including the city of Těšín.

The men enjoyed the relative calm that followed. At this time the Polish-Czechoslovak dispute was under consideration at the Paris Peace Conference, and the representatives of the two governments, Poland and Czechoslovakia, were engaged in talks. Both sides laid claim to parts of Silesia: as Jan understood it, the Czechoslovak government claimed Austrian Silesia on the grounds of historical right—Silesia had belonged to the lands of the Czech Crown since the fourteenth century. Since 1526 the Czech lands, including Silesia, had been part of the Habsburg-ruled Austrian Empire. The Poles, on the other hand, claimed Silesia as Polish by reason of having the majority of the population; in 1919 more Poles lived in Austrian Silesia than Czechs. (As far as Jan could find out, depending on which areas were included, there were over 400,000 Poles, over 200,000 Czechs, and about 150,000 Germans living in the disputed Těšín Silesia at that time.)

On February 7 Božena arrived in the Těšín area to consult with Jan on the details of the impending move from Vienna to Bratčice. Jan was about to leave with a regimental detail for Trenčín to pick up food supplies for the regiment, and Božena went with them. In that way she and Jan had almost two days together to discuss and decide many important matters. From Trenčín Božena returned to Vienna and Jan to the Polish border area with the food supply team. Three weeks later, on February 28, Božena had sold the food store and arrived in Bratčice with all their furniture, household goods, and belongings, exactly as planned. She was back in her childhood home with her parents and small daughter, the trying weeks in Vienna safely behind her. Except for vivid, painful memories of crossing the border....

Božena Moves from Vienna, February 11 – 18

The store and the apartment that Božena and Jan had rented since 1914 were modest. Božena was determined to keep only those items in their possession that were worth keeping and to sell or give away the rest. But how could she not keep the beautiful inlaid furniture that Jan had made?

Selling the store was a different matter. By February 1919 store shelves were half empty, and the normally well-stocked supply room behind the store was almost bare. But the store was still a going concern, well-established, well-known, well-situated, surrounded on all sides by apartment houses whose tenants were Božena's steady, loyal customers. It would not be too difficult to find a buyer, but how would she manage the payment? The move from Vienna was permanent. She could not accept a promissory note. Cash was preferable, but the almost worthless Austrian crowns had no value whatsoever outside Austria. As luck would have it, Heidi, one of the two dependable girls who worked part-time for Božena during the war and took over when she needed to be absent, came forward with an offer to buy the store. She managed to persuade her relatively well-to-do father that in those difficult times it was a good investment and he should buy the store for the family. He paid Božena what she considered a fair price in cash, in silver coins.

To this Božena added the modest savings which she had accumulated during the war, also in silver coins. The grand total was not much, but it might be at least a down payment on another store wherever they settled next in Czechoslovakia, once Jan returned from Slovakia.

A moving van owned by Jan's friend Ernst delivered Božena's goods to the railway station, and Ernst and his helper deposited them in a boxcar where Božena had reserved space on the emigrant train. Finally, early in the morning of February 27, the train, fully loaded without an inch to spare, pulled out of the station and headed for the Austrian-Czechoslovak frontier. At the border a group of Austrian passport and customs officials was waiting to board the emigrant train. They examined documents cursorily, but they searched everybody and everything in the most minute detail. Nothing escaped their attention. Clearly, they were looking for family treasures, anything of value such as gems, jewelry, articles of gold or silver, works of art, antiques, coins, bullion...the emigrants were at their mercy. All valuables were confiscated, those in clear view as well as those hidden in the most personal, ingenious places. This was no border inspection. It was outright looting.

Could these have been genuine Austrian passport and customs officials? No one knew for sure. Afterwards, Jan and Božena discussed the incident. The unrest and turmoil of the times in defeated Austria, stormy and explosive with public disorder that spilled over from Vienna into the countryside, were fed by deep popular despair. In this climate of violence and credible threats of a Red revolution, would it be impossible for a group of frustrated men, perhaps even despondent war veterans expecting rich rewards, to put on the uniforms of passport and customs officials and rob a train? It had happened before. The Czechoslovak consular officer who accompanied the emigrant train from Vienna was livid but powerless to do anything.

It was dark when the train moved again, crossing the border into Czechoslovakia. The consular officer stayed behind to return to Vienna to lodge the strongest possible protest with the Austrian authorities. Božena entered her new homeland with her furniture and her household goods intact, but minus the money from the sale of the store and without any of the couple's hard-earned savings.

* * * *

Meanwhile in Silesia, late on February 9, the two segments of Jan's howitzer regiment were ordered to reunite again, to move jointly to the Teachers' Institute building and a large yard in Těšín, and await orders there. Jan resumed his post as duty officer of the Second Battery. There was talk, unconfirmed, that the border dispute with Poland had been resolved, more or less, with Czechoslovakia losing part of Silesia and perhaps half of the town of Těšín itself to Poland; and that the Hungarians, who had ruled Slovakia over a millennium, were about to start an offensive in earnest on a wide front, the purpose of which was to keep at least southern Slovakia an integral part of Hungary.

For the next two weeks, Jan's artillery regiment kept at the ready, engaging mostly in various guard duties. The men were rested, well fed, clean, and relaxed, and their howitzers and equipment shone. It was a relatively quiet period for them. More and more their major concern was the future—where they would settle, what they would do, and how they would fit into the new and unknown social, economic, and political order of the Republic once they returned home. Optimism prevailed, but a few worries lingered on. Once the euphoria of victory, liberation, freedom, and democracy faded, the questions of day-to-day life surfaced. Would there be jobs, housing, security? They could only hope, but they could not be certain.

On February 26 the regiment was ordered to help to evacuate the towns of Jablunkov and Frýdlant located, respectively, southeast and southwest of Těšín. The regiment rode and marched west through the town of Frýdek to Sedliště, a small place between Frýdek and the city of Ostrava, the future capital of Czech Silesia, and stayed there for another two weeks, engaged essentially in the same guard activities as in Těšín and waiting for developments at the Paris Peace Conference (Map VIII).

By the middle of March, the border dispute between Poland and Czechoslovakia appeared to have been settled, not really to the satisfaction of either party, it was rumored, but to the satisfaction of the Allied Powers. Jan found out later that Czechoslovakia and Poland had been unable to come to an agreement. Upon persistent prodding by the Allies at the Paris Peace Conference, however, they did finally agree to submit the dispute for arbitration to the Conference of Allied Ambassadors, an arm of the Allied Powers, and to accept the verdict as a decision binding on both parties. In July 1920 the Ambassadors announced their finding. The new border represented neither a substantive gain nor a significant loss for either party, but it did favor the Czechs. In addition, an area located northwest of Těšín, the county of Hlučín, formerly part of Prussian Silesia, was transferred to Czechoslovakia as well. The city of Těšín was divided between Poland and Czechoslovakia along the river Olše/Olza. According to the 1921 Czechoslovak census, the total population of Silesia within the borders of Czechoslovakia amounted to over 672,000 people.

Back in Slovakia, March 18 – September 15

On March 15 the regiment was ordered to move back to Slovakia, this time to Bratislava, the capital of historic Slovakia, located on the left bank of the Danube River, to challenge the Hungarian occupation forces reportedly moving into the area. The three batteries first took up a position at the Bratislava castle overlooking the city and the Danube; later, they transferred to "Dynamitka," the munitions factory Dynamit-Nobel within the city proper; and still later, they were to move into Velký Žitný ostrov (the Great Rye Island), an 80 kilometer long, oval-shaped, diluvial plain on the Danube between Bratislava and the towns of Nové Zámky and Komárno, a rich, grain-producing area (Map VIII). The three municipalities—Bratislava, Nové Zámky, and Komárno—had been occupied by Czechoslovak forces in January. The prevailing view at the battery and at the regiment concerning the Legion's mission in Slovakia was that it was yet another police action. They were there to establish and enforce law and order; to help set up a new, loyal civilian administration on all levels, from local to national, including an effective and loyal police force; and to assist in organizing a more efficient economic order. From what the men had seen since their arrival in January, Slovakia certainly needed all of the above, and soon.

Unfortunately, a very different turn of events ensued. On March 20, according to the officers of the battery, the Allied and Associated Powers, impatient with the Hungarian government's procrastination in completely withdrawing from the territories of its three neighbors—Czechoslovakia, Romania, and Yugoslavia—issued an ultimatum: the Hungarian forces were ordered to withdraw behind a new demarcation line with Slovakia some 50-80 kilometers farther into Hungarian territory than stipulated in the original Allied order in 24 hours or suffer the consequences. "We must expect to move to the new demarcation line soon. Be ready to respond at a moment's notice," the officers warned the men.

And, indeed, early in April, on General Piccione's orders, the howitzer group, again in concert with the Legion's infantry regiments, prepared to move to the area between the town of Komárno, an important port on the Danube, and Nové Zámky, on the bank of the river Nitra some 30 km north of Komárno. They were to advance there with care, occupying the territory on the Slovak side of the new Allied-ordered demarcation line, area by area and district by district. They expected only limited interference from the Hungarian forces, who were already deeply involved elsewhere in defending their new borders with Romania. By the middle of April Piccione's legionnaires succeeded in securing the area in question. In eastern Slovakia, by April 15 the French legionnaires commanded by General E.Ch.A. Hennocque had occupied Subcarpathian Ruthenia (Podkarpatská Rus), a former much-neglected Hungarian province of some 600,000 people, that the Allies had ceded to Czechoslovakia at the request of the Ruthenian National Council.

However, on April 30 the Hungarians launched a surprise night attack on the Komárno front. Artillery and heavy machine gun fire supported a large infantry contingent advancing on the Czechoslovak forces, but the attack failed. In any case, no one at the battery viewed that assault as anything more than a serious probe of the Czechoslovak positions, certainly not as the opening salvo of a war in Slovakia.

The legionnaires' complacency was short-lived, however. According to the officers of the battery, General Piccione had made a serious mistake. The Romanians had advanced deep into Hungary and pushed the retreating Hungarians far beyond the Allied-ordered line of demarcation, thereby creating a sizable no-man's-land bordering on the designated Czechoslovak section. Abhorring a power vacuum, Piccione ordered the Czechoslovak troops to cross the demarcation line, advance into the vacant area, and secure it. He could foresee all kinds of problems—disorder, lawlessness, pillage, and even pogroms—in a vacant territory that was not occupied. Therefore he decided to take the risk.

Reacting immediately, the Hungarians lashed out at the Czech trespass of their territory, a "lawless violation" of the Allied demarcation line, and prepared for swift retaliation. What next?

What Jan did not know then but found out later was that the Hungarians had mobilized their forces in March and April; they were ready to attack the Czechoslovak forces whenever a legitimate reason presented itself. Unwittingly, General Piccione supplied it.

Looking back on these events, Jan was able to see the rationale of what had transpired. The Allied ultimatum to the Hungarians of March 20, which pushed the demarcation line much deeper into Hungarian territory than the original Allied order, had shocked the Hungarian nation. They were outraged to be humiliated in this fashion. The Hungarian president, Count Mihaly Karolyi, resigned on the spot. In a bloodless coup d'état a Hungarian-born Soviet agent,

Béla Kun, was appointed the new prime minister. Kun promised prompt, armed Soviet assistance against Hungary's "voracious" neighbors and called the nation to arms to liberate the "stolen" Hungarian hereditary territories.

The desperate, stunned nation received Béla Kun's appeal, socialist in spirit but nationalist in form, with enthusiasm. Both the radical socialists and revolutionaries on the left and the Hungarian nationalists on the right could unite on this issue. By the end of March they were ready when Béla Kun called for volunteers and began to mobilize the recently demobilized Hungarian troops. On May 20 Béla Kun launched a well-prepared, well-supplied, well-orchestrated offensive against the Czechoslovaks along the whole Slovak-Hungarian demarcation line. From a police action, this "armed provocation" by General Piccione had escalated into war. Unprepared for such a sudden and fierce attack along the whole front, the Czechoslovak forces turned tail and ran. Before the middle of June almost two-thirds of eastern Slovakia was in Hungarian hands (Map C).

But not southwestern Slovakia. Against all odds, in the Nové Zámky-Komárno area Jan's howitzer regiment, together with the attached infantry regiments, stood their ground. Faced with the repeated fury of the enemy assaults, the resolute defenders eventually managed not only to halt the determined Hungarians from advancing and breaking through but ultimately chased them back on June 4 across the Danube. Casualties were high, but by June 7 the dangerous Hungarian penetration of southwestern Slovakia in the direction of Nové Zámky, Žitný ostrov/Rye Island, and Bratislava was arrested.

In the middle of these dramatic events, on June 1 General Maurice Pellé, the chief of the French Military Mission in Czechoslovakia since February 1919, replaced General Piccione with French General Eugène Mittelhauser. The sudden change was awkward and even embarrassing for the men at the battery, who had always felt that General Piccione understood and supported them. As recently recruited legionnaires, they had looked up to him as their first Commander in Chief, and their loyalty to him was unquestioned. Jan suspected that General Piccione was a victim of unfortunate circumstances, perhaps even behind-the-scene intrigues in these unsettled times.

In any case, General Mittelhauser made a difference. He introduced martial law and instant court-martials; cashiered incompetent officers and commanders; prohibited unauthorized retreats; improved the troops' rations; reintroduced military pay and made it retroactive; and somehow coaxed military supplies, heavy weapons, and airplanes from the French government, and ammunition and stronger moral support for the troops from the Czechoslovak government.

At the same time there was heavy and sustained Allied pressure on Béla Kun. The luck that avoided General Piccione was with General Mittelhauser. Confronted with the angry Allied threat of all-out war if Béla Kun did not cease and desist in his "illegal aggression," the powerful Hungarian offensive petered out by June 8. By June 15 the war was virtually over. (On June 18 remnants of several Hungarian units operating in the area attacked Nové Zámky once again, but that was the enemy's last gasp.) On June 24 an armistice was signed, and after that the Hungarian army began to withdraw from Slovakia in earnest. By July 4 reportedly not a single Hungarian soldier was left on the Slovak side of the new demarcation line put in place by the Allies. Slovakia was free, and Subcarpathian Ruthenia was liberated some six weeks later (Map D).

Back on the demarcation line in Komárno, Jan's battery and regiment were no longer on strict alert, but neither were they able to go home as yet. Once all their guns, animals, weapons, equipment, uniforms, and personal gear were spic and span again, they had time to enjoy some limited leisure and recreation. One night Jan stood guard duty with several other men from the battery. Imagine their astonishment when General Mittelhauser, in person and alone, came to check on them. What a scrupulous and conscientious Commander in Chief! Unfortunately, none of the men spoke French. But the General wished them good night in Czech, "Dobrou noc," and shook their hands. The men saluted like never before.

Now that Jan and his friends had time to ponder their situation in Slovakia, they tried to understand the logistics of the Slovak campaign. Just about everything that seemed to go right for the Hungarians had gone wrong for the Czechs and Slovaks, they concluded. The Hungarian troops were highly motivated. The nationalists viewed Slovakia as an integral part of Hungary. The revolutionaries saw Slovakia as a fresh new link in the chain of socialist revolutions that were about to liberate the world. The Hungarian troops, well trained and led by experienced World War I officers, had a wealth of war material and supplies left behind by both the German-Austrian armies and the Hungarian Imperial forces. While the Romanians were occupied fighting the Ukrainians, the Hungarian troops had time to engage fully in Slovakia.

For the Czechoslovak forces, on the other hand, the Great War had ended over six months before. Czechoslovakia was now an independent, sovereign country, a respected friend and ally of the powerful Allied and Associated Powers, the victors of the war.

Occupied or not, as part of the new Czechoslovak state Slovakia was a legitimate, established, and internationally recognized fact of life. So what was the point of the high drama on the Slovak border?

The front, hundreds of kilometers long, was difficult to defend, whether in the North Carpathian Mountains, which form the greater part of Slovakia, or in the southern part of the lowland, the Slovak plain, where Jan's regiment was located. Contrary to expectations, the Slovak population was not hospitable to its liberators. Mostly indifferent and not particularly patriotic, they were not supportive. They did not seem to value the troops' sacrifices on their behalf, kept their distance, and most of the local officials—Magyar or Magyarized administrators, police, business, church, and civic leaders—were outright hostile. "But, after all, we should not forget," writes Jan, "that Slovakia had been an integral part of the Kingdom of Hungary for a millennium."

By late spring 1919 the loose volunteers—the former Austrian soldiers, Czechs and Slovaks recruited after the war; students; members of youth organizations; Sokol; and the Workers' Gymnastic Union—were less than enthusiastic about fighting in serious military encounters. The Italian and French legionnaires were tired of the war, too. Without military pay, often hungry, they wanted to go home. It was not just battle fatigue; they felt unappreciated. Not only were the Slovaks cool to them, but the Czech public seemed to be ignoring them as well. The Czechs in Bohemia and Moravia viewed the war in Slovakia as unimportant by then, uninteresting and distant. They had much more pressing worries occupying them in a new country emerging from the war with an uncertain future. The soldiers were depressed. They felt that the longer they stayed in Slovakia without any really good reason, the fewer the jobs available for them at home when they returned to take care of their families.

General Piccione and his largely Italian staff had viewed the mission of the heterogeneous army under their command in much the same way as the men of Jan's battery and regiment had, namely, as a simple operation intended to open the country to freedom and self-government. Since the general did not expect any appreciable resistance and certainly not a war, his advance into Slovakia had been casual. He had no overall strategy, no reserves, no dependable system of communication, and no intelligence regarding the enemy. His army, advancing at a leisurely pace, walked straight into the Hungarian trap.

Perhaps most important of all, the legionnaires in Slovakia were chronically short of equipment and supplies, especially of ammunition and heavy weapons; air support was almost non-existent. The men were told that the new Czechoslovak bureaucracy, inexperienced and unprepared for the task of large military procurement, had no funds at its disposal for the purpose. The resulting strain on the armed forces in Slovakia became critical.

Small wonder, then, that by the end of May 1919 the motley Czechoslovak armed forces in Slovakia found themselves enveloped in a fog of misunderstanding and disorder on many levels. The war had been mercifully short—it was over in six weeks—but it was nasty. Almost 1,000 men, mostly Czechs but Slovaks as well, had been killed, many more were maimed or wounded, and almost 2,000 were missing in action. The men were ready to go home, not for a leave but forever. As volunteers they had enlisted in the Czechoslovak Army with enthusiasm. Now their hearts were no longer in it.

Jan, too, was tired, restless, and disillusioned. His original dedication to the legionnaire cause had been waning with the length of the experience. Like most of his compatriots, he was ready to be demobilized and become a civilian again.

Discharged from Service. A New Life Begins.
Olomouc, November 3, 1919

Starting in late July and in August, the operations of Jan's battery, now the Second Battery of the First Group of Heavy Howitzers of the Czechoslovak Army Corps from Italy, were gradually terminated in western Slovakia, and legionnaires over forty years old were demobilized. In September the rest of the Group was moved in several stages to a garrison in Brno, the capital of Moravia (Map VIII). Finally, on November 3 Jan, together with most other men in the Group, was demobilized. The Great War had been over for more than a year. The ceremony took place in Olomouc, on the same parade grounds where Jan had been first sworn into the Austro-Hungarian army three long years ago on November 22, 1916.

The same parade grounds, but a world apart. The world was different, the country was different, the army was different, and Jan himself was different. Nothing had so profoundly affected his life as the war. At 29 he felt old, weary, drained, used up, and branded for life. The buoyancy and confidence of his youth had vanished forever, it seemed. He carried the war inside him. The worst symptoms were the horrible, sweaty nightmares, whose absurd abnormalities returned regularly to penetrate his sleep night after night. He tried to rid his mind of the poison of his wartime fears and traumas, to banish the memories of bloody massacres from his head, but peace of mind remained elusive. Jan's only hope was that time would bring relief and sanity. It did, but the healing took longer than Jan had expected.

Eventually he did mend, but he was never the same. Scars remained, not only mental and emotional but physical as well. For the rest of his life he suffered the impaired hearing of a cannoneer; burning stomach pains which often woke him up coughing at night; and persistent migraine headaches, which he could not relieve with aspirin because his stomach could not tolerate it.

Only a few of his friends stayed on with the Group (now the Reserve Battery of the Czechoslovak Mountain Artillery Regiment) to become professional soldiers in the armed forces of the new Republic. The rest quit. The future was uncertain, but to a man they were sick of army life. They had had enough of the surreal existence of soldiers.

After the demobilization ceremony Jan wanted to leave for Bratčice to be with Božena and little Božena as soon as possible. But with his mother and brothers in the immediate vicinity (his sister Josefa, "Pepi," had moved to Prague), how could he turn his back on them? Only some 50 km from Olomouc was the countryside where Jan was born, had gone to school, and learned his trade. And it was from Olomouc that he had departed, a certified cabinet-maker, to seek his fortune in Vienna. He knew he was not likely to return this way soon once he reached Bratčice.

So right off Jan decided to drop in on his oldest brother, Karel, the one who had been severely wounded on the Serbian front early in the war. It was Karel and his family with whom Božena had stayed when she visited Jan during those first months of his basic training with the Infantry Landwehr Regiment No. 13. Karel's right knee had remained stiff and unbending, but he still worked for the Olomouc railway station, now as a train dispatcher. The visit was short but joyous.

A friend of Karel took Jan to the nearby town of Litovel, where Jan visited briefly with his youngest brother, Ludvík, a born entrepreneur, who had been instrumental in Jan's becoming an artilleryman in January 1917 (Map VIII). Ludvík introduced him to the mayor of Litovel, who on the spot offered Jan the job of chief of the town's police as soon as he could return. Jan thanked the mayor for the attractive offer and promised to think it over and let him know.

After hitching several rides, Jan reached Klopina, his village birthplace, to surprise his mother and his second oldest brother, František, who was taking care of his mother and working the family farm. Neither Ludvík nor František had married as yet. Suddenly, as if by arrangement, Jan's good friend Franz Dubový appeared with his bride Marie, Božena's younger sister, who lived in Pískov, the village just over the next hill where Jan was first apprenticed fifteen years earlier. After warm embraces all around, Jan recounted the many times that Franz, master sergeant at the regimental slaughterhouse, had showed up out of the blue bringing welcome gifts of food just when Jan was losing all hope of eating again. "Remember, Franz, when I ate not only the strudel but the newspaper that Božena had wrapped it in? Or how you caught me counting lice? Or how fast I could devour a whole loaf of bread?" Everyone laughed, savoring the joy of being alive and together again.

Miraculously, all the brothers had survived the war, as had Božena's brother Alois, the master electrician, skilled fisherman, and gourmet cook from Vedronza, whom Jan was looking forward to seeing in Bratčice soon. Marie told him that Alois had just opened an electrical supply shop near Bratčice in Golčův Jeníkov (Map VIII).

From Klopina Jan made his way by train to Bratčice to rejoin his wife and child. These short visits with the family had given him the emotional relief he needed more than anything else. He was ready to meet Božena and get on with his life. He was thirsting for normal civilian existence, in which he and his wife could make their own decisions about their own lives and their own future. He wanted and needed to be part of a community of people like himself. He was ready and willing to start from the bottom up, but on his own terms.

As always, Božena was ahead of him. She already had a plan. Why not move to Prague, the capital of the new state of Czechoslovakia, and open a food store again? She had the experience, she liked the person-to-person relationship with customers, who liked her, too, and she was sure that she and Jan could make a good living. They had little to start with, but they could borrow money. They were young—Jan was 29, Božena 25— healthy and hard-working, and Jan was a respected veteran. Why not give it a try?

Why not, indeed? Jan liked Božena's energetic and insightful arguments. He had heard them before. He had some reservations though; he thought of his training and experience in cabinet-making, which he enjoyed very much and was good at, and of the tempting offer from the mayor of Litovel to become the head of the town's police, "a good steady job with a decent pension...." But in the end he agreed with Božena. They would be working together, side by side, and the hard work and devotion to duty would pay off. Božena wanted another child and promised him a son. How could he refuse?

Two days later Jan and Božena took the train to Prague, some 70 kilometers from Bratčice. They would return later to pick up little

Božena as soon as they found a place to live and had settled in. They were on their way to start anew, older, wiser, perhaps, but with faith in the future and determined to make a good life for themselves and their children.

And they did succeed in creating a good life in Prague—until the next upheaval twenty years later, World War II.

VI
EPILOGUE

The Great War Reconsidered

World War I changed the world. Nothing like it had ever happened before in the history of humankind. In *scope* the armies of World War I numbered in tens of millions; conservative estimates put the number at 65 million men. Due to advances in technology, communication, and transportation brought about by the rapid expansion of industry and the many scientific and technological breakthroughs before 1918, huge numbers of soldiers were clothed, fed, housed, armed, transported, and rapidly deployed with a degree of efficiency never before possible. The combatants were no longer the professional-mercenary soldiers of the past, but civilians in uniform, able-bodied men liable for regular army service through universal conscription. Because of the inclusiveness of popular enlistment, almost every family in the belligerent countries saw their sons, brothers, and fathers leave home to fight in the war.

Nor was World War I like any earlier war in *intensity*. Due to new, revolutionary weapons, the huge armies facing each other across a no-man's-land sacrificed mobility for firepower. The result was trench warfare, the most characteristic—and deadly—feature of the First World War. Hundreds and even thousands of massed guns blasted a path for the infantry's frontal attack of a few hundred yards ahead, only to have the infantry wiped out by a counterblast of hundreds and even thousands of massed enemy grenades, shrapnel, and bombs before the infantrymen had time to reach the enemy trenches.

Artillery was extraordinarily effective. It was larger in proportion to infantry than ever before, its ranges were longer, its high explosive shells, including gas shells, were more lethal and its rolling barrages lasted longer. Guns and mortars, hidden for the first time behind hills and mountains that shielded them from hostile flat trajectory fire and ground observation, shot faster and with greater accuracy than was ever before possible. As a consequence, while the deadly combination of machine guns and barbed wire entanglements in the no-man's-land forced the infantry into trenches, the efficient field guns, the howitzers, and mortars kept them there.

Neither side could win. On the one hand, the artillery bombardments along all the fronts could not destroy all the machine guns and barbed wire entanglements or kill all the soldiers in trenches. On the other hand, the attackers could not overrun all the enemy barbed wire, all the machine guns, and all the elaborate trenches, even with the heaviest artillery support. The defense won out over the offense again and again, and the price was human life.

Given the huge numbers of fighting men facing each other over a swath of no-man's-land, backed by a large arsenal of sophisticated killing machines for a period of over four years, the number of *casualties* was extraordinarily high. In fact, World War I was the bloodiest war ever in the history of humankind: no earlier war comes even close to World War I in terms of the sheer magnitude of human pain, suffering and tragedy. According to conservative estimates, the casualties were historically unprecedented. In round numbers about 8 million men were killed, 7 million were permanently disabled, 15 million were seriously wounded, and about 8.3 million were taken prisoner or were missing in action. The large number of men, their concentration in relatively small areas, the defensive nature of the war, the new technologies of mass destruction, and the war's long duration thus made for a quantum leap in the intensity of the fighting and the number of casualties. The intensity affected civilians, too. Some 5 million civilian casualties (excluding Russians) were directly related to the war. (Russia, Serbia, and Bulgaria suffered greater civilian losses than military.)

In addition, the belligerent governments regimented the daily lives of their citizens, women as well as men, by aggressively manipulating their respective national economies. Production, distribution, transportation, prices, income, and labor were under strict government control. Governments also used censorship and propaganda in new, intrusive ways, turning the war on the home front into a fury of unprecedented mass hatred against the enemy, aimed at his swift annihilation "for what he has done to us" and at the destruction of his "sick and predatory" way of life. World War I came close to becoming what World War II in fact was, *a total war*.

The war was waged by both sides as a prolonged battle that had to be won unconditionally. No other outcome but complete and total victory was even considered. Compromise was unthinkable. As to the cost of such a victory, no leader seemed to care. It was this relentless pursuit of a total victory at any price that ruined Europe. It drove the losers into humiliation and despair and the victors into bankruptcy.

In *significance* the Great War was a watershed and a sea change from previous conflicts. It may not have been a world war in the sense that World War II was, but it involved a great many countries and peoples. It started as a European war to restore the balance of power in the world, but the participation of colonies in Asia and Africa and the interventions of Turkey, the United States, and Japan made the war more than just another European power struggle. The war was fought by sixteen countries and their colonies on three continents. If countries that declared war but did not fight were included, then some 93 percent of the world's population was formally at war.

Writers over the years have attempted to pinpoint what made this war different. Attempting to capture its nature and significance, they have variously described the war as "a static savagery of the trench lines," "a nightmare of grotesque horror," "the anguished end of an age," "an act of lemming-like self-destruction," "a self-inflicted death blow," "a death blow to European civilization." Indeed, with the war a way of life died. Europe lost its dominant and exclusive leadership in world affairs, but nothing replaced it. There were no victors in this war; all lost in one way or another.

Could the disaster have been prevented? Some historians blame reckless and inadequate political leaders and their lack of imagination. Others criticize the preponderance of military over political decisions; the military was fighting by the rules of the offensive wars of the past, not the defensive war at hand. Still others fault the aristocratic landed gentry, who assumed that the peasant-soldiers were as expendable as the cattle on their estates, to be sacrificed in ever greater numbers in the hope of rapid victory. The fact remains that for four long years, employing obsolete tactics and strategies, staggering numbers of men in highly concentrated formations waged battles with the most powerful firepower in the history of warfare. It is true that towards the end of the war, tanks, aircraft, and submarines began to change the mix and the tempo, but by then it was too late to alter the outcome.

* * * *

The Italian front, the front of my father's war, was not a major theater of World War I; the Eastern and Western fronts were. Other lesser fronts included the Southern (Serbian) front; the Caucasus front; the Dardanelles and Gallipoli; Mesopotamia (Iraq); Salonika; and Palestine and Syria. (Fighting also took place in East, Central, North, and South-West Africa. Japan's contribution to the Allied cause was its 1914 capture of the German naval base and colony of Tsingtao in China's Shantung Province.) But the Italian front was significant: the large numbers of fighting men and the blood spilled and the casualties suffered (for Italy, 1,351,000 killed and wounded in action and 561,000 prisoners of war and missing in action; for Austria-Hungary, 1,420,450 killed and wounded and 653,449 POWs and MIA) add up to an intensity of warfare under adverse conditions that was extraordinary. In addition, the outcome of the war for both belligerents was disastrous, fatal for Austria-Hungary and humiliating and seriously debilitating for Italy. Defeated, Austria-Hungary came apart, and its disintegration changed the map of Europe. Italy, the economic weak sister of Europe before the war, came out of the war weaker still, ripe for the Fascist plucking that followed.

Italy and Austria were hereditary enemies of long standing. History, as is so often the case in territorial disputes, made them into *prima facie* rivals. In the Wars of Italian Independence, the Habsburgs lost Lombardy, Tuscany, Modena (1859) and then Venetia (1866) to Italy. However, as early as 1814 Austria had forcibly annexed Trentino, a north Italian region bordering on Austria. Most of the population of Trieste, a Habsburg-ruled Mediterranean port located over 100 km east of Venice, was more Italian in culture and in spirit than Austrian.

Although the two countries may have been enemies, neither of them was ready for war. Both had high hopes, however, that if war came, it would be short, and they would be victorious. Both were among the weakest links in their respective wartime alliance systems. The principal allies of each were strong, supportive, and reassuring. Thus when Italy, courted by France and Great Britain with promises of many rewards, declared war on Austria (though not on Germany), the two old rivals entered into and waged a war which was separate from the major confrontations of World War I. For all practical purposes it became a private war between the two old antagonists. For Italy the chief enemy was Austria-Hungary, and for Austria-Hungary, which Germany had rescued from certain defeat in Russia, Italy became the principal enemy. The chief enemy of the Allied Powers was Germany, not Austria-Hungary, and the major enemies of the Central Powers, excluding Austria-Hungary, were Russia, France, Great Britain, and later the United States, not Italy.

In the Italo-Austrian sideshow, both junior partners had to be rescued by their mentors—the Austrians by the Germans at the battle of Caporetto and the Italians by the French and British at the battle of the Piave. They both, for better or worse, became *de facto* dependencies of their powerful allies.

* * * *

Before the war most Czech patriots had high hopes that eventually the Austrian government would acknowledge the necessity of reforming the obsolete political structure of the Empire, an outmoded relic of the past, and opt for a federal system of government of national and ethnic provinces. The fact that there were 29 million subordinate "minorities" in the Empire and only 22 million of the ruling "majorities" —12 million Austrians and 10 million Hungarians—was a persuasive argument in favor of reform. Even Tomáš G. Masaryk, the great Czech patriot, philosopher and deputy in the Vienna Parliament, advocated at first only a greater political autonomy for the Czechs within the confines of the Dual Monarchy, not an independent Czech state.

It was after the outbreak of the war, in July 1915 in Zurich, that Masaryk for the first time called for "the liberation of Czechoslovakia from Habsburg oppression." Following that declaration, Masaryk and his friends abroad began to lobby the Allied governments to permit Czech and Slovak volunteers to join the Allied armed forces in order to fight against the Central Powers. Ultimately, the Allies agreed, and the Czechoslovak legions—in France, Russia, and Italy—came into existence. They fought alongside the Allied troops and suffered many losses.

Toward the end of the war, there were almost 100,000 Czech and Slovak legionnaires in the Allied armed forces. Within the more than 42 million Allied troops, the legionnaires represented a very small drop in a very large ocean. As a dramatic statement and powerful symbol, however, of the deep desire of the Czech and Slovak people for freedom and independence from the authoritarian rule of the Dual Monarchy, the Czechoslovak legionnaires were an impressive force. The Allies valued them for what they stood for and rewarded them with national independence and sovereign statehood.

The Great War and the Twentieth Century

World War I was the existential great divide between the idyllic half century of peace before the war and the violent century that followed. In fact, it may not be an exaggeration to say that to a significant degree World War I and its aftermath, having initiated developments unparalleled in history, have defined much of the twentieth century. The disappearance of colonialism and imperialism distinctly altered the map of the world; nation-states, more than one-third of which are now democracies, came to dominate the world's landscape; and a global market economy, which has challenged the sovereignty of nation-states, brought unheard-of technological changes and developments to the world at large, though not without a price. Last but not least, World War I, "the war to end all wars," ushered in the most turbulent century in human history.

Without World War I there would not have been communism in Russia, fascism in Italy, or Nazism in Germany. All three were born of the deep social unrest, fiery political turbulence, and hopeless economic depression that occurred during the war and its aftermath, the breakdown of the Versailles world. There would have been no Italian invasion of Ethiopia in 1935; no German, Italian, or Soviet intervention in the Spanish Civil War in 1936-1939; no Pact of Steel, the so-called Berlin–Rome–Tokyo Axis, in 1937; no German annexation of Austria in 1938; and no German occupation of Czechoslovakia in 1939. Most historians view World War II as the continuation of World War I, which ended leaving too many issues unresolved. The communist revolution in China, the Cold War, the Korean War, the wars in Vietnam, Afghanistan, Bosnia, and Chechnya, the Arab-Israeli war, and many other wars and conflicts—including nationalist and ethnic strifes and civil wars in Asia, Africa, and Latin America—can be linked to World War I.

Many historians maintain that World War I ushered in war and violence as the defining characteristics of the twentieth century—a single, discrete epoch in which much of the world was engaged in violence, recovering from violence, or preparing for violence. More people have been killed in the twentieth century—in wars, revolutions, civil strife, and mass genocide—than in any previous century.

This frenzy of massive violence has produced another phenomenon of a magnitude unknown in the past, an attribute so painfully dramatic that many social historians consider it the most telling symbol of the twentieth century: namely, refugees, displaced people in flight. In sheer numbers the twentieth century is in this respect number one in human history. During and after World War I and World War II, some 70 million people were uprooted by wars, revolutions, civil strife, forcible displacements, and various forms of persecution. In 1996 there were still over 15 million people displaced from human-caused disasters, "the migrants of misery," facing increasing internal as well as international indifference. Both the League of Nations and the United Nations have tried valiantly to cope with the problem of international homelessness, but unless the international community is willing to deal with the causes as well as the consequences of violent displacement of people, the problem will only get worse.

The major ideological strands unleashed by the First World War—the rise and application of nationalism, the decline of imperialism and colonialism, the growth of socialism as well as capitalism, the birth and spread of totalitarianism, and the initial proliferation of democracy—have partitioned the world community into social, economic, political, and ideological blocs unknown in their universalist absolutes before World War I. More recently, however, with the impressive growth of nation-states, the demise of the Soviet Union, the flowering of democracy and capitalism, and the advent of economic globalism, the world has become more pragmatic, more pluralist and decentralized, more fragmented, more diverse, more complex, and smaller.

Anti-colonialism, Nationalism, and Democracy

World War I initiated a trend of national state-building unmatched in history. In 1918 President Wilson called for the national self-determination of all dependent peoples everywhere; Pope Benedict XV advocated a territorial settlement that would take into account, above all else, the wishes of the people concerned; and Lenin demanded "the elimination of imperialism, the last stage of monopoly capitalism." Empires began to topple. The German Hohenzollern empire, the Austro-Hungarian Habsburg empire, the empire of the Romanov tsars in Russia, and the Turkish Ottoman empire were the first to go. With the spread of nationalism in the colonies, other empires followed suit, principally the British, French, Dutch, Belgian, and Portuguese. Eventually, the Soviet empire collapsed, too.

While European civilization was disintegrating in the trenches of World War I, the oppressed peoples of the world, from Central Europe to Asia to Africa, were discovering a new opportunity; they were beginning to search actively for ways and means to weaken, blunt, or even cripple the privileged authority of the aristocratic, imperialistic rulers who had dominated them for so long. In Europe several new or enlarged nation-states appeared on the post-World War I map—Czechoslovakia, Poland, Romania, Yugoslavia, Finland, Albania, Lithuania, Latvia, and Estonia. The slogan "For each nation a state, for each state a nation," proclaimed, hailed and fought for by nationalist intellectuals in the nineteenth century, began to be applied seriously and with determination by men and women in cities, towns, and even villages everywhere.

The Third World was born on the battlefields of World War I. For the colonial soldiers it was a revelation to discover, in the trenches where they fought side by side with their invincible white masters, how fallible, weak, and mortal their mentors in fact were. With Europe in ruins, it became clear that the colonial powers had lost much of their authority, legitimacy, and capacity to rule and control their colonies. Home from the war, the veterans of World War I, knowledgeable and bitter, became the leaders and supporters of anti-colonial movements, fighting for independence in Egypt,

India, West Africa, Kenya, Indonesia, Indochina, Algeria, the British West Indies, Morocco, and Tunisia.

World War I loosened the ties between the colonial powers and their colonies, and World War II severed these ties for good. At the same time, however, the colonial powers, as nation-states, served as models to the colonies for their own national development, independence, and statehood. The colonials discovered that, in fact, they themselves were members of "nations" simply on the basis of their peoples' traditional commonality of race, religion, ethnicity, language, creed, color, tribe, clan, culture, or shared experience. They, too, were entitled to self-government and independent statehood.

The "we" versus "they" mentality has been around since time immemorial. But it was only at the end of the 18th century during the French and American revolutions that a new, popular spirit and widely shared passion for the universal rights of man (and woman) and the sovereignty of like-minded people emerged as a powerful, widely shared view of the good life in a well-ordered, just society. In the 19th and 20th centuries this dynamic, comprehensive, populist call for the supreme unity of "people like us" spread like wildfire in Latin America, Europe, Asia, and Africa. Historians named it the Age of Nationalism.

But it was World War I that triggered the universal triumph of nationalism. Thanks to World War I the 18th and 19th century revolutionary idea of nationalism led to the 20th century's overwhelming proliferation of national states; and nationalism has turned out to be the single greatest ideological determinant of our time.

Nationalism is a complex, ambiguous, inconsistent, and contradictory concept, but it has been the most powerful political force of the twentieth century. Its aim is self-determination, and its goal is independent statehood. The cultural, political, social, and economic components of nationalism endow the nation-state with meaning, legitimacy, authority, and power. In this multiple sense, a nation-state is sovereign.

A number of the nation-states that replaced not only colonies but most of the former communist party-states as well, have had to assimilate subnational, second-wave, separatist, and minority national groups. Some of these groups are seeking fulfillment of their aspirations through peaceful accommodation; others, using violence, demand separation; and still others are not sure. Examples of such varied subnational minorities are Muslims in the Philippines, Eritreans in Ethiopia (who won their war of independence in 1991), Muslims in Lebanon, and South Moluccans in Indonesia. In Rwanda, Hutus butchered some 500,000 Tutsis; in Sri Lanka, being Tamil or

Sinhalese may be the cause of death. In Kashmir, Muslim separatists fight the Hindus; and after almost fifty years religion is still the *casus belli* for India and Pakistan. Turkey continues its scorched-earth drive against the Kurdish rebels; the Russians have major problems with the Chechens and vice versa; the Chinese occupation forces are harassing the Tibetans; the governments of Guatemala and Mexico are trying to suppress their indigenous peoples by force; Chinese ethnics are pushing for domination in Malaysia; the Khmer Rouge fight other Cambodians; the military ruling clique in Myanmar/Burma is trying hard to suppress its indigenous ethnic groups—the Karen, Rakhine, Shan, Mon, and many smaller minorities; the Palestinians are standing up to the Israelis; Muslims are fighting Christians in Sudan; and Muslim fundamentalist forces are fighting Muslim moderates in Afghanistan and Algeria. The list is by no means complete.

The story of Yugoslavia, the land of the South Slavs, is instructive: Yugoslavia emerged from World War I as a new nation-state, the Kingdom of Serbs, Croats, and Slovenes, composed of formerly Habsburg-ruled Slovenia, Croatia, Bosnia-Herzegovina, and formerly independent Serbia, which included Montenegro and Macedonia. In 1929 the country became the Kingdom of Yugoslavia. Under Tito, in 1945 Yugoslavia became a Federal People's Republic, a communist but independent national state. Today, after almost 80 years of independence and after years of civil strife, which began in 1991, Yugoslavia is in shambles, with losses of between 20 and 50 thousand lives, because Serbian and Croatian nationalists sought dominance over each other and over the Bosnian Muslims (and briefly over Slovenia, too).

In a similarly instructive case, that of Czechoslovakia, a nation-state which also emerged out of the ruins of World War I, its two constituent peoples, the Czechs and the Slovaks, parted company in 1992 after almost 75 years of unity (excluding the Nazi-imposed separation in World War II). The divorce, however, was amicable and peaceful. The dissolution of a nation-state can clearly go either way (Map E).

Before World War I governments professing to be *democracies* existed only in Europe, the two Americas, Australia, and New Zealand. Since World War I the number of democracies has increased steadily. According to the non-partisan Freedom House, in 1996 there were some 80 democracies in the world, and about 60 additional countries were not too far off the mark. This development is the direct offshoot of both the rise of nationalism and the decline of imperialism: among many dependent peoples, democracy as a reinforcement and legitimization of nationalism became increasingly associated with demands for self-determination.

Democracy has not been a dependable cure for nationalist ills, however. By itself, it has not been a sure guarantee of the peaceful resolution of nationalist disputes. Some democracies are more limited than others, especially in terms of citizen participation, human rights, and fairness of the judicial process. The issue of nationalism is a potent vote-getter; it thrives on the "we versus they" dichotomy. In multinational democracies, parochial nationalism tends to fracture the general consensus. Also, democracies have not always been peace-loving. Classical Athens, republican Rome, 19th century Britain, 19th and 20th century United States, and Israel—have all been at one time or another bellicose and aggressive.

But democracy can offer a level playing field and can exercise a restraining influence against excesses on both the nationalist forces as well as on the government. Nationalist pressure may lead to democratic power-sharing, and often does; or it may lead to bloodshed. Nationalists have challenged democratic governments in Canada, France, Germany, Belgium, Spain, Northern Ireland, Italy, and India, but not in Switzerland.

Nationalism as a battle cry is indeed ambiguous, and must be judged case by case. It may be the last refuge of scoundrels, as Samuel Johnson remarked about patriotism, or it may be the bastion that saves the heart and soul of an oppressed people. But it is a troubling, polarizing issue in the world of nation-states that we live in.

Globalization of the World Economy

The structural changes in the political constellation of international relations after World War I have initiated a process which, after World War II, has been variously called globalization, Westernization, or even Americanization of the world. Europe was the loser in World War I, but it took some time before the United States, the Third World, democracy, and the new nation-states established themselves as winners. Then yet another major force appeared, ready to challenge the emerging new world order in general and the nation-state system in particular: a new global market culture, an economic and technological civilization composed of multinational corporations and international companies, the new carriers of global cosmopolitanism, the very antithesis of nationalism. While nation-states demand sovereignty and borders, multinationals demand global freedom of movement and *laissez-faire*. And herein lies the problem.

Domination of the strong over the weak is as old as the world. Its history is linked to the spread of civilization. Whether called empires, hegemonies, spheres of influence, mandates, or trusteeships, the strong have always dominated the weak. Such domination used to pay off. Empires and hegemonies were once the best instruments to gain wealth and power abroad—to acquire, by force, markets, raw materials, cheap labor, and investment opportunities for surplus capital. But that kind of domination is no longer cost-effective. Large multinationals can achieve many of the same results faster, cheaper, more efficiently, and without the high risk involved in the use of force and violence. They raise capital where it is least costly, hire labor where it is abundant and cheap, sell finished products where the prices are high, and pay taxes, if they must, where taxes are low. Nothing is overlooked. Their production, distribution, and consumption of goods and services, organized, coordinated, and super-modern, are as integrated and efficient on a world-wide basis as are their products and marketing.

Multinational companies, whose growth has been spectacular, are post-World War II phenomena. They could not have developed earlier because they require two modern conditions: (1) a network of communication and transportation that is efficient, rapid, and all-inclusive, and (2) a well-developed form of corporate organization capable of spawning corporate subsidies abroad. Multinational corporations, a particularized form of the general dynamics of modern world economic affairs, represent a rational response to the perceived need for production and distribution on a global scale; they transport capital, technology, services, and knowledge through world-wide organizations with their own expertise, strategy, and management culture. Many of them are huge, rich, and powerful—some more powerful than many nation-states, e.g., Mitsubishi (Japan); Royal Dutch/Shell Group (Netherlands, U.K.); General Motors (U.S.); Exxon (U.S.); Itochu Corp. (Japan); Toyota (Japan); HSBC group (U.K.); General Electric (U.S.); Nestle (Switzerland); IBM (U.S.); Daimler Benz (Germany); Unilever (Netherlands); ENI (Italy); Renault SA (France); etc. These corporations use their capabilities as leverages for their demands vis-à-vis nation-states. The problem is inherent in the relationship.

Multinationals depend on nation-states, of course, and could not operate world-wide without their cooperation; but they are not dependencies of nation-states. Just the opposite. By imposing their standards on nation-states, multinationals tend to dominate states. As a result nation-states are no longer the principal engines of economic progress and technological advancement that they used to be; the global enterprises are. Nor do nation-states initiate in that realm; they tend to respond and conform. Both governments and corporations know that the two—nation-states and multinationals—are on a collision course. Forging new partnerships is a challenge for both of them because they do need each other.

Multinationals threaten the sovereignty of nation-states, and the nation-states' defense of their sovereignty grates on multinationals. While governments struggle with global issues such as foreign trade, pollution, human rights, health, welfare, technology, food production, and drug trafficking, they cannot afford to lose sight of the responsibility to protect their own peoples' particular identities and needs. But can nation-states ignore multinational corporations?

The Costs and Benefits of Globalism

Costs: The globalization of the world, however beneficial, has been eroding the independence of nation-states, endangering their national borders, and polluting their environment. Sovereign states are no longer as sovereign and independent as they were before the advent of globalism. They have been penetrated in countless ways, and the *pluralism of penetration* is the rule, not the exception for countries large and small, rich and poor, developed or not. Important decisions concerning labor relations, jobs, unemployment, interest rates, the value of money, stock markets, the prices of goods, and so on are often taken away from the states' control and decided elsewhere. This penetration may be beneficial to some groups and harmful in other ways to others, but it is a fact of life today.

In 1950 there were about 2.7 billion people in the world. For the year 2000 the current demographic projection is a world population of more than 6.3 billion. The world population will thus have more than doubled in fifty years (and tripled—to more than 8.1 billion—by the year 2020). Unless the disparity between the rich and the poor of the world is alleviated, an almost impossible task, it is bound to result in large-scale, continuous, sustained *migrations* of the poor to the countries of the less poor. According to predictions of the World Bank, this migration will be the largest ever in the history of humankind. Nothing will stem the tide of the poor immigrants—not sophisticated border fences, not walls, not border guards, not electronic devices, not jails. Frontiers are losing their former separating and protective significance. Already the less fortunate are moving in on the more fortunate all over the world. Unless migrants are accommodated and integrated into the host countries' population and work force, they will destabilize the host countries, certainly in the short run.

Global development and modernization contribute to *global pollution*, and the cost of cleaning up the environment can be prohibitive. The cost of coping with the consequences of acid rain, ozone depletion, global warming, and of disposal of nuclear wastes and even non-biodegradable garbage is more than many nation-states can afford. The destruction of the universal, world-wide ecological system is now, for the first time, possible. Václav Havel, the president of the Czech Republic, has stated that progress may not be worth the price, "unless calibrated progress and respect for the environment go together, hand in hand, as a moral imperative."

Benefits: Multinational enterprises may run the world economy, but they need the support of their own home states to do so. And their home states can no longer perform fully without the support of their own global corporations. The two systems, economic and political, need each other and bolster each other. Nation-states help "their" multinationals with tax breaks and incentives; privileged access to contracts (in defense, telecommunication, transportation, health, and such); regulatory support; favorable legislation; protection from competition at home (in communication, robotics, data processing, aerospace, shipping, chemical industries); and other special assistance to compete better abroad.

Global enterprises, on the other hand, help their home states with technological innovation for home industries; socio-economic promotion and development (research foundations, scholarships, schools, cultural endowments) and job creation. They provide abundant funds for corporation-friendly political candidates, national as well as local (increasingly, foreign corporations participate in national political fund-raising activities as well); economic and technological visibility abroad; and preservation and enhancement of the home states' standing and prestige in the world.

Still, this symbiotic relationship between corporations and their home states is not equally beneficial to both parties. While multinationals are constantly growing in power by entering into cooperative agreements, takeover bids, and restructuring, states are being weakened by the transfer of their economic power to the global enterprises. And the states' own scientific, technological, and economic development is no longer subject to the exclusive control of their governments. The profit basis of the world market tends to prevail.

Meeting the Challenge

Even the most powerful nation-states often find it difficult to mitigate the sustained pressure of their global enterprises' special interests. The opposing forces are often too strong or too slippery or too threatening. One way for nation-states to cope with predatory globalism may be to *join other nation-states*, either *ad hoc* or as members of one or more overlapping cooperative associations, global, regional, or functional, of various shapes and sizes. These associations, while preserving some freedom of maneuver for their members, could assist them in exploiting external opportunities as well as in protecting their own economies, polities, societies, and environments from external dangers. But membership in such cooperative organizations may require some surrender of sovereignty, too. Examples are trade associations, labor organizations, common markets, monetary organizations, investment banks and credit societies, ecological unions, and anti-drug cooperatives. The General Agreement on Tariffs and Trade, International Labor Organization, European Union, Andean Common Market, Lome Convention Association, NAFTA, ASEAN, International Monetary Fund, International Bank for Reconstruction and Development, Organization for Economic Cooperation and Development, the Food and Agricultural Organization, UNESCO, and the World Health Organization are a few of the cooperative arrangements that are often beneficial for nation-states as well as for subnational ethnic groups looking for protection.

The global economic interdependence brought about by the growing internationalization of nation-states' economies, makes it increasingly difficult for individual states to control their own separate destinies alone. Who are the major culprits responsible for the chaotic, archaic, and anachronistic state of the international order, the world market, where only the fittest survive? The profit-hungry multinationals are not alone to blame. The nation-states must share the blame. The responsibility for remedying the situation is theirs as well. The global companies have not created the global market; they are just very good at exploiting it and preying on it. But the states' economic malaise is real. The time for them to neglect international economic relations is over. Most of them have mastered nationalism. Now they have to *master internationalism*—which includes comprehensive, orderly, and equitable economic relations among nation-states—as well.

But there is still more for nation-states to worry about. A growing number of economists argue that the next stage of international development, which is already emerging, will be the globalization of world financial markets. The economists claim that the available world-wide capital formation is now so vast and so mobile that it is poised to seek immense new opportunities for the highest profits anywhere in the world. That development is bound to affect negatively the sovereignty of the nation-states even more than did the globalization of goods, services, and labor in the last few decades. A case in point was the sudden collapse of several Asian national economies and the panic it triggered worldwide.

It is hard to believe that much of the complexity of the world we live in has its roots in World War I. But it is a fact that the universe of nation-states has brought about not only an ever-increasing number of democracies in the world, thus further ratifying and legitimizing their sovereignty, but also the powerful multinational enterprises and mega-corporations that systematically—and successfully—undermine that sovereignty. If my father were alive today, he would be perplexed. He would not understand the incredible proliferation of nation-states in the world; the shocking speed of change; the number, gravity, and priority of global problems and issues on all levels; the magic instancy of communications; the smallness of the world, on the one hand, but also its growing incomprehensibility; and the inescapable interdependence of all peoples. Knowing my father, I think he would probably worry that we may all suffocate under the weight of the fantastic technological paradise we have created but failed to master as yet.

In Sum

The people of this planet are no longer separable. It is no longer possible or preferable to go it alone. No countries, regions, or continents are islands unto themselves any longer. The systematic, rational cooperation of all with all is now both inevitable and essential.

As we witness the sad events in Bosnia, Northern Ireland, Israel, Lebanon, Algeria, North Korea, Sri Lanka, Kashmir, Cambodia, China, Burma, Iran, Iraq, Zaire, Rwanda, Sudan, Burundi, Liberia, and Afghanistan, World War I seems closer to us than eight decades ago. It defines the twentieth century for us and brings the conflict home. We are still part of it. In November, 1995 President Clinton reported: "A few weeks ago, I was privileged to spend some time with His Holiness John Paul II when he came to America. At the very end of our meeting, the Pope looked at me and said, 'I have lived through most of this century. I remember that it began with a war in Sarajevo. Mr. President, you must not let it end with a war in Sarajevo."

I, too, have lived through most of this century. And I, too, stood in Sarajevo on the very spot where Archduke Franz Ferdinand and his wife were shot. Having lived in Prague, the heart of Europe, for almost the first one-third of my life, I remember well the joys as well as the sorrows of the 1920s and the 1930s: I grew up in a loving family within a flourishing democracy, which I took for granted. As a teenager I became aware of the rise of Nazism and the shame of the Munich Pact. On my way to school the morning of March 15, 1939, from the window of the streetcar I saw the first German soldiers march into Prague. When World War II came, unlike my father, who was forced to serve in the Austrian army in World War I, I was not subject to conscription in the German army; that "honor" was denied to young Czechs, who were not deemed worthy of it. But we were punished in other ways. I myself was sent to a Nazi forced labor camp in Eisenach, Germany.

After the war democracy returned to Czechoslovakia. Germany was defeated, and we were free again. Our universities, closed by the Germans, were open once more, and we students studied and lived with abandon, as if there were no tomorrow. The idyll ended in February 1948, when the Soviet-orchestrated communist coup d'état terminated that brief, glorious postwar interlude. With the secret police at my heels, I managed to escape from the country and begin a new life.

I experienced the first part of the century through my father. His precious legacy, the war diary, became almost an obsession with me when I started working on it. My father could not have known that the war stories he spun for me when I was a boy would remain with me for a long, long time. When my own two sons came of draft age, I was thankful that their generation would not have to risk their lives on a battlefield. They were only the second generation in my family, as far as I know, to escape military service.

I came to the diary late in life, but I was ready for it. Translating it, editing it, and learning all I could about my father and his war brought him back to life. The endeavor awakened in me questions I regret I had never thought to ask him while he was still alive. Writing this book intrigued me more than any other book I have published.

Like my father, I, too, am a product of my time, place, background, experience, and station. When I started to work on the manuscript, I had no idea where it would take me. It has been an absorbing adventure.

Bugler in Sokol uniform, Olomouc, fall of 1908, age 18.

Journeyman cabinet maker, Olomouc, July 1910, top row, second from left.

Private (*Soldat*), basic training, Infantry, Olomouc, December 16, first row, third from left.

Private First Class (*Vormeister*), Mountain Artillery, on leave, Vienna, August 1917.

Sergeant (*Zugsführer*), with Božena,
on leave, Vienna, July 1918.

Sergeant (*Četař*), Czechoslovak Legion from Italy, now Czechoslovak Army Corps from Italy, Heavy Field Howitzers Group No. 1, in Slovakia, 1919.

With other Czechoslovak legionnaires from Italy in Slovakia, 1919, seated, first from right.

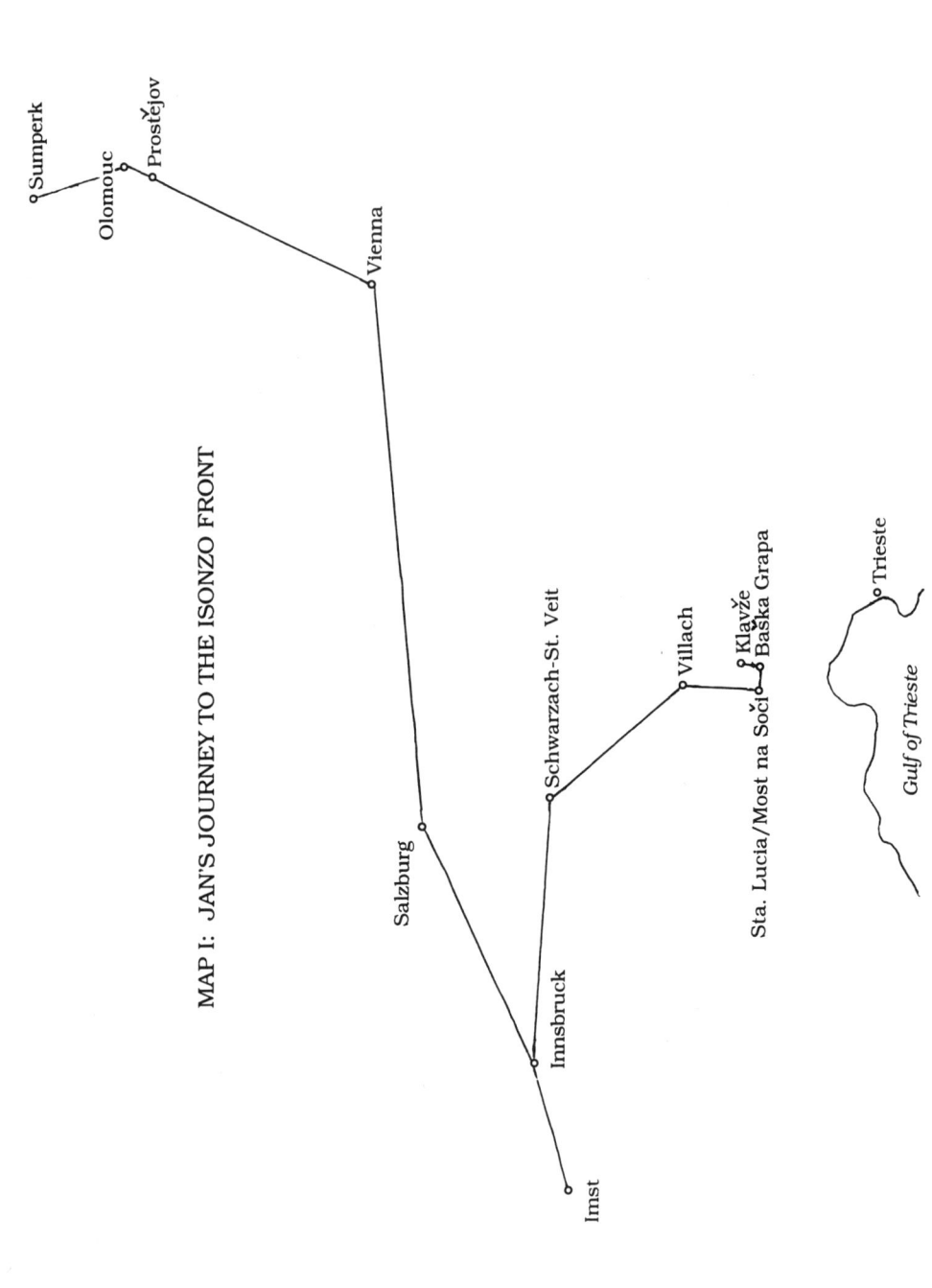

MAP I: JAN'S JOURNEY TO THE ISONZO FRONT

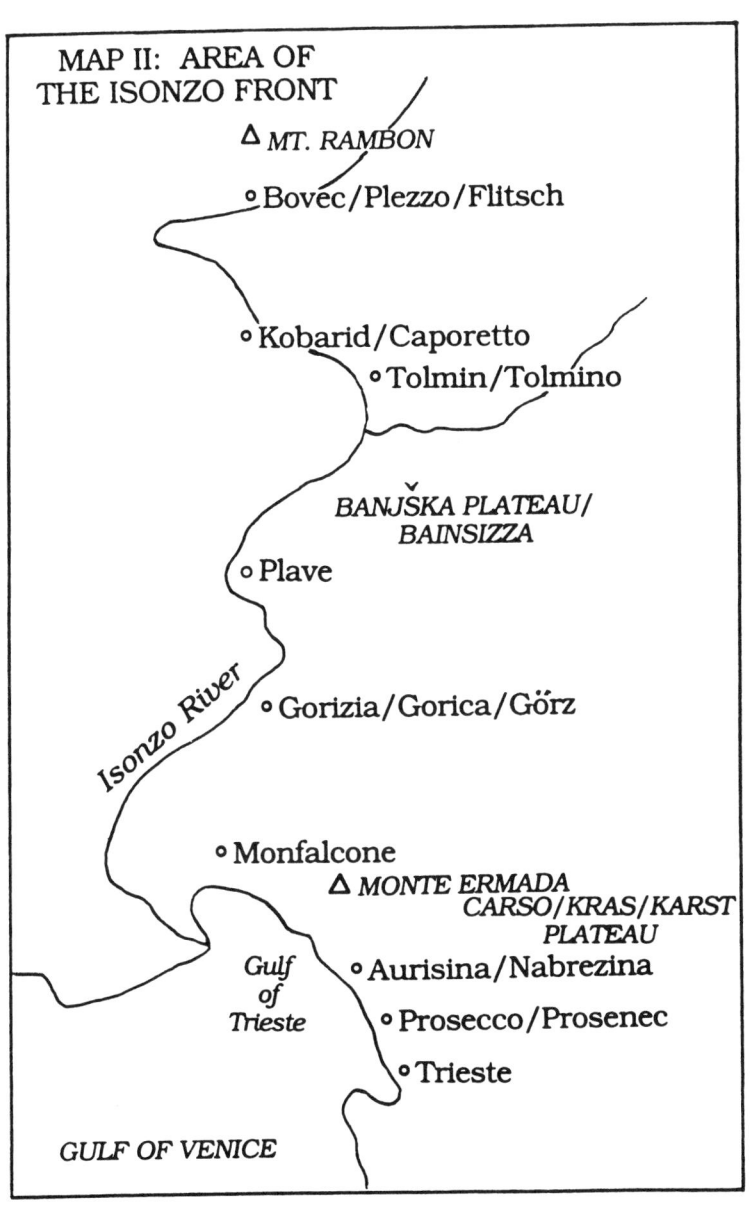

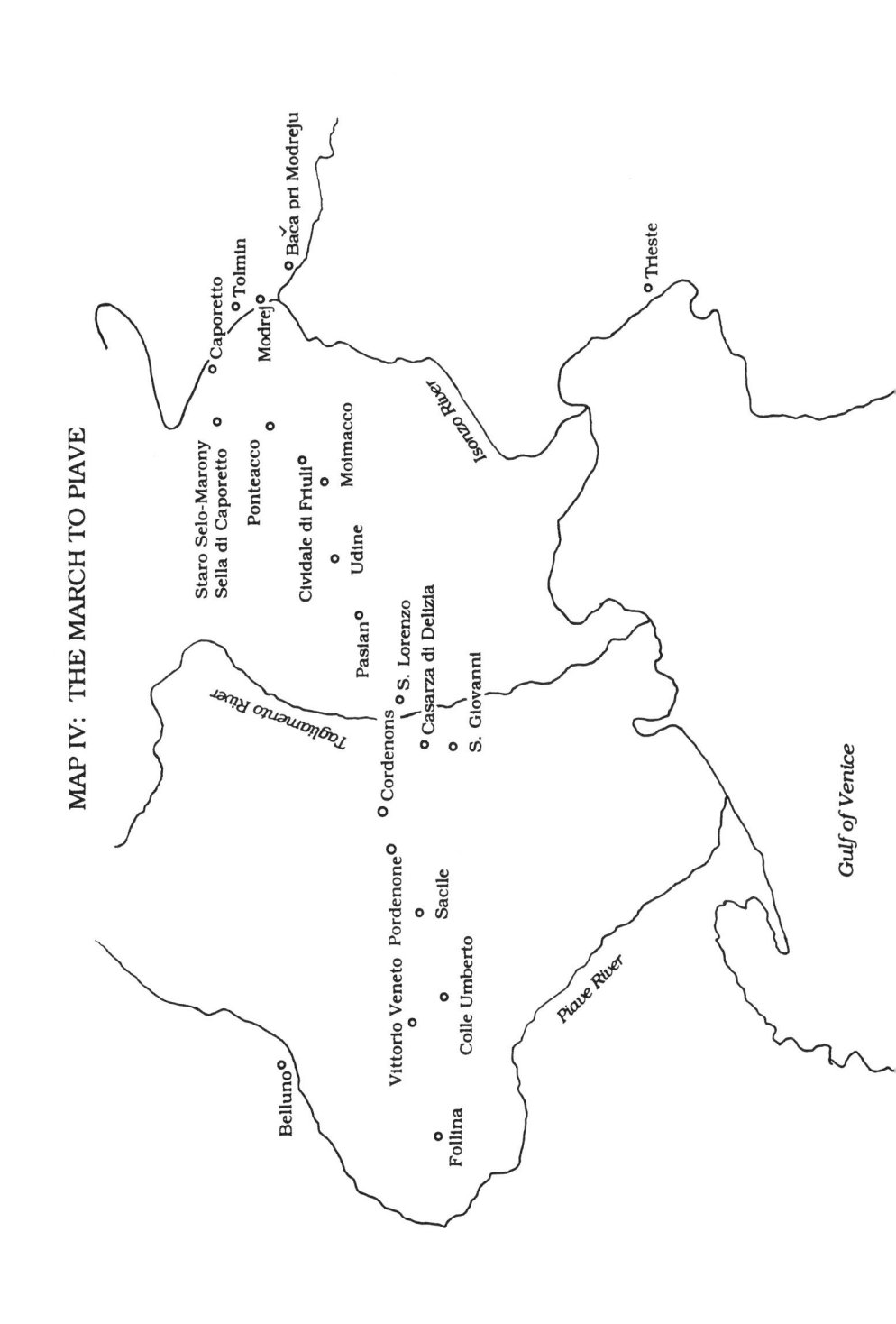

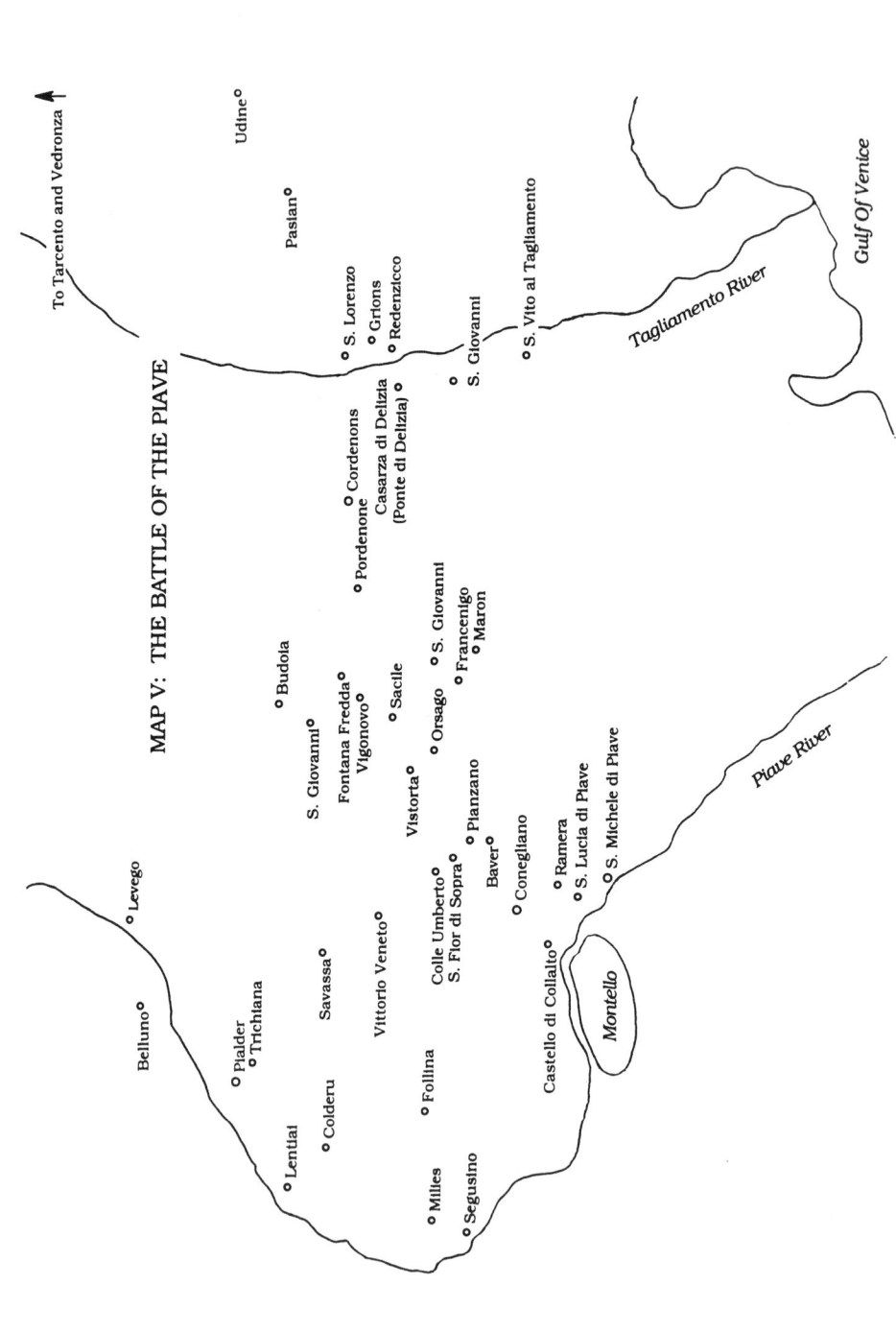

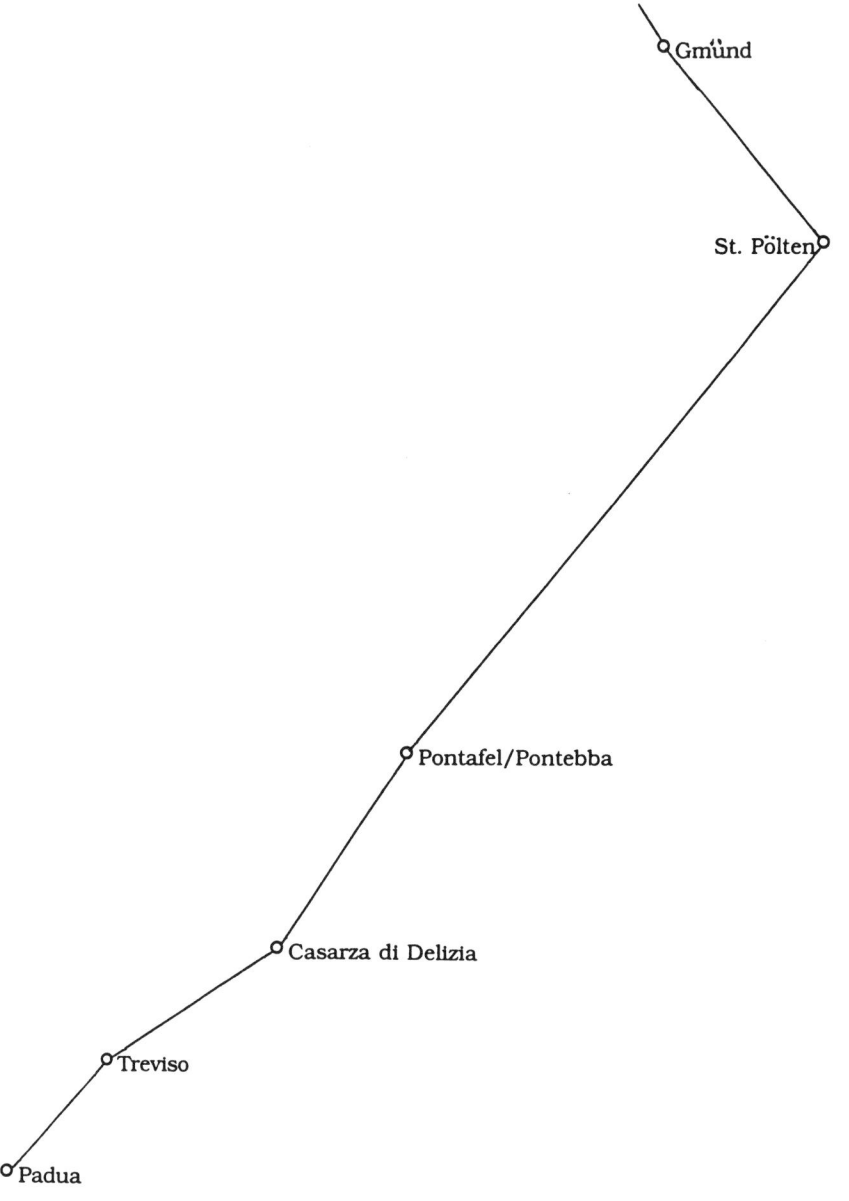

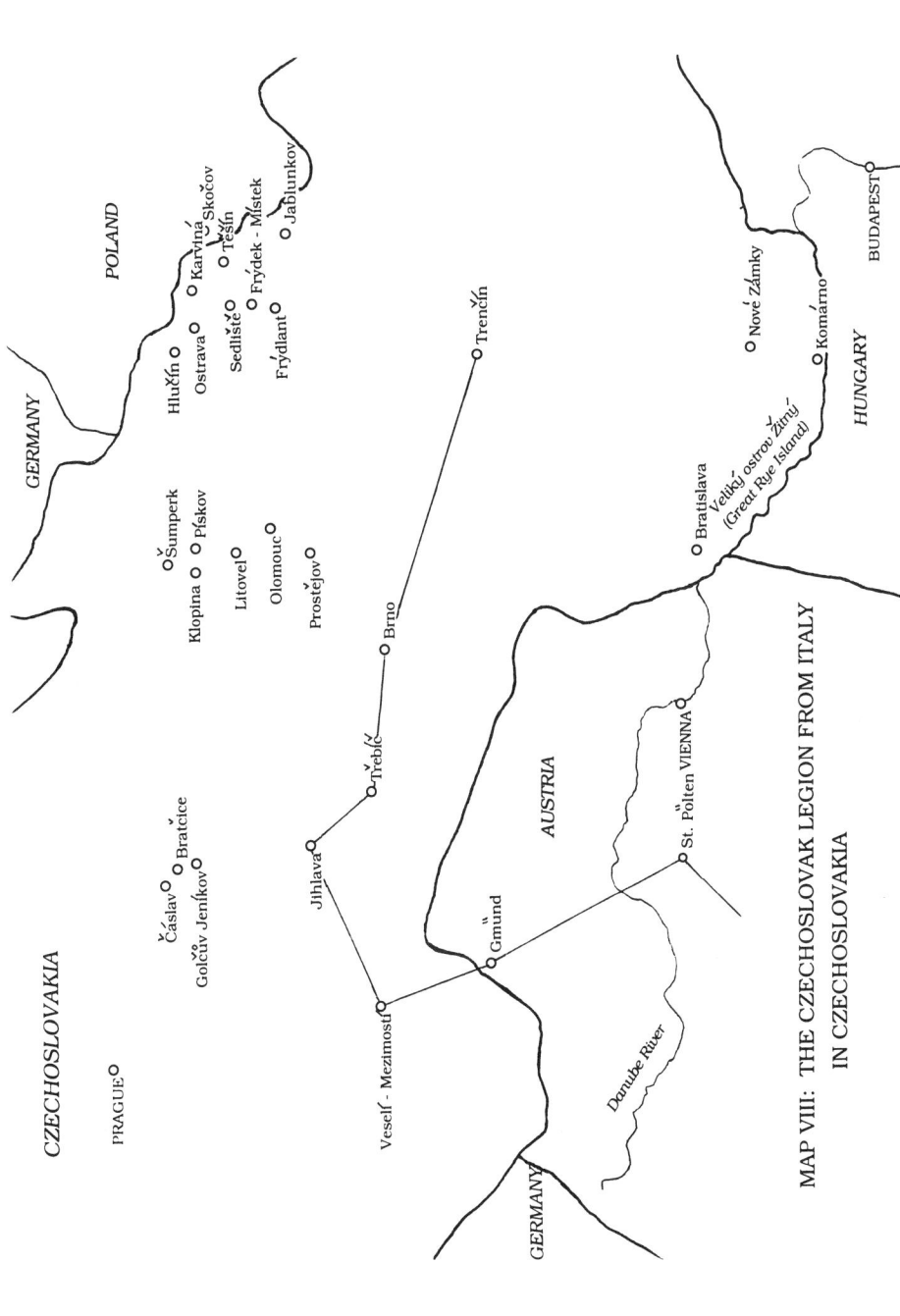

MAP VIII: THE CZECHOSLOVAK LEGION FROM ITALY IN CZECHOSLOVAKIA

Map A: East Central Europe, 1910

Historical Atlas of East Central Europe

Map B: World War I, 1914-1918

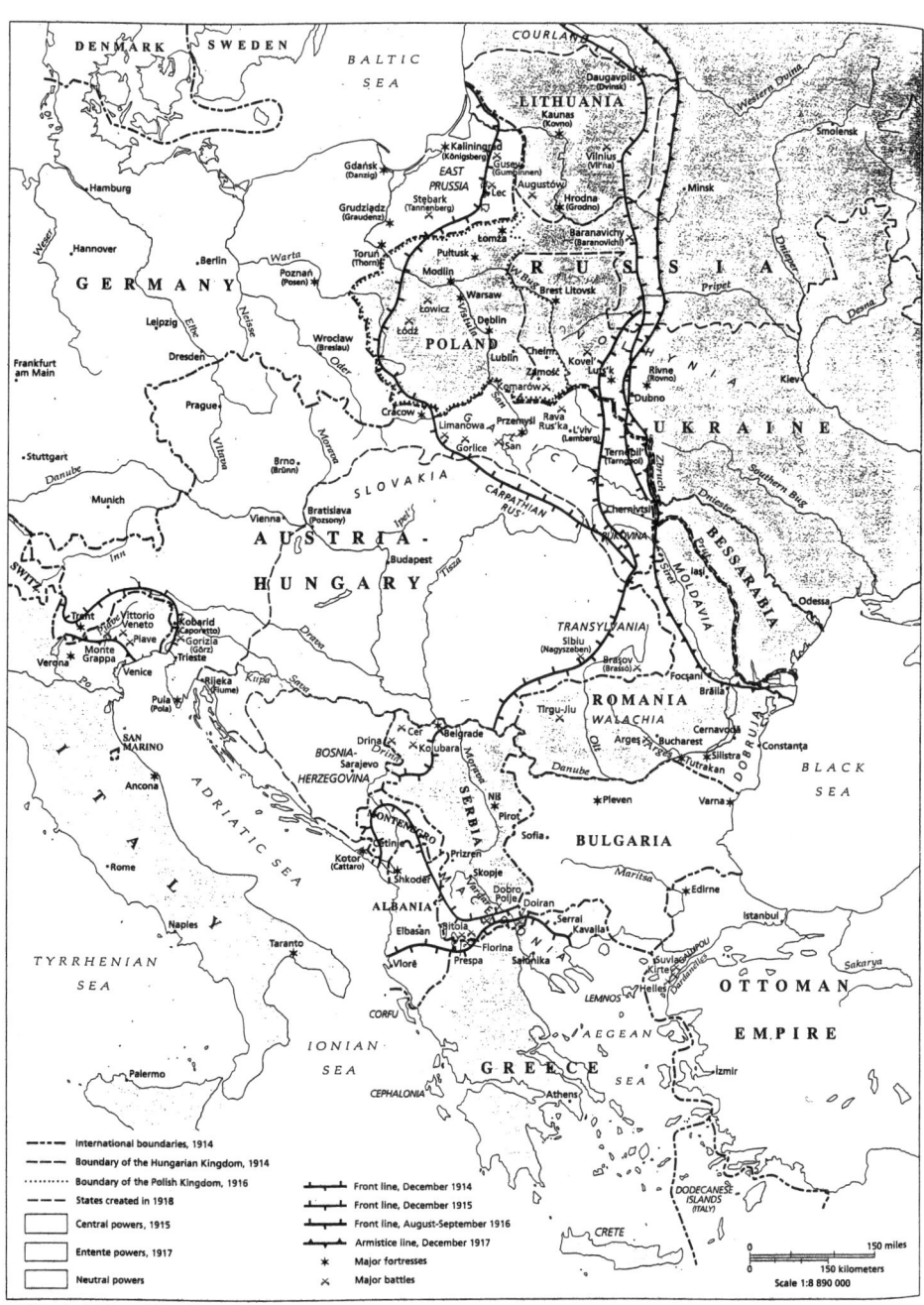

Historical Atlas of East Central Europe

Map C: East Central Europe, 1918-1923

Historical Atlas of East Central Europe

Map D: East Central Europe, ca. 1930

Historical Atlas of East Central Europe

Map E: East Central Europe, 1992

Historical Atlas of East Central Europe

Select Bibliography

Abernethy, David B. "The Dynamics of Global Dominance: European Overseas Empires, 1415-1980." Unpublished manuscript, 1996.

Angell, Norman. *The Great Illusion.* New York: G.P. Putnam and Sons, 1910.

Barker, Pat. *Regeneration.* New York: Dutton, 1992.

———. *The Eye in the Door.* London: Viking, 1993.

———. *The Ghost Road.* London: Viking, 1995.

Bernardi, Mario. *Di qua e di la dal Piave.* U. Mursia editore SPA, Milano, 1989.

Bruce, Anthony P.C. *The Illustrated Companion to the First World War.* London: Michael Joseph, the Penguin Group, 1989.

Burgwyn, H. James. *The Legend of the Mutilated Victory.* Westport, CT: Greenwood Press, 1993.

Clodfeter, Michael. *Warfare and Armed Conflicts*, Vols. 1 and 2. Jefferson, NC: McFarland, 1992.

Collins, Randall. "The Micro Contribution to Macro Sociology," *Sociological Theory*, Vol. 6 (Fall) 1988: 242-253.

Cork, Richard. *A Bitter Truth. Avant-Garde Art and the Great War.* New Haven, CT: Yale University Press, 1994.

Cru, Jean Norton. *War Books: A Study in Historical Criticism.* Stanley J. Pincetl, Jr., ed. San Diego State University Press, 1988.

Cruttwell, C.R.M.F. *A History of the Great War 1914-1918.* Second edition. Oxford: Clarendon Press, 1936.

Dastrup, Boyd L. *The Field Artillery: History and Source Book.* Westport, CT: Greenwood Press, 1994.

Edmonds, Sir James E. *A Short History of World War I.* London: Oxford University Press, 1951.

Edmonds, Sir James E., and H.R. Davies. *Military Operations, Italy 1915-1919.* London: H.M. Stationary Office, 1949.

Eulau, Heinz. *Micro–Macro Dilemmas in Political Science*. Norman: University of Oklahoma Press, 1996.

Falls, Cyril. *The Battle of Caporetto*. Philadelphia: J.B. Lippincott, 1966.

Faulks, Sebastian. *Birdsong*. London: Hutchinson, 1993.

Ferro, Marc. *The Great War 1914-1916*. Transl. by Nicole Stone. London: Routledge & Kegan Paul, 1973.

Fleming, D.F. *The Origins and Legacies of World War I*. Garden City, NY: Doubleday, 1968.

"Freedom in the World." *Freedom House News*, December 18, 1996. New York: 120 Wall Street, 10005.

Fussell, Paul. *The Great War and Modern Memory*, London: Oxford University Press, 1975.

Galbraith, John Kenneth. *A Journey through Economic Time*. Boston: Houghton Mifflin, 1994.

Giddens, Anthony. *New Rules of Sociological Method*. Second edition. Stanford, CA: Stanford University Press, 1993.

Gilbert, Martin. *Atlas of the First World War*. New York: Oxford University Press, 1994.

———. *The First World War: A Complete History*. New York: Henry Holt, 1994.

Gladden, Norman. *Across the Piave*. London: H.M. Stationary Office, 1971.

Gray, Randall. *Chronicle of the First World War*. New York: Facts on File, 1990.

Gregorovič, Miroslav. *První československý odboj: Čs. legie 1914-1920*. Prague: Panorama dějin, 1992.

Gudmundsson, Bruce I. *On Artillery*. Westport, CT: Praeger, 1993.

Guide Turistiche Regionali. *Friuli Venezia Giulia*. Novarra: Istituto Geografico de Agostini SPA, 1979.

Guide Turistiche Regionali. *Trentino Alto Adige*. Novarra: Istituto Geografico de Agostini SPA, 1977.

———. *Veneto*. Novarra: Istituto Geografico de Agostini SPA, 1978.

Hobsbawm, Eric. *The Age of Extremes 1914–1991: The Short Twentieth Century*. London: Michael Joseph, 1994.

Honzík, Miroslav. *Legionáři*. Prague: Novinář, 1990.

Horsman, Mathew. *After the Nation-State*. London: Hammersmith, 1994.

Howe, Geoffrey. *Nationalism and the Nation-State*. Cambridge University Press, 1995, 23pp.

Ignatieff, Michael. *Blood and Belonging: Journeys into the New Nationalism*. New York: Farrar, Straus, and Giroux, 1993.

Il Feltrino Invaso, Vol. 1, *Testimonianze* dagli scritti di Don Antonio Scolpel et al.; Vol. 2, *Immagini* a cura di Luigi Zannin et al. Rasai de Seren del grappa: Edizioni DBS, 1993.

Kagan, Donald. *On the Origins of War and the Preservation of Peace*. New York: Doubleday, 1994.

Karlický, Vladimír. *Československé dělostřelecké zbraně*. Prague: Naše vojsko, 1975.

Keating, Michael. *Nations against the State*. New York: St. Martin's Press, 1996.

Kennon, George F. *At a Century Ending*. New York: W.W. Norton, 1996.

Kennedy, Paul. *The Rise and Fall of the Great Powers*. Random House, 1988, Fontana Press, 1989.

Kiszling, Rudolf. *Österreich-Ungarn Anteil am Ersten Weltkrieg*. Graz: Stiastny verlag, 1958.

Klavora, Vasja. *Blaukreuz: Die Isonzofront, Flitsch/Bovec 1915-1917*. Klagenfurt: Hermagoras/Mohorjeva, 1993.

———. *Schritte im Nebel: Die Isonzofront, Karfreit/Kobarid, Tolmein/Tolmin 1915-1917*. Klagenfurt: Hermagoras/Mohorjeva, 1995.

Klípa, Bohumír. "Československá legie v Itálii," *Historie a vojenství*, Vol. 42, No. 1, 1993: 17-97.

Krofta, Kamil. *Dějiny československé*. Prague: Sfinx, B. Janda, 1946.

Livesey, Anthony. *The Historical Atlas of World War I*. New York: Henry Holt, 1994.

Lokay, Miroslav. *Československá legie v Itálii*. New York: Czechoslovak Society of Arts and Sciences, 1970.

Lucas, J.S. *Austro-Hungarian Infantry, 1914-1918*. London: Almark Publishing 1973.

McClure, William. *Italy's Part in the War, 1918*. Florence, 1918.

McEntee, Girard L. *Italy's Part in Winning the World War*. Princeton University Press, 1934.

_____. *Military History of the World War*. New York: Charles Scribner's Sons, 1937.

Magenschab, Hans. *Der Krieg des Grosväter 1914-1918*. Second edition. Vienna: Österreichische Staatsdruckerei, 1989.

Mansfield, Edward and Jack Snyder. "Democratization and War," *Foreign Affairs*, Vol. 74, No. 3 (May-June, 1995): 79-97.

Marwick, Arthur. *The Deluge*. Boston: Little Brown, 1965.

_____. *War and Social Change in the Twentieth Century*. New York: St. Martin's Press, 1974.

Maynes, Charles W. "The New Pessimism," *Foreign Policy*, No. 100, Fall, 1995: 33-49.

Morando, Pietro. *Uomini e Giganti*. Rovereto: Museo Storico Italiano della Guerra, 1988.

Nolte, Claire E. "Every Czech a Sokol!" *Center for Austrian Studies*, University of Minnesota, Vol. 24, 1993: 79-100.

_____. "Our Task, Direction and Goal. The Development of the Sokol National Program to World War I." *Die slawische Sokolbewegung: Beitrage zur Geschichte von Sport und Nationalismus in Osteuropa*. Diethelm Blecking, ed. Dortmund: Forschungsstelle Ostmitteleuropa, 1991: 37-52.

Novotný, Jan. *Sokol v životě národa*. Prague: Melantrich, 1990.

Ostry, Sylvia, and Richard R. Nelson. *Techno-Nationalism and Techno-Globalism*. Washington, DC: Brookings Institution, 1995.

Peroutka, Ferdinand. *Budování státu*, Vol. 1, 2, 3, 4. Third edition. Prague: Lidové noviny, 1991.

Pichlík, Karel, Bohumír Klípa, and Jitka Zabloudilová. *Českoslovenští legionáři 1914-1918*. Prague: Mladá fronta, 1996.

Pieri, Piero. "Italian Front," in *A Concise History of World War I*. Vincent J. Esposito, ed. New York: Frederick Praeger, 1964.

Pignotti, Lamberto. *Figure d'Assalto*. Rovereto: Museo Storico Italiano della Guerra, 1985.

Remak, Joachim. *The Origins of World War I 1871-1914*. Holt, Rinehart & Winston, 1967.

Roth, Jack J., ed. *World War I: A Turning Point in Modern History*. New York: A.A. Knopf, 1967.

Rommel, Erwin. *Infantry Attacks*. London: Greenhill, 1990.

Sartre, Jean Paul. *The Roads to Freedom*. 3 vols. New York: A.A. Knopf, 1947-1951.

Schaumann, Walther, and Peter Schubert. *Isonzo 1915-1917: Krieg ohne Wiederkehr*. Bassano del grappa: Ghedina & Tassotti, 1993.

_____. *Piave: Un Anno di Battaglie 1917-1918*. Bassano del grappa: Ghedina & Tassotti, 1991.

Schneigert, Zbigniew. *Aerial Tramways and Funicular Railways*. Trans. by Edward Jakobwicz and Wladyslaw Iwinski, Eng. trans. edited by Zygmunt Frenkiel. Oxford: Pergamon Press, 1966.

Slovník prvního československého odboje. Prague: Hermes, 1993.

Tainter, Joseph A. *The Collapse of Complex Societies*. Cambridge University Press, 1988.

Vaněk, Otakar, and František Bednařík. *V boj! 1915-1918*. Prague: Za svobodu, 1927.

von Albertini, Rudolf. "Impact of Two World Wars on the Decline of Colonialism," *Journal of Contemporary History*, Vol. 4, No. 1, Jan. 1969: 17-36. Special issue.

Winter, Jay and Blaine Baggett. *The Great War and the Shaping of the 20th Century*. New York: Penguin Studio, Penguin Books, 1996.

Zweig, Arnold. *Education before Verdun*. New York: Viking Press, 1936.